T0305168

The Asian Tsunami

26 December 2004

Over 220 000 men, women and children in poor countries in Asia were swept away in the great Asian tsunami of 2004.

This book is dedicated to their memory.

The Asian Tsunami
Aid and Reconstruction after a Disaster

Sisira Jayasuriya

Professor of Economics, School of Economics and Finance, La Trobe University, Melbourne, Australia

Peter McCawley

College of Asia and the Pacific, Australian National University, Canberra, Australia

In collaboration with Bhanupong Nidhiprabha, Budy P. Resosudarmo and Dushni Weerakoon

A JOINT PUBLICATION OF THE ASIAN DEVELOPMENT BANK INSTITUTE AND EDWARD ELGAR PUBLISHING

Edward Elgar
Cheltenham, UK • Northampton, MA, USA

Published by
Edward Elgar Publishing Limited
The Lypiatts
15 Lansdown Road
Cheltenham
Glos GL50 2JA
UK

Edward Elgar Publishing, Inc.
William Pratt House
9 Dewey Court
Northampton
Massachusetts 01060
USA

A catalogue record for this book
is available from the British Library

Library of Congress Control Number: 2010922139

Mixed Sources
Product group from well-managed
forests and other controlled sources
www.fsc.org Cert no. SA-COC-1565
© 1996 Forest Stewardship Council

FSC

ISBN 978 1 84844 692 2

Printed and bound by MPG Books Group, UK

Contents

Contributors

Nisha Arunatilake is Research Fellow, Institute of Policy Studies of Sri Lanka, Colombo, Sri Lanka.

Sisira Jayasuriya is Professor of Economics, School of Economics and Finance, La Trobe University, Melbourne, Australia.

Peter McCawley is Visiting Fellow, Arndt-Corden Division of Economics, College of Asia and the Pacific, Australian National University, Canberra, Australia and was formerly Dean, ADB Institute, Tokyo.

Suahasil Nazara is Professor, Faculty of Economics, University of Indonesia, Depok, Jakarta, Indonesia.

Bhanupong Nidhiprabha is Associate Professor, Faculty of Economics, Thammasat University, Bangkok, Thailand.

Budy P. Resosudarmo is Associate Professor, Arndt-Corden Division of Economics, College of Asia and the Pacific, Australian National University, Canberra, Australia.

Paul Steele is Environment Advisor, Asia and Pacific Regional Centre, Bangkok, Thailand and was formerly Associate Research Fellow, Institute of Policy Studies of Sri Lanka, Colombo, Sri Lanka.

Dushni Weerakoon is Deputy Director, Institute of Policy Studies of Sri Lanka, Colombo, Sri Lanka.

Foreword

Natural disasters of various kinds are an ever-present risk in most countries in Asia. It is usually the poor who are at highest risk, particularly in developing countries, because the places where the poor live and work tend to be especially vulnerable when disasters strike.

In recent years, a number of megadisasters have struck the Asian region that have incurred very heavy costs in terms of human lives: the 2004 Asian tsunami (causing a loss of nearly 230 000 lives); cyclone Nargis in Myanmar in 2008 (over 130 000 lives); the earthquake in Sichuan in the People's Republic of China in 2008 (over 80 000 lives); and the earthquake in the Kashmir region of India and Pakistan in 2005 (over 70 000 lives). In addition, there are numerous other natural disasters which are less serious in terms of human lives lost but which have high localized economic costs and disrupt the lives of millions of people: regular widespread flooding in major cities such as Jakarta and Manila and across Bangladesh, typhoons in the People's Republic of China and Viet Nam, and severe droughts in India and Pakistan are but some examples.

One of the consequences of the 2004 Asian tsunami was a sharply heightened awareness across developing countries in Asia of the need to give higher priority to disaster risk reduction programs across the region. Multilateral action has supported measures to give greater attention to disaster risk reduction issues at the national and local level. The Hyogo Framework for Action adopted in Kobe in early 2005 urged all countries to make major efforts to reduce the risk of disasters by 2015. There was increased awareness of the need to pay attention to pre-disaster programs as well as strengthen capacity to respond in the post-disaster period. More recently, in 2009, the United Nations issued *Risk and Poverty in a Changing Climate*, the first biennial assessment of global disaster risk.

This book is a study in the response to the largest natural disaster in Asia in recent history. The assistance provided by communities, governments, multilateral agencies, and non-government organizations following the Asian tsunami was an extraordinary humanitarian effort. It was also a very large aid program which involved thousands of different organizations. Indeed, as a collective effort, it was one of the largest single aid efforts that the international community has ever joined in for a natural disaster affecting developing countries. In looking to improve disaster risk reduction programs across Asia in the future, therefore, there are valuable lessons to be learnt from the experience of the regional reconstruction following the 2004 Asian tsunami.

Through the production of studies of this kind, ADBI is committed to a program of research and capacity building that supports the Asian Development Bank's overarching goal of promoting poverty reduction in the Asia-Pacific region.

Masahiro Kawai
Dean, Asian Development Bank Institute

Preface

This book grew out of the idea that national researchers in Asia should be provided with an opportunity to critically examine the emergency relief humanitarian response and reconstruction efforts in their respective countries to the great Asian tsunami of 2004. A series of natural disasters have struck several countries in Asia since then – most recently an earthquake in Padang in West Sumatra in Indonesia (October 2009) as this preface is being written – highlighting the importance of developing effective strategies to cope with such disasters.

Following the tsunami, a huge, complex and region-wide aid program quickly got underway. The effort involved thousands of agencies from Asian national governments, foreign governments, multilateral donor agencies and non-governmental organizations. Before long, a vast number of reports, surveys, and evaluations were prepared. But inevitably, much of this material was prepared by international aid workers with limited local experience in the field in Asia. It seemed appropriate to invite local research workers to write about the response to the disaster from a national perspective so that international views could be supplemented by views from the region.

The resulting book draws on several aspects of the contemporary literature in the international development debate. This book is a product of joint efforts. The individual country studies were authored primarily by national researchers. The Indonesia chapter was co-authored by Suahasil Nazara and Budy P. Resosudarmo, the Sri Lanka study by Dushni Weerakoon, Sisira Jayasuriya, Nisha Arunatilake and Paul Steele, and the Thailand chapter by Bhanupong Nidhiprabha.

The issues in the book need to be considered with reference to the literature on disasters – and especially the extensive discussion that has been taking place in recent years about responses to disasters in developing countries. The Asian tsunami itself dramatically highlighted the terrible risks that megadisasters in poor countries pose to human security in the region, especially the security of people who live in poor and vulnerable communities. The disaster led to a sharp increase in awareness across Asia of the need to strengthen disaster risk reduction policies. It should be mentioned here at the outset that in carrying out research for this study we have benefited from many reports from international agencies and researchers including the hundreds of reports of project work implemented in the field by numerous donor agencies. Many of these reports are excellent. They provide detailed accounts of the work done by thousands of workers in the field. In what follows, we have sought to draw on them and complement their analyses and findings.

The book is also a study of aid delivery. It thus draws on the international literature about aid and development. The response to the tsunami – by the Asian regional governments and communities as well as the international community – was a very large and unanticipated aid effort. Indeed, as a collective endeavour, the indications are that a national and international aid program amounting in total to perhaps US$17 billion or more was organized to support relief, rehabilitation and reconstruction projects following the tsunami. It was widely observed that this represented one of the largest disaster response programs ever undertaken in developing countries. Many issues of aid policy and delivery arose as thousands of individual aid activities were implemented in the hope of ensuring that the US$17 billion would be used effectively.

We should emphasize that this study has not been prepared with the aim of finding fault with the response to the 2004 tsunami. Doubtless some mistakes were made, and doubtless not every single one of the very large number of aid projects undertaken under very difficult circumstances in the field was successful. Rather, our aim has been to review the overall response following the 2004 tsunami disaster and to consider what broad lessons for policy might be drawn from the experience.

One of our main conclusions is that in the circumstances, the initial emergency relief effort can be considered a major achievement, due in large measure to the often spontaneous responses of local communities and measures taken by national governments. We also believe that the major assistance program supported by both Asian national governments and the international community was very successful in achieving the goal of providing widespread help following the 2004 tsunami. But another of our conclusions is that donor governments and aid agencies do not coordinate their activities well – with each other or with the national government – when disasters occur; in this respect, the international community should aim to do better. And perhaps the most important conclusion we reach is that much greater priority needs to be given to pre-disaster programs in developing countries in Asia; both regional governments and the international community need to give much higher priority to strengthening *local preparedness* across the region so that when disasters strike, local communities are themselves able to respond quickly to minimize the harm that is done.

Many people have helped prepare this book. We wish, particularly, to thank our colleagues in the ADB Institute in Tokyo who have given us strong support. We also wish to acknowledge the invaluable contributions from the research workers and our colleagues at the University of Indonesia in Jakarta, the Institute of Policy Studies in Sri Lanka, and Thammasat University in Bangkok, and numerous officials from governments and donor agencies. Lee Smith provided excellent editorial assistance in completing the book.

And, of course, we are most grateful to our spouses, Sreeni Jayasuriya and Anne Willoughby, for their forbearance while we have been working on this book.

Sisira Jayasuriya
Peter McCawley

Abbreviations

ABAS	Aceh Barat Selatan
ACFID	Australian Council for International Development
ADB	Asian Development Bank
ADPC	Asian Disaster Preparedness Centre (Bangkok)
AIPRD	Australia-Indonesia Partnership for Reconstruction and Development
ALA	Aceh Leuser Antara
ANAO	Australian National Audit Office
AusAID	Australian Agency for International Development
Bappeda	*Badan Perencanaan dan Pembangunan Daerah* or Regional Development Planning Agency
Bappenas	*Badan Perencanaan dan Pembangunan Nasional* or National Development Planning Agency
BBB	Build Back Better
BOP	Balance of Payments
BPN	*Badan Pertanahan Nasional* or National Land Administration Agency
BPS	*Badan Pusat Statistik* or Central Statistics Agency
BRR	*Badan Rekonstruksi dan Rehabilitasi* (Agency for the Rehabilitation and Reconstruction of Aceh and Nias)
CFW	Cash for work
CGI	Consultative Group on Indonesia
CIDA	Canadian International Development Agency
CIFOR	Center for International Forestry Research
CNO	Centre for National Operations
DAC	Development Assistance Committee (of the OECD)
DAD	Donor Assistance Database
DART™	Deep Ocean Assessment and Report of Tsunami
DDPM	Department of Disaster Prevention and Mitigation
EC	European Commission
ECHO	European Commission Humanitarian Aid Office
ECLAC	(United Nations) Economic Commission for Latin America and the Caribbean
EIB	European Investment Bank
ETESP	Earthquake and Tsunami Emergency Support Project

EU	European Union
FAO	Food and Agriculture Organization
FFEM	French Global Environment Fund
GAM	*Gerakan Aceh Merdeka* or Free Aceh Movement
GDP	Gross Domestic Product
GND	Grama Niladhari Divisions
GoI	Government of Indonesia
GOSL	Government of Sri Lanka
GPP	Gross Provincial Product
HFA	Hyogo Framework for Action
HPG	Humanitarian Policy Group (of the ODI)
IADB	Inter-American Development Bank
ICT	Information and communication technology
ICTA	Institute for Construction Training and Development
IDLO	International Development Law Organization
IDP	Internally displaced person
IFAD	International Fund for Agricultural Development
IFI	International Financial Institution (such as WB and ADB)
IFRC	International Federation of Red Cross and Red Crescent Societies
ILO	International Labour Organization
IMF	International Monetary Fund
INCOSAI	International Congress of Supreme Audit Institutions
INGO	International non-government organization
INTOSAI	International Organization of Supreme Audit Institutions
IPS	Institute of Policy Studies (Sri Lanka)
IPS-TS	Institute of Policy Studies – Tsunami Survey, 2005 and 2006
ISDR	International Strategy for Disaster Reduction
JBIC	Japan Bank for International Cooperation
LIBOR	London Inter-Bank Offer Rate
LPEM	*Lembaga Penyelidikan Ekonomi dan Masyarakat* or Institute for Economic and Social Research
LRRD	Linking Relief, Rehabilitation and Development
LTTE	Liberation Tigers of Tamil Eelam
MDF	Multi Donor Fund (of the World Bank, for Aceh and Nias)
MFAR	Ministry of Fisheries and Aquatic Resources
MOF	Ministry of Finance
MoU	Memorandum of Understanding
NAD	Nanggroe Aceh Darussalam
NDTF	National Development Trust Fund
NDWC	National Disaster Warning Center
NEER	Nominal effective exchange rate

NGO	Non-government organization
NZAID	New Zealand Agency for International Development
OCHA	UN Office for the Coordination of Humanitarian Affairs
ODA	Official development assistance
ODI	Overseas Development Institute
OECD	Organisation for Economic Co-operation and Development
Perpres	*Peraturan Presiden* or Regulation of the President
Perpu	*Peraturan Pemerintah Pengganti Undang-Undang* or Regulation in Lieu of Law
PP	*Peraturan Pemerintah* or Government Regulation
PRC	People's Republic of China
P-TOMS	Post-Tsunami Operation Management Structure
PTSD	Post-traumatic stress disorder
RADA	Reconstruction and Development Agency
RALAS	Reconstruction of Aceh Land Administration System
RAND	Recovery Aceh-Nias Database
REER	Real effective exchange rate
RMIT	Royal Melbourne Institute of Technology
Rp	Rupiah (Indonesian currency)
Satker	*Satuan Kerja* or Work Unit
SET	Security exchange index (in Thailand)
SIDA	Swedish International Development Cooperation Agency
SLR	Sri Lanka Rupee
SMEs	Small and medium-sized enterprises
SMERU	SMERU Research Institute (Jakarta)
SPAN	*Sensus Penduduk Aceh dan Nias* or Aceh and Nias Population Census
TAFLOL	Task Force for Logistics, Law and Order
TAFOR	Task Force for Relief
TAFREN	Task Force for Rebuilding the Nation
TAFRER	Task Force for Rescue and Relief
TEC	Tsunami Evaluation Coalition
TGLL	Tsunami Global Lessons Learned
THRIS	Tsunami Help and Recovery Information System
TICA	Thailand International Development Cooperation Agency
TWS	Tsunami warning system
UN	United Nations
UNCTAD	United Nations Conference on Trade and Development
UNDP	United Nations Development Programme
UNEP	United Nations Environment Programme
UNFPA	United Nations Population Fund
UNORC	UN Office of the Recovery Coordinator for Aceh and Nias

UNOSE	United Nations, Office of the Special Envoy for Tsunami Recovery
USAID	United States Agency for International Development
USGAO	United States Government Accountability Office
WB	World Bank
WCDR	World Conference on Disaster Reduction
WHO	World Health Organization

Note: Throughout this book the term 'billion' refers to 1000 million and 'trillion' refers to 1000 billion.

1.   The tsunami

Early in the morning of Sunday 26 December 2004, Boxing Day, just before 8 am local time, an earthquake rumbled in the deep in the sea off the coast of Northwest Sumatra. Immense geological pressures triggered the earthquake. The Indian Ocean tectonic plate moved abruptly against the Eurasian plate causing a 100 foot bulge on the seabed along a plate more than 600 miles long. The sea bed rose by up to 5 metres in places, displacing a phenomenal volume of water. A series of smaller aftershocks followed.[1]

The main earthquake prompted immediate warnings in geological centres around the world. The energy of the earthquake generated giant waves travelling at speeds of up to 1000 km per hour across the Indian Ocean over a giant area. But there was very little time for countries in the region to act. In any case, rapid-response warning systems in most poor countries across Asia were non-existent or ineffective. There was, in fact, very little that could be done.

In the largest nearby provincial town in Indonesia, Banda Aceh at the tip of North Sumatra around 300 km from the epicentre of the main quake, thousands of people rushed into the streets. Buildings and houses across the town rocked. Much local damage was caused by the earthquake. But worse, far worse, was to come. As teams of people in Banda Aceh began to organize immediate assistance after the quake, giant shockwaves from the deep sea earthquake were spreading outwards from the epicentre. In the deep waters of the open ocean, shockwaves of this kind are barely noticeable. But as the shockwaves reach shallow water, the height of the waves quickly builds up. The people in the streets of Banda Aceh had no idea that a tsunami was on the way.

Around half an hour after the earthquake, while large crowds were working in the streets of Banda Aceh to cope with devastation across the city caused by the quake, a huge surge of water began to build up from the sea. At first, the water receded in a very strange way as if the lowest of low tides was occurring. And then a series of waves surged forwards as if the tide was rushing back in. Twenty-metre waves burst across the foreshores of the town. But just as damaging was an astonishing surge that, like an unimaginable high tide with tremendous power, swept up the creeks and

inlets and into the streets of Banda Aceh, pushing and sweeping and crush-
ing all that lay before it. Nothing could resist the immense tide. Boats and
cars and trucks were carried along; houses were pushed aside; children
were plucked as nothing from their mothers' arms; thousands of people
were carried away in just a few minutes. Within perhaps one hour of the
initial earthquake deep under the sea, over 160 000 Indonesians had died.

This was just the beginning. The tsunami arrived as a series of waves.
The waters retreated and advanced in cycles of over thirty minutes
between each peak. In most places, the third wave was the most powerful,
occurring about an hour and a half after the first wave. Smaller tsunamis
continued for a number of hours. And then, after the destruction in Banda
Aceh, during the next few hours a great natural disaster unfolded across
more than a dozen poor countries in Asia as the waves sped out across the
Indian Ocean. As one report put it (TGLL 2009: 3 and 16), 'the magnitude
and scope of the destruction ranks it as one of the greatest natural disasters in recent history . . . . when the tsunami was finished, it was the most
destructive disaster of its kind in history.'

As the tsunami spread outwards around the tip of North Sumatra and
quickly outwards to Thailand, South Asia, and eventually even to Africa,
many thousands more were swept away. Even five years later the precise
death toll and the full catalogue of physical disaster is uncertain. The exact
death toll will never be known. However it is clear that almost 230 000
people died, well over one million people were displaced (Table 1.1) and
over US$10 billion in damage was caused to infrastructure, houses and
other property.

There was an unprecedented response to the disaster. Nearby local
communities reacted first, helping in every way they could, using whatever resources could be mobilized. This was followed by a fast national
response, and later a huge global response. Governments, international
agencies and millions of people across the world donated to help communities devastated by the tsunami. As one survey of the disaster (Bernhard
et al. 2005: 82) observed:

> The nature of the tragedy, combined with the clear and constant communica-
> tion through the media, led hundreds of millions of individuals around the
> globe to donate funding to various national and international charities and
> relief organizations. An outpouring of this magnitude from individuals has
> never been witnessed before for a single event.

Most of the affected countries were entirely unprepared for the disaster.
This was not surprising. Countries like Sri Lanka had not experienced an
event of this kind for millennia.[2] Even Indonesia, which frequently experiences serious natural disasters, was caught unprepared by the scale of the

Table 1.1   2004 Asian tsunami: estimated deaths and displacements

Country	People lost	Displaced
Indonesia[a]	167540	566898
Sri Lanka	35322	519063
India	16269	647599
Thailand	8212	n.a.
Other (10 countries)	555	34700
Total	227898	1768260

Note: (a) Includes Nias earthquake.

Source: USAID Fact Sheets (estimates).

disaster.[3] The tsunami subjected the affected countries and communities to unprecedented stress in terms of disaster management. Local communities and national governments immediately organized emergency relief operations and, helped by international agencies quickly provided food, clean water, basic health services, and temporary shelter. This initial relief effort has been widely described as remarkably successful given the circumstances. The high-profile international effort to help reconstruction and recovery was also widely hailed for its scale and generosity (Schwartz 2006: 6):

> Tsunami recovery represents the largest ever mobilisation of donor funds for an emergency and reconstruction effort. All over the world, governments, international agencies and multilateral donors, non-government organizations (NGOs) and individuals supported the provision of humanitarian relief and reconstruction to affected areas. NGOs and the Red Cross movements alone raised over $5 billion, alongside $8 billion pledged by governments and others for recovery and reconstruction.

The promised funding initially appeared to be more than adequate to cover both initial relief and reconstruction. Indeed the expected flow of international assistance was such that – as incorporated explicitly into the reconstruction plans in Indonesia – the aim was not simply to replace destroyed housing and infrastructure but to 'build back better'.

By the end of 2005, towards the end of the first year after the tsunami, the response effort supported by international aid programs seemed to have been a resounding success. There was satisfaction – and more than a whiff of self-congulation – in many of the early assessments based on progress reports prepared by national agencies and major international organizations. The observation by Inderfurth et al. (2005) captured the mood of many of these reports:

> While full reconstruction may take five years or longer, if the level of commit-
> ment demonstrated by the international community is maintained, the tsunami
> will be remembered as a model for effective global disaster response, not just as
> a disaster. Because of the speed and generosity of the response, its effectiveness
> compared to previous (and even subsequent) disasters, and its sustained focus
> on reconstruction and prevention, we give the overall aid effort a grade of 'A'.

However these early ultra-rosy assessments seemed rather overblown even
then. They certainly failed the test of time.

In fact, soon after relief operations began, problems with the relief and
reconstruction effort began coming to light. During 2005 there were widespread reports of inefficiencies in the distribution of funds, unsatisfactory
plans for the rebuilding of houses, slow progress in reconstruction, allegations of corruption, cost escalations, funding gaps following the slow disbursement of funds, and coordination failures. A report presented to the
Prime Minister of Sri Lanka in December 2005 by the Institute of Policy
Studies (IPS) of Sri Lanka highlighted the coordination problems that had
emerged following the influx of large numbers of donors including many
'new' NGOs. The report (Jayasuriya et al. 2005: 17) noted that 'Many
NGOs lack experience and local knowledge, and in their haste to spend
monies disregard local circumstances and community needs.'

In July 2006 a major study prepared by the Tsunami Evaluation
Coalition (TEC) reviewed the experience of the international relief and
reconstruction efforts. The study (Telford et al. 2006: 93) observed that:

> some international agencies managed well; but many did not . . .. Local contexts,
> institutions and contributions were frequently neglected. Affected people's will
> and capacity to move from reliance on handouts to rebuilding their lives were
> inadequately exploited . . . They were marginalized, even undermined, by an
> overwhelming flood of international agencies controlling immense resources.

The IPS Report from Sri Lanka also raised the issue of the costs of the
rehabilitation and reconstruction efforts. The study (Jayasuriya et al.
2005: 53) warned that 'cost blowouts will almost certainly create funding
gaps, make reconstruction tasks difficult and impose further strains on
government fiscal expenditures'.

Subsequent developments confirmed that problems persisted despite
substantial progress with reconstruction in both Sri Lanka and Indonesia.
By early 2007 the impact of unexpected inflation in costs was being widely
acknowledged. In a report to Congressional Committees in February
2007, the United States Government Accountability Office described the
impact on its tsunami aid projects in the following terms (USGAO 2007:
Highlights):

Although both of its signature projects – one in Indonesia and one in Sri Lanka – are under way, USAID has increased initial cost estimates, reduced or canceled some project activities, and may extend completion dates . . . In Indonesia, estimated construction cost per mile increased by 75 percent . . .; USAID reduced the length of road to be built by over one third . . .

In December 2007 the World Bank tsunami website reported (World Bank 2007) that in Sri Lanka:

The Tsunami Emergency Reconstruction Program I . . . ended on March 31, 2007. At completion, there are still about 15,000 families in need of permanent housing. These are primarily landless families, and due to this increase in housing needs, with only about US $8 million remaining, additional funding would be required to complete all units of the housing program.

The World Bank tsunami website also reported (in December 2007) – citing sources from the Indonesian Reconstruction and Rehabilitation Agency (*Badan Rekonstruksi dan Rehabilitasi*, or BRR) – that 30 000 houses remained to be built. In both Indonesia and Sri Lanka there were reports not only of cost escalations producing funding gaps but also of institutional and procedural bottlenecks hindering the use of available funds.[4] These problems led to delays in reconstruction and prolonged the suffering of affected groups. Nevertheless, the reconstruction effort continued to make headway and five years after the tsunami the restoration of the major physical infrastructure in most of the severely affected regions of Indonesia, India, Sri Lanka and Thailand was largely complete. The many thousands of aid workers who participated in the tsunami relief effort – both from within the affected countries and from overseas – can certainly be proud of what was achieved. They confronted major problems and overcame them to the best of their ability. It needs to be recognized that the response, unprecedented in its scale and scope, was remarkable not because it proceeded without any problems but because it was able to address problems as they emerged. The effort was an immense undertaking which involved communities, aid workers, governments and the wider international community.

It is no exaggeration to describe some elements of the logistics of the aid effort as similar in scope to a series of prolonged military operations. Just as analysts consider it useful to consider the aims and achievements of military exercises, so it is useful to ask broad questions about objectives and outcomes of the tsunami aid effort across Asia. The tsunami was not the first megadisaster to strike in poor countries in Asia, nor, unfortunately, the last as more recent events show (see Table 2.1). How the world responded to the 2004 tsunami should be examined so that all possible

lessons can be drawn and applied in the effort to cope with the continuing threat of natural disasters. This is a daunting task; discussion about
the lessons of the tsunami has already generated a significant literature,
primarily in the form of reports but also as journal articles and other documents, and is likely to present a major field of research for many years to
come (ISDR-BIBLIO 2006; Cosgrave et al. 2009).

AIM OF THE STUDY

The broad aim of this study is to make a contribution to the task of
improving disaster risk reduction policy in Asia by examining several
aspects of the delivery of tsunami aid in three countries (Indonesia, Sri
Lanka and Thailand). We recognize that the rapid delivery of emergency
assistance – of food, water, medicine, sanitation and shelter – in the immediate aftermath of a disaster is the single most critical issue in minimizing
the human costs of disaster. However, as development economists, our
comparative advantage is not in the analysis of the logistics of the delivery
of emergency services and technical aspects of disaster mitigation. Our
focus in this volume therefore is just as much on the subject of the links
between shorter-term relief assistance and longer-term development.

The subject of linking relief, rehabilitation and development (LRRD)
has received increasing attention in recent years. It was the main focus
of the major *A Ripple in Development?* report on post-tsunami assistance
prepared with the support of the Swedish aid agency, SIDA (Brusset et al.
2009) as well as other studies on the delivery of tsunami aid (Masyrafah
and McKeon 2008). This book will thus give much attention to the institutional and economic policy issues raised in different stages of the relief and
reconstruction effort, to the role of international assistance provided by
the global community, and to how a more productive partnership can be
established between local and international agencies to enable communities to better undertake disaster risk reduction.

In the following chapters we look at the main factors which had a
bearing on institutional responses to the provision of aid following the
tsunami. Some of these key factors, for example, influenced the speed
and mode of delivery of assistance. There were other factors which actually hampered inter-agency coordination. We draw on economic theory
to shed light on why reconstruction efforts triggered unexpectedly high
localized inflation, particularly in the form of rapid construction cost escalation, which generated substantial funding gaps. We review the overall
responses to the tsunami disaster from all involved parties – international,
national and local, public and private – paying particular attention to

the international aid effort. A special focus of the study is that we draw on analytical perspectives from the viewpoint of research workers in the affected countries. We conclude with thoughts on what lessons might be drawn from this remarkable experience.

Several themes are taken up in the studies in the book. The different stages of the relief and reconstruction process must be clearly recognized. Each stage requires a different response. Another clear theme that emerges from the 2004 tsunami experience highlights the critical role of local communities. Local communities responded quickly in each of the three countries to the huge challenge of providing emergency assistance in the immediate aftermath of the disaster – the period most important in terms of saving lives. It takes time for even national level assistance to arrive at a disaster-hit location – and a significantly long time when the affected location is remote. It takes even longer for international assistance to arrive. Local communities must be at the centre of any viable disaster management strategy.

A third theme focuses on the international aid effort. In one sense, much of this book is a study in aid effectiveness. The role of international assistance in global disaster management is acquiring major significance. The size of the international aid response program was one of the most striking aspects of the relief and reconstruction efforts following the 2004 tsunami. There was an outpouring of sympathy across the world. Overall, the offers of aid from the international community came to around US$14 billion in total assistance (though, as we discuss later, the precise amount of actual disaster-related assistance is difficult to determine). In any case, it is clear that the scale of this international aid effort dwarfed any previous similar disaster relief assistance program and the promised aid was deemed adequate to cover the entire cost of reconstruction. Indeed, the fact that local and national agencies pledged several billions more sometimes went almost unnoticed. Against this background, we focus on key issues such as the following:

- Who promised what?
- Were the promises fulfilled to a satisfactory extent?
- What are the lessons learned?

As noted in Chapter 3, the original promises from aid donors were frequently vague. It was often not easy to determine the actual amount of new assistance to the country targeted for tsunami reconstruction. Further, the different suppliers of assistance were inclined, consciously or unconsciously, to set their own criteria for judging success in aid delivery – and indeed, were inclined to adjust the criteria from time to time to fit in with circumstances.

From the earliest stages, the relatively large scale of the international aid program and the involvement of numerous actors raised difficult coordination challenges. Coordination was difficult not simply because of the number of actors of various types but also because they had a multiplicity of objectives and modes of operation. This is a recurring theme that runs throughout our discussions: actors in the international aid arena have multiple, and often quite complex, objectives. The *real* objectives of major actors are often not what they say their *nominal* objectives are. Their nominal objectives are the goals that they publicly proclaim. But the real objectives of policy may, and indeed often do, encompass both humanitarian objectives and other important goals. As will be seen below, for various reasons donors had especially strong motives for providing help in the case of the Asian tsunami – motives which have been absent in the case of some other recent disasters. This aspect of donor aid policy, often tactfully left unmentioned in the international aid literature, is dramatically illustrated by the sharp contrast between the response of the international community to the Asian tsunami in 2004, on one hand, and to the disaster of cyclone Nargis in Myanmar in 2008 on the other.[5] And even when donors said that they were committed to cooperating closely with other agencies, individual donors had specific agendas which made it difficult, sometimes nearly impossible, to coordinate aid efforts and to maximize the effectiveness of the delivery of aid. These difficulties of coordination applied just as much to the activities of NGOs as to the programs of governments.

Donors often tended to be supply-oriented rather than demand-responsive. As shown in the case of various housing construction projects, the tendency of donors to deliver their preferred form of aid raises particularly difficult issues when donor agencies are not responsive to local customs and cultural sensitivities. Mechanisms are needed to ensure that local communities affected by natural disasters have opportunities to outline their priority needs. Mismatches between donor and community views can lead to friction, and sometimes even open conflict.

Most importantly, the tsunami experience highlights the need for substantial amounts of aid to be delivered quickly. But there are many institutional constraints that hinder speedy responses from assistance agencies. Recognizing this need to provide assistance quickly, we also examine the issue of whether aid should be delivered as cash or in-kind and argue that in some circumstances there is a strong case for providing cash assistance to disaster affected communities at an early stage in the relief effort.

Yet another theme discussed is the need to allow for significant construction cost increases when large reconstruction programs are implemented in places where construction materials and labour are in short supply. The underlying economic forces that generate 'Dutch Disease' effects are discussed in Chapter 7. It is important to recognize that the jump in prices of construction costs – resulting from sharp increases in the demand for construction inputs in short supply – is likely to far exceed the inflationary impact that might be caused by the injection of aid funds into the economy. These sharp increases in costs were not anticipated by reconstruction agencies following the Asian tsunami. In both Aceh and Sri Lanka, construction costs nearly doubled and resulted in funding gaps; significantly, this phenomenon was not an important issue in Thailand where there were fewer supply constraints. There is a potential trade off between the pace of reconstruction and the effective use of funds. There is therefore a need to prioritize construction activities when problems of this kind arise.

The book is structured as follows. Chapter 2 provides a broad overview of the issues which need to be considered in reaching judgements about the effectiveness of tsunami aid. Chapter 3 looks at the financial aspects of the global assistance program in some detail. The three chapters that follow discuss the country experiences of Indonesia, Sri Lanka and Thailand; national researchers were primarily responsible for preparing these chapters. The final chapter sets out the main conclusions and summarizes the main findings.

NOTES

1. A useful briefing can be found on Wikipedia, *2004 Indian Ocean earthquake*, http://en.wikipedia.org/wiki/2004_Indian_Ocean_earthquake, accessed 31 July 2009.
2. Sri Lanka, for example, was completely unprepared for the tsunami. Sri Lanka experiences periodic droughts, floods, landslides and the occasional cyclone. But the nation had never experienced a tsunami, or indeed any other type of natural disaster of this scale in recorded history. Even the tsunami generated by the great Krakatoa eruption of 1883 in Indonesia had lost much of its power by the time it reached Sri Lanka. While minor earth tremors are not uncommon, no serious earthquake has occurred for three centuries. Historical records indicate that a major earthquake in 1615 inflicted serious damage with large numbers of casualties (http://www.lankalibrary.com/geo/portu/earthquake.htm). Sri Lanka had no effective domestic hazard warning system, and had not felt the need to be part of international early warning systems, such as the Tsunami Warning System (TWS) in the Pacific (with 26 member countries).
3. Indonesia has since experienced several seriously destructive natural disasters although none have approached the scale of the 2004 tsunami.
4. According to the same World Bank website, BRR has consistently under-spent its budget allocations: 'However, with the vast amount of reconstruction required to be completed, BRR has not yet managed to disburse its annual budgets fully in the year required, leaving much work still to be done'. In Sri Lanka, 'while individual agencies varied in performance, the bilateral and multilateral agencies had spent on average 29 per cent and 32 per cent, respectively, of committed funds by end 2006' (Weerakoon et al. 2007: 22).
5. Both were megadisasters in poor countries in Asia, with Nargis accounting for well over

100 000 (by some counts, up to 140 000) deaths. Yet the international donor response was entirely different: in contrast to the US$14 billion or so provided to tsunami-affected countries, Myanmar received something less than US$500 million following cyclone Nargis. One obvious reason for the difference, of course, is that the Government of Myanmar was not cooperative with the international donor community in receiving aid. But this was not the whole story. Many donor countries linked offers of aid to Myanmar with specific conditions that were likely to be rejected.

REFERENCES

Bernhard, Richard, Y.Yritsilpe and O. Petchkul (2005), 'Corporate philanthropy in Thailand', in *Philanthropy in Disasters: Tsunami and After*, Conference Proceedings of the Asian Pacific Philanthropy Consortium, Kenan Instutute, Phuket, 28–30 November.

Brusset, Emery, M. Bhatt, K. Bjornestad, J. Cosgrave, A. Davies, Y. Deshmukh, J. Haleem, S. Hidalgo, Y. Immajati, R. Jayasundere, A. Mattsson, N. Muhaimin, R. Polastro and T. Wu (2009), *A Ripple in Development? Long Term Perspectives on the Response to the Indian Ocean Tsunami 2004*, Stockholm: SIDA, www.sida.se/publications, accessed 20 August 2009.

Cosgrave, John, E. Brusset, M. Bhatt, L. Fernandez, Y. Deshmukh, Y. Immajati, R. Jayasundere, A. Mattsson, N. Muhaimin and R. Polastro (2009), *A Ripple in Development? Document Review*. Annotated Bibliography prepared for the Joint Follow-up Evaluation of the Links between Relief, Rehabilitation and Development (LRRD) in Responses to the Indian Ocean Tsunami, Stockholm: SIDA, www.sida.se/publications, accessed 10 September 2009.

Inderfurth, Karl F., D. Fabrycky and S.P. Cohen (2005), 'The tsunami report card', *Foreign Policy,* The Carnegie Endowment for International Peace, http://www.foreignpolicy.com/, accessed 21 September 2008.

ISDR-BIBLIO (2006), 'Tsunami', Geneva: ISDR, http://library-isdr.unog.ch/cgi-bin/Pwebrecon.cgi?v1=2&ti=1,2&CNT=50&Search%5FArg=tsunami%20%2B%20ISDR%2DBiblio&Search%5FCode = FT%2A&Search%5FCode = FT%2A&PID = ZnuCNzK2OwDx3hW7qdnFkrPY8fTb&SEQ = 20090929092212&SID =1, accessed 24 September 2009.

Jayasuriya, Sisira, P. Steele and D. Weerakoon (2005), *Post-Tsunami Recovery: Issues and Challenges in Sri Lanka*, Report presented to the Prime Minister of Sri Lanka, Institute of Policy Studies, Colombo, November.

Masyrafah, Harry, and J.M.J.A. McKeon (2008), *Post-Tsunami Aid Effectiveness in Aceh: Proliferation and Coordination in Reconstruction*, Wolfensohn Center for Development Working Paper 6, Washington: The Brookings Institution, http://www.brookings.edu/~/media/Files/rc/papers/2008/11_aceh_aid_masyrafah/11_aceh_aid_masyrafah.pdf, accessed 26 September 2009.

Schwartz, Eric (2006), 'Responsibilities and challenges', July, UNOSE website, http://www.tsunamispecialenvoy.org/default.aspx, accessed 27 September 2006.

Telford, John, J. Cosgrave and R. Houghton (2006), *Joint Evaluation of the International Response to the Indian Ocean Tsunami: Synthesis Report,* London: Tsunami Evaluation Coalition.

TGLL (Tsunami Global Lessons Learned Project) (2009), *The Tsunami Legacy: Innovations, Breakthroughs and Change*, TGLL Project Steering Committee, http://

www.reliefweb.int / rw / rwb.nsf / db900sid / MUMA-7RF7PQ ? OpenDocument, accessed 26 August 2009.

USGAO (2007), *Foreign Assistance: USAID Signature Tsunami Reconstruction Efforts in Indonesia and Sri Lanka Exceed Initial Cost and Schedule Estimates, and Face Further Risks*, Report to Congressional Committees: Washington, www.gao.gov/cgi-bin/getrpt?GAO-07-357, accessed 23 July 2009.

Weerakoon, Dushni, S. Jayasuriya, N. Arunatilake and P. Steele (2007), *Economic Challenges of Post-Tsunami Reconstruction in Sri Lanka*, Tokyo: Asian Development Bank Institute, http://www.adbi.org/files/dp75.sri.lanka.post. tsunami.reconstruction.pdf, accessed 17 September 2009.

World Bank (2007), Sri Lanka Tsunami Recovery website, http://www.worldbank.lk/ WBSITE / EXTERNAL / COUNTRIES / SOUTHASIAEXT / SRILANKAEX TN/0,,contentMDK:21594465~menuPK:232812~pagePK:2865066~piPK:286 5079~theSitePK:233047,00.html, accessed 13 January 2009.

2. Response to disaster: issues

INTRODUCTION

The response to a megadisaster such as the 2004 Asian tsunami raises many issues. And the response can be considered in various ways. The assistance provided by communities, governments and NGOs following the Asian tsunami was a remarkable humanitarian effort which needs to be considered within the extensive literature that has grown up in recent years about the need for better disaster response programs in developing countries. But the response was also a very large and unanticipated aid program. This aid program involved, under conditions of extreme stress, thousands of national, regional and international organizations. Indeed, as a collective endeavour, it was one of the largest single aid efforts that the international community has ever joined in developing countries. The effort therefore needs to be considered from the point of view of international aid policy as well. This chapter considers these issues.

LITERATURE REVIEW

In recent years the international community has spent much time discussing ways to improve policy responses to natural disasters in developing countries. As the 2009 Global Assessment Report on Disaster Risk Reduction issued by the United Nations noted, 'Global disaster risk is highly concentrated in poorer countries . . . Particularly in low and low–middle income countries with rapid economic growth, the exposure of people and assets to natural hazards is growing at a faster rate than risk-reducing capacities are being strengthened, leading to increased disaster risk' (ISDR 2009b: 3).

Developing countries in Asia are particularly exposed to risks from natural disasters. Of the ten major natural disasters with the highest death tolls across the world since 1975, six have occurred in developing countries in Asia (Table 2.1).

At the global level progress has been made in strengthening policies but, as is usual with international discussions about worldwide issues, the

Table 2.1   Natural disasters with more than 50 000 fatalities, 1975–2008

Date	Place	Event	Deaths	Comment
1984–85	Ethiopia	Drought	300 000	
1976, July	PRC, Tangshan	Earthquake	242 000	Unofficial toll up to 700 000
2004, Dec	Asia regional	Tsunami	227 898	More than a dozen countries
1983	Sudan	Drought	150 000	
1991, April	Bangladesh	Cyclone	138 866	Cyclone Gorky
2008, May	Myanmar	Cyclone	133 655	Cyclone Nargis
1981	Mozambique	Drought	100 000	South Mozambique
2008, May	PRC, Sichuan	Earthquake	87 476	
2005, Oct	India, Pakistan	Earthquake	73 338	Kashmir region
2003	Europe	Heat wave	56 809	Various countries

Source: United Nations, ISDR (2009a: 4); Table 1.1 for Asian tsunami.

whole is dependent on the parts.[1] Much depends on what can be done by individual countries. Often the capacity of developing countries to implement the ambitious goals agreed to at international conferences is quite limited.

At the international level, the annual *World Disasters Report* issued by the IFRC (International Federation of Red Cross and Red Crescent Societies) is an important source of information and commentary which helps strengthen global coordination of disaster risk reduction policy. Within Asia, perhaps because of an acute awareness of the risks of natural disasters at home, Japan has played a major role in encouraging increased attention to issues of disaster risk reduction.[2] In 1994 at an international meeting near Tokyo, the Yokohama Strategy for a Safer World set down guidelines for natural disaster prevention, preparedness and mitigation. The Yokohama Strategy was drawn up as a plan of action. A decade later in early 2005, the World Conference on Disaster Reduction in Kobe, Japan, reviewed progress made under the Yokohama Strategy. In Kobe, five priorities for action were adopted:

- Ensuring that disaster risk reduction is a national and local priority
- Identifying disaster risks and enhancing early warning systems
- Building a culture of safety using knowledge and education
- Reducing the underlying risk factors
- Strengthening disaster preparedness.

In the wake of the 2004 Asian tsunami there was sharply increased awareness in poor countries in Asia of the high economic costs of disasters. One World Bank study, for example, has estimated that economic losses due to natural disasters are 20 times greater as a proportion of GDP in developing countries than in developed countries (Parker et al. 2007). And a recent AusAID report noted that 'Over 95 per cent of people killed by natural disasters are from developing countries' (AusAID 2009: 7).

The Hyogo Framework for Action (HFA), adopted in Kobe in early 2005, urged all countries to make major efforts to reduce their disaster risk by 2015.[3] And in addition to the discussions about the HFA in Kobe, it is clear that following the tsunami disaster, policy makers in developing Asian countries began to pay considerably more attention to disaster management planning.[4] There was increased awareness of the need to pay attention to pre-disaster action programs as well as strengthen capacity to respond in the post-disaster period (Marianti 2007: 13). In 2009, the United Nations issued *Risk and Poverty in a Changing Climate*, the first biennial assessment of global disaster risk (ISDR 2009a). The central message of the report was that there is a close link between disaster risk and poverty, and that 'reducing disaster risk can provide a vehicle to reduce poverty, safeguard development and adapt to climate change' (ISDR 2009a: v). The key findings listed in the report emphasized the need to identify the underlying factors which exacerbate disaster risk in developing countries and to adopt policies to reduce the risks (Box 2.1).

At the national level in developing countries in Asia three proposals, in particular, have attracted attention from policy makers when considering how to implement the advice set out in the various reports issued following international conferences about disaster risk reduction:

- Establishing new national institutions
- Mainstreaming disaster reduction policy
- Establishing a national network of local disaster organizations

Implementation of each of these proposals is constrained both by resources and, to some extent, by different views as to the best policy. In practice, resource constraints impose tight limits on what governments can do. Surprisingly, the resource constraints faced by governments in developing countries in Asia receive little attention in the international literature about disaster risk reduction policy in the region. In the absence of resource constraints, it is easy enough to agree that it would be a good idea to establish new national institutions to implement national disaster policy. One suggestion sometimes made is that developing countries

BOX 2.1   UNITED NATIONS 2009 *RISK AND POVERTY IN A CHANGING CLIMATE*: KEY FINDINGS

- Global disaster risk is highly concentrated in poor countries.
- Most disaster mortality and asset destruction is intensively concentrated in very small areas exposed to infrequent but extreme hazards. But low-intensity damage to such things as housing, local infrastructure and agriculture, which erodes livelihoods, is extensive in many countries.
- Key factors contributing to high levels of disaster risk in poor countries are poor urban governance, vulnerable rural livelihoods, and declining ecosystems.
- Poorer communities suffer a disproportionate share of disaster loss.
- Weather-related disaster risk is expanding rapidly. Climate change is already changing the nature of weather-related hazards.
- Progress towards reducing disaster risk is mixed. In some directions, such as strengthening capacities and institutional systems, many countries are making significant progress. But in other areas such as the mainstreaming of risk reduction considerations into overall policies, there is much less progress.
- Governance arrangements for disaster risk reduction in many countries do not encourage the mainstreaming of disaster risk factors into overall policy considerations. As a result, countries have difficulty addressing the key factors that contribute to high levels of disaster risk.
- Using specific policy tools, such as microfinance, microinsurance, and index-based insurance, helps tackle the underlying drivers of disaster risk that impact on the poor.
- A failure to address the underlying drivers of disaster risk will result in dramatic increases in disaster risk and associated poverty outcomes.

Source: ISDR (2009b).

should establish a high-level national disaster council to determine policy which might, in turn, be supported by a national development management office to focus on implementation.[5]

And, indeed, sometimes institutions of this kind are established on paper. But because many developing countries in Asia are short of both money and skilled staff to support new organizations, the results of these initiatives are often disappointing. There is limited value in establishing institutions which are poorly resourced.[6]

Issues of policy are not necessarily easy to address either. For one thing, bearing in mind that the institutions to implement policy are often not strong in developing countries in Asia, there is a limit to the number of cross-cutting issues that can be mainstreamed in an effective way at any time. The agenda of issues which the international community often suggests for policy mainstreaming in developing countries is already quite extensive – gender, environment along with related issues of climate change, health and safety, and a range of social issues such as those relating to minority groups, the aged, disabled citizens, and so on – so proposals to mainstream disaster risk reduction issues are, in effect, competitive with suggestions to mainstream many other issues as well.

For another thing, there is not always agreement as to what extent particular administrative structures are likely to provide the best outcomes. Recommendations to place responsibility (and, what is just as controversial, resources) in the hands of national governments do not receive universal support. A survey of the different models adopted in Latin America (Freeman et al. 2003) reported 'There is . . . disagreement in the literature regarding the advisability of depending on national government as the appropriate foundation for a comprehensive program [because] . . . focusing natural disaster policy through existing government systems enhances narrow power structures and draws away from local concerns and initiatives.'

Commenting on the advantages of a decentralized approach, one Indonesian observer (Marianti 2007: 19) noted that 'Proponents of this view prefer community-based projects and programs that are developed by NGOs. Although this way cannot guarantee the quality of risk management, it is closer to affected people (thus more likely to capture their needs) and can directly empower the local populations.'

Certainly there are pros and cons. Certainly some institutional capacity is needed to support policy-making and implementation at the national level. But in later chapters of this study it will be argued that the highest priority in developing countries in Asia needs to be given to strengthening local preparedness to respond to disasters.

SUPPLY SIDE ISSUES

The broad scope of issues discussed in literature about the provision of humanitarian aid often focuses on the supply side of aid delivery. But the demand side – what the people affected by disasters want, and what their perceptions of the aid provided are – needs attention as well. It will be useful to consider the tsunami aid program within the context of this supply and demand framework.

One set of issues on the supply side of the provision of humanitarian assistance concerns objectives of aid – the goals of donors, promises made, and the conditions that donors set down in offering aid. Because of the complex nature of aid policy, it will be useful as background for the discussion in the following chapters to note one key aspect of the objectives which often influence the activities of aid agencies: the difference between the nominal and the real objectives of humanitarian aid policy.

The generally stated motive for the supply of humanitarian relief – and the motive usually given much emphasis by donor governments and other donor institutions – is to help the affected populations. The Principles and Good Practice of Humanitarian Donorship endorsed by major international donor governments in Stockholm in 2003, for example, stated that 'The objectives of humanitarian action are to save lives, alleviate suffering, and maintain human dignity during and in the aftermath of man-made crises and natural disasters, as well as to prevent and strengthen preparedness for the occurrence of such situations' (International Meeting on Good Humanitarian Donorship 2003).

This statement of objectives (and the many similar statements made by donors) may be regarded as a statement of the *nominal* policy of humanitarian aid programs. But in practice, *real* policy is influenced by other important considerations as well. Indeed, the mix of factors that influences donor policy, including decisions as to when and how to provide humanitarian aid, is complex. As a report prepared by the Tsunami Evaluation Coalition (TEC) noted, aid agencies are generally accountable to three main groups of stakeholders (Cosgrave 2007: 23):

- The donor public, the media and taxpayers (which involves 'upward' accountability)
- Other agencies or the common standards agreed by agencies ('lateral' accountability)
- The affected populations ('downward' accountability).

And it might be added that for many official bilateral agencies in donor countries (which are major sources of international funding), issues of upward accountability invariably involve also reporting to ministers, parliaments, and other powerful public sector agencies who have interests in the determination of international aid policy.

Of these three main stakeholder groups, the *realpolitik* of the situation is that it is the first and the third groups which tend to be seen as being the most important within significant policy-making circles. And indeed it is the first group which is generally given high priority, as Bill Clinton, in his role as UN Secretary-General's Special Envoy for Tsunami Recovery observed (Clinton 2006a: 4): 'Typically, demands for accountability come loudest from donors – private and institutional – and implementing agencies are more likely to focus on this kind of upward accountability. Too often, the less organized voices of the survivors are not heard, and this equally vital downward accountability is given second-priority at best.'

It is therefore useful to think of humanitarian aid policy as often having the Janus-like quality of being obliged to look in two directions at once – towards the needs of affected populations ('downwards') and simultaneously towards the wishes of the donors ('upwards').[7] Commenting on the pressures on different actors involved in the supply of aid following the tsunami, the TEC survey (Cosgrave 2007: 11) observed that 'huge amounts of [aid] funding encouraged a virtual obsession with "upward" accountability to donors, the media, and the public in donor countries. This discouraged accountability to disaster-affected populations and "lateral" accountability to other agencies and the governments of affected countries.'

Nominal policy pronouncements make much of the needs of affected populations following disasters. However in practice, real policy often strongly reflects the preferences of ministers, parliaments and the media in donor countries (Drury et al. 2005).

Coordination

Apart from these issues of broad policy, important practical aspects of the aid effort concern the delivery of aid. An extremely challenging problem following the Asian tsunami, right from the start, was the coordination of aid work in the field.

It is in the nature of responses to megadisasters in developing countries that the coordination of responses is likely to be difficult. On one hand, the international community usually wishes to play a significant role, offering assistance with various degrees of enthusiasm reflecting, amongst other things, policy considerations in donor countries. On the other hand, recipient governments and local institutions will be closely involved as well, working to provide assistance through their own national channels.

Recipient governments and local institutions will not always be able to set aside the resources which international agencies expect to be available. Further, discrepancies between international offers of aid and the capacity to absorb the aid are sometimes exacerbated by the marked differences in capacity between international donor organizations and national agencies within recipient countries. It was to be expected, therefore, that many issues of coordination would complicate the delivery of tsunami aid.

One main challenge was how to coordinate the activities of international donors, on one hand, and numerous national relief agencies, on the other. There were problems of coordination both within each group, and between these two rather different types of agencies. As the discussion in the country studies below illustrates, the arrangements made for coordination varied from country to country depending on the local situation. Issues of coordinating the activities of foreign agencies were particularly complicated in countries such as Indonesia and Sri Lanka where foreign programs were relatively large and where many national and international NGOs (INGOs) quickly established relief programs (Scheper et al. 2006: 30):

> During the first two months, an estimated 300 INGOs arrived in Aceh to assist in the relief effort. As most of these agencies lacked local experience and facilities, they spent the first three months providing relief supplies, conducting need assessments and building their own staff and infrastructural capacity, often by attracting the best and the brightest staff from local organisations. The lack of contextual knowledge limited their ability to assess local capacities. Dozens left after the first few months, having completed their work or lacking institutional resources to match the scale of recovery operations.

In Indonesia, the establishment of a new body with considerable authority, the *Badan Rekonstruksi dan Rehabilitasi* (Agency for the Rehabilitation and Reconstruction of Aceh and Nias, or BRR), played a major role in helping improve overall coordination of the relief and reconstruction effort. Nevertheless, the influx of foreign emergency specialists and other consultants into the disaster zones certainly imposed strains on local administrative systems. Commenting on the phenomenon, UN Special Envoy Bill Clinton (Clinton 2006a: 6) noted that problems in delivering aid could sometimes be 'compounded by a post-disaster influx of new assistance providers who have little knowledge of the context in which they are operating, including structures of inequality, chronic poverty, and vulnerability.'

Many of the newcomers were experienced in the management of emergency assistance in the field, but some were not. There was inevitably an element of excessive enthusiasm on some occasions as relatively inexperienced relief workers turned up in droves.

   Another feature of the post-disaster coordination environment was the establishment, often (probably usually) without any consultation with local authorities in the region, of a large number of tsunami-related websites. Many of these were established as parts of the existing websites of large development or humanitarian agencies (such as the United Nations, IFRC, World Bank, and so on). But many others were established in an *ad hoc* way by NGOs or enthusiasts who hoped that the use of new web-based technology would be helpful in responding to the disaster.

   This phenomenon is of some interest. The Asian tsunami appears to be the first megadisaster in a developing country which has prompted an intense activity in the electronic website world. Hovanesian and Cox (2007: 2–3) provided a summary of some of the main challenges of applying ICTs (information and communication technologies) in the disaster environment following the tsunami:

> The most important differentiating factor of an implementation of ICT solutions in post-disaster situations in comparison with those in a normal environment is the timing of the deployment; solutions in post-disaster situations have to be deployed in an extremely short period of time. . . . the environment can grow increasingly more difficult as *ad hoc* structures and overseeing entities are created for implementing and coordinating the reconstruction, while workflow processes are adapted to the situation as the reconstruction is progressing. . . . Across the tsunami-affected countries, over a thousand donor agencies and implementing partners have been participating in online data sharing, directly providing up-to-date information on the progress of their reconstruction works. In the absence of information sharing during the initial rehabilitation phase, the sheer number of organizations involved threatened to overwhelm the capacity of the government to absorb such a large volume of information on aid.

No evaluation of the family of tsunami-related websites appears to have been carried out. But several aspects of the activity are notable. One is that it seems that there was a problem of sustainability because quite a few of the websites were not well maintained. Within six months or so of the tsunami disaster, perhaps one-third of the sites appeared to have become neglected. Further, as time went on, even some of the main websites supported by the major international organizations began to develop problems. For example, by mid-2009 it appeared that the website established by the UN to support the work of Bill Clinton as Special Envoy for Tsunami Relief had been taken over by a commercial firm for sales distribution purposes. Others were difficult to access or had been replaced by alternative websites (sometimes containing the same data as the original sites, sometimes not). On the other hand, some of the websites, especially those established by some of the larger international donor agencies and international NGOs, provided a great deal of information about the tsunami relief effort. While many of the items carried on these websites were public relations materials, many other items were substantial reports published by international and national agencies and by NGOs.

It should also be noted that some of the websites were specifically established for coordination purposes (Hovanesian and Cox 2007). The UN-supported RAND (Recovery Aceh-Nias Database), for example, was established to facilitate the improved reporting of expenditure by donor agencies on tsunami-related activities.[8] This RAND database, in turn, supported a more broadly based 'Tracking Tsunami Resources and Results' database which provided data from a number of tsunami-affected countries.[9] In addition, a very large number of documents relating to the tsunami aid effort have been made available on the web. The major *A Ripple in Development?* evaluation study of links between relief, rehabilitation and development (LRRD) supported by SIDA (Brusset et al. 2009a) was underpinned by the preparation of an extensive annotated bibliography of which over 92 per cent of the documents cited were recorded as having web links (Cosgrave et al. 2009: 14). Presumably the flow of this remarkable amount of information contributed to better overall coordination because of the relative ease of access to reports and data about activities that different donors were concentrating on.

A third feature of the numerous coordination issues across the region was the competition, and indeed open friction, sometimes evident between different parts of the aid industry. One example is that of unexpected tensions between organizations supporting foreign doctors and nurses working in the field. Shortly after the relief effort had begun in Indonesia, the *New York Times* carried a story (Perlez 2005) highlighting the work done by physicians working in emergency conditions in Banda Aceh. The report was sharply criticized by the Center for Nursing Advocacy (2005), a US organization representing nurses. The Center argued that the story demonstrated 'physician-centric bias' because:

> the article ignored the work of nurses, and gave readers the impression that only physicians were providing care of any significance in Aceh province, and by implication, elsewhere in the tsunami disaster zone. . . . the Perlez piece failed to note or explain the absence of local health workers or nurses generally in Aceh. It simply focused on the exploits of foreign physicians as if it were self-evident that only they mattered.

A frank exchange of views quickly followed. One of the physicians in the Banda Aceh team issued a statement defending the *New York Times* story as accurate. The Center for Nursing Advocacy, in turn, continued to insist that the whole affair illustrated the way that contributions by nurses were undervalued. This particular exchange between doctors and nurses is perhaps not important in itself. However the incident serves to illustrate the sorts of frictions which bubbled to the surface when teams of emergency workers were attempting to deliver aid in the field under difficult circumstances.

Finance

Issues of financial management also presented difficult challenges on the supply side of aid delivery. As noted earlier, in overall terms the tsunami aid effort was one of the largest single aid efforts ever supported by the international community. But to view the aid effort in this way immediately gives rise to the question of whether it is best to consider the activity as one project – or as many projects. Funds were provided in many different ways, from national and international sources and through public and private channels. These funds were in turn spent in many different ways in accordance with many different administrative requirements.

The advantages and disadvantages of arrangements of this kind are discussed in more detail in the country chapters below. However in many cases, the management of the finances associated with project activities posed three challenges: the establishment of effective financial controls including checks against corruption; avoiding unreasonable delays in spending; and ensuring that arrangements for the tracking of expenditure and transparent accountability were satisfactory.

From the beginning of the tsunami aid effort, both international and national agencies had considerable concerns about the need for reliable financial control systems. These concerns were heightened by the focus on risks of corruption in international aid programs in recent years as well as the reputation of Indonesia as a corruption-prone country. The Australian National Audit Office, for example, referred to these issues in a report prepared in 2006 on the Australian aid program established to assist Indonesia immediately after the tsunami (ANAO 2006: 66):

> Fraud and corruption are recognized risks in many countries in which AusAID works. This is the case in Indonesia, where corruption is reported to be a widespread problem. . . . International development banks also report that Indonesia's procurement system is inherently weak. Problems include:
>
> - collusion between bidders;
> - supply of poor quality materials and equipment, insufficient quantities or substitution of materials (eg., wood for steel); and
> - requests for unjustified contract amendments.

Numerous other donors had similar concerns about programs in Indonesia and elsewhere. In response, the governments of the main tsunami-affected countries quickly acknowledged the need to put adequate safeguards in place. Numerous meetings were held with donor agencies to discuss arrangements. In Indonesia, for example, an International Conference on Promoting Financial Accountability in Managing Funds Related to Tsunami, Conflict and Other Disasters was held in April 2005 at which Indonesian President Susilo Bambang Yudhoyono explained (ANAO 2006: 67):

> I have declared my commitment in fighting against corruption as a national movement in December 2004. We will press on as hard as we can in the fight against corruption. We have registered encouraging progress in dealing with corruption in this country. We are strongly determined and committed to ensure that there will be no corrupt practices in the spending of these rehabilitation and reconstruction funds.

As a result of these concerns of the international donor community, a notable feature of the overall tsunami assistance effort across the region was a focus on measures to minimize opportunities for corruption.

But there are trade-offs to be made in imposing stricter financial controls. One disadvantage of stricter controls was that approvals to spend funds were sometimes delayed. These delays, in turn, slowed the delivery of aid in some programs. Donors sometimes justified the delays in the delivery of aid by emphasizing the need for controls over the quality of assistance. But stakeholders in the program – both contractors supplying aid in the field and recipients of the aid – were nevertheless disappointed when activities took longer to complete than expected.

The overall tracking of expenditures, and transparent accountability, were other issues which financial managers needed to address. The indications from the very large number of individual program reports that executing agencies have made publicly available are that these things were generally managed well at the individual activity level. What has been much more difficult to obtain is reliable aggregate data for the tsunami assistance effort. These issues are discussed in more detail later in this study. Chapter 3 shows that there are matters concerning the tracking of expenditures and the transparency of accounting which the donor community might usefully address.

Response Stages

In all of the main tsunami-affected countries, the response to the disaster passed through three stages – relief, rehabilitation, and reconstruction (Figure 2.1). Although the division between the stages is not clear-cut, it is useful to take note of the differences between them. For one thing, the priorities that needed to be addressed and the role of different actors changed as time went on. Another reason for distinguishing between the stages is that the impact of the overall assistance program on local economies varied greatly over time. Many communities devastated by the tsunami experienced, first, a collapse of almost all local economic activity and a period of heavy dependence on emergency assistance in the period following the tsunami (De Silva and Yamao 2007). Later, as large-scale rehabilitation and reconstruction programs got underway, there was evidence of local Dutch Disease effects (discussed below) as the prices of local non-tradable goods (such as housing and some types of labour) rose markedly.

There is also another stage that needs to be considered. The transitional period of a return back to longer-term stability for local communities which occurs after assistance activities have largely been completed has so far received little attention in discussions about the response to the tsunami (Rice 2007). But as the main assistance programs come to an end, local demand for many goods and services tends to fall away. When this happens, regional policy makers are faced with the challenge of finding ways to assist local economies adjust to a new, post-assistance, economic environment. Discussing the transition to the new environment, the World Bank (2009) observed that:

> Growth in Aceh's non-oil and gas economy declined sharply in 2008 as the reconstruction effort winds down. . . . As many reconstruction actors (NGOs, GoI) wind down or significantly scale down their operations in the province, sectors linked to the reconstruction effort that had led growth in Aceh since 2005 registered low or negative growth.

The overall result of these various changes was particularly marked in Aceh where the World Bank noted that 'Aceh's economy has suffered tremendous shocks over the past few years.'

Cross-cutting Issues

International donors and national agencies agreed that a range of cross-cutting issues needed to be addressed in the delivery of the post-tsunami aid program.[10] Of the wide range of cross-cutting issues which, in principle, might have been seen as needing attention, the main ones given priority in the post-tsunami assistance programs included peace-keeping issues, gender, attention to children and aged persons, community participation, environmental concerns, and the sustainability of the aid activities.

The incorporation of these cross-cutting issues into post-tsunami assistance programs complicated the process of delivering aid. Indeed

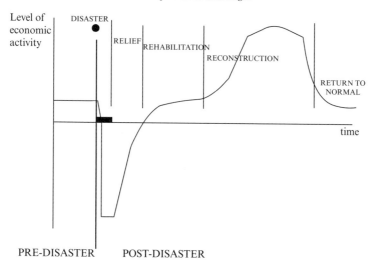

Figure 2.1   Stages of response following a disaster

requirements on the part of some international agencies that attention to particular cross-cutting issues be built into the project that they were supporting amounted, in effect, to a form of conditionality. And requirements of this kind inevitably touched, to some extent, on the question of to what extent the quality of aid was important rather than the quantity or the speed of delivery.

It is inevitable, for example, that the incorporation of cross-cutting issues into program designs takes time and requires additional care. Often specialist staff need to be recruited to provide sectoral advice. Projects may need to be significantly changed to ensure that the key cross-cutting issues receive appropriate attention. This is no bad thing, of course. Certainly poorly designed projects should not be allowed to go ahead. But in practice an unavoidable consequence of adopting this approach was that projects were somewhat delayed.

A number of European donors, especially, were concerned that there should be a strong focus on peace-keeping and post-conflict programs.[11] These programs were seen as important, especially, in Aceh and Sri Lanka, where difficult and prolonged periods of regional civil conflict had taken a heavy toll in the years preceding the tsunami (He and Reid 2004; Aspinall 2007). European peace-keeping negotiators had been actively promoting discussions between protagonists in the period before the tsunami. They took the view that in the terrible wake of the tsunami it was possible that perhaps a window of opportunity might open up to promote peace (Brusset 2009a: 37–40). They hoped that there might be an increased desire amongst surviving communities to set aside differences and concentrate on building peace in the post-tsunami environment.[12] In the event, in both Aceh and Sri Lanka there was an impetus towards peace in the period following the tsunami. In Aceh, negotiations were successful and a peace agreement was reached. In Sri Lanka, the truce between protagonists was temporary because after a period of peace, fighting between forces of the Government of Sri Lanka and the separatist Tamil Tigers resumed.

Another cross-cutting issue to which many international agencies gave priority was the impact of tsunami recovery activities on women. A survey by the Tsunami Evaluation Coalition around one year after the tsunami recorded that the recovery and reconstruction program appeared to have various negative effects on women. Scheper et al. (2006: 41) listed the following as key issues:

- Inflexibility in the humanitarian system which failed to make exceptions for the specific situations of affected women, particularly female-headed households
- Insufficient protection in the IDP (internally displaced persons) camps which made them unsafe for women and girls
- Insufficient international legal assistance with respect to land tenure, inheritance and guardianship disputes, often complicated by traditional Shari'a law interpretations
- Loss of access to sustainable livelihoods and limited access to economic recovery programs which appeared to have been particularly pronounced for women
- Limited access to information because information channels had tended to remain male-dominated, and
- Limited opportunities, capacity and leadership amongst women's grassroots and advocacy organizations which, in turn, hindered their ability to influence mainstream relief and reconstruction activities.

Nowak and Caulfield (2008) survey the literature on gender issues and disasters in considerable detail and also report on field surveys which they undertook in India and Indonesia following the Asian tsunami. They emphasize that 'women and men experience, perceive, and respond to disasters in different ways'. One main finding from literature surveys which they note is that 'Women and children are disproportionately affected by disasters . . . Despite gender and gender relations being important organizing principles in social arrangements and structures, humanitarian organizations frequently ignore gender-specific issues in disaster management' (2008: 6).

They also report that various authors are critical of the processes of the delivery of humanitarian aid which create a situation where 'disaster management is often a male-dominated, top-down process, which employs an authoritarian style' (Nowak and Caulfield, 2008: 12). One of their main conclusions (ibid.) is that 'the culture and attitudes of humanitarian agencies need to change in order to achieve gender equity in relief programmes'. Other field surveys of problems faced by women after the tsunami (Oey-Gardiner 2005; Fulu 2007; IDLO and UNDP 2007) also suggest that women often faced particular problems (legal restrictions on land rights and inheritance, and domestic violence) to which aid agencies tended to give low priority.

In addition, there were sometimes differences of views about environmental priorities between the agencies who were providing aid and the recipient communities. In Aceh, for example, some international environmentalist groups were concerned that housing projects would encourage illegal logging both in the province of Aceh and in the nearby province of North Sumatra.[13] UNEP urged that more attention be given to environmental issues in the plans prepared for reconstruction in Aceh after the tsunami (UNEP 2007). But survivors of the tsunami living in temporary accommodation were less concerned about the problems caused by illegal logging because they were eager to see housing projects completed as fast as possible. They took the view, in any case, that illegal logging had long been a problem in the area and that it was unreasonable for environmentally inclined INGOs to use the leverage that aid programs provided to delay them access to promised housing.

The issue of long-term sustainability of activities supported by assistance programs was also a controversial issue. The major *A Ripple in Development?* LRRD evaluation report prepared with the support of SIDA and released in early 2009 discussed this matter in considerable detail (Brusset et al. 2009a). The promotion of the broad sustainability of activities supported by humanitarian assistance programs is not an issue which the international aid community has learnt to deal with effectively. It is true that the international aid community has given much attention to challenges of sustainability in the context of environmental issues. However, the global aid industry has found it much harder to ensure that international aid activities, including humanitarian aid activities, are sustainable in the broad sense of remaining viable once donor support stops.

When responding to megadisasters such as the Asian tsunami, the international donor community tends to focus on priorities such as supplying consumable items needed for immediate use or large-scale housing or infrastructure projects. While the provision of items of this kind is extremely helpful in responding to priorities in the wake of a disaster, it is not always the case that the broader issues of long-term sustainability receive attention within these types of programs. In fact, even five years after the tsunami it is not clear how sustainable many of the projects supported by the large tsunami assistance program might be.

The long-term effectiveness of many of the larger projects will not become clear, perhaps, until ten years after the tsunami disaster. And by then, the donor community will have left. It will be up to the local communities themselves in the tsunami-affected countries to tackle the difficult issues of long-term sustainability of development in the wake of the disaster. In the meantime, project reports prepared by units such as the World Bank-supported Multilateral Donor Fund, which was established to help promote development in Aceh, suggest that the sustainability of reconstruction investments is likely to be a problem (Multi Donor Fund 2008).

Trade-offs in Delivery: Speed versus Quality

The issues of the physical delivery of assistance, financial management and attention to cross-cutting issues discussed above are reflected in the dilemma that most assistance agencies faced when providing aid following the tsunami – whether to supply aid quickly, or whether to spend more time ensuring that the quality of aid, however measured, was of a high standard.

There are arguments for each approach. Those who emphasized the need for speed pointed to the acute needs that local communities had in the wake of the disaster. Following the tsunami in Asia, there was widespread damage and destruction of many assets (infrastructure, buildings, boats, crops). Because local economies collapsed, virtually all of the usual daily income-earning opportunities disappeared as well. Many thousands of tsunami survivors not only lost family members but were left destitute. A further reason for supplying assistance quickly was that as time passed, it became clear that the strong preference of the consumers of the aid programs – the tsunami survivors – was that assistance be provided more quickly.

However many of the agencies supplying aid – and especially international agencies – were more cautious. They pointed to the problems which arise when inappropriate types of aid are provided, of the risks of financial mismanagement, and of the need to ensure that assistance programs were properly designed. They also noted that unless the detailed procurement and audit processes set down by their headquarter agencies were complied with, embarrassing criticisms of their aid programs were likely to appear in the media in donor countries. It was partly because of concerns of this kind that a 'build back better' approach which emphasized quality rather than speed was adopted by many aid providers in the communities devastated by the Asian tsunami.

But there was another, broader reason why some members of the international aid community urged that a 'build back better' approach be followed: a concern that in the rush (as some saw it) to deliver humanitarian assistance quickly, longer-term development issues would tend to be overlooked. This view was clearly represented, for example, in *A Ripple in Development*, the report on LRRD issues released in 2009. *A Ripple in Development* argued (Brusset et al. 2009b: 7) that humanitarian aid should

> not be applied just towards immediate recovery, but towards making the affected societies socio-economically stronger, more resilient to future risks. Return to the pre-tsunami status quo was not, therefore, a benchmark of success, since it did little to overcome development issues that made the region so vulnerable in the first place.

This approach, it needs to be noted, sets a high bar in terms of standards for the delivery of tsunami aid. It assumes (or at least hopes) that donors will take a long-term point of view, that a complex range of cross-cutting issues will be addressed, and that somehow the weak state and non-state institutions which support government and governance in the tsunami-affected countries will be able to provide good services once aid donors leave the scene. The approach also implicitly reflected a longer-term time horizon than tsunami-affected communities themselves often appeared to prefer.

DEMAND SIDE ISSUES

It is appropriate for the purposes of this study to consider the recipients of tsunami aid as the consumers of the assistance. But it should be borne in mind that, as noted above, international aid programs often have a Janus-like quality of being designed to respond to the interests of stakeholders in both aid-recipient countries and in donor nations. Depending on the political-economy framework within which the overall aid effort is placed, the final consumers of tsunami aid also included the taxpayers who paid for the provision of the goods and services supplied by the assistance programs – that is, taxpayers in both donor countries and in the countries affected by the tsunami.

However, since it is the outcome of the action in the field which is generally regarded as the best single measure of effectiveness of the aid effort, the views of recipients cast important light on how the overall effort should be evaluated. There is a very extensive literature on the views of people in communities affected by the tsunami.[14] It is clear that the speed of response was one of the most important aspects of the aid program from the point of view of recipients. And as noted above, agencies providing assistance faced something of a dilemma in trying to respond, on one hand, to the wishes of aid recipients but on the other hand, meeting the quality standards implied in the 'build back better' motto.

But speed was not the only thing that was important for aid-recipient communities. Depending on who was consulted, issues such as the supply of housing and the lack of livelihood opportunities were noted as matters which aid recipients were concerned about. A survey conducted by the Fritz Institute in October 2005, nine months after the tsunami, provided an unusual insight into what local communities in the tsunami-affected areas thought of the assistance that they had received (Fritz Institute 2005). Their views on the effectiveness of the support provided were quite mixed. In terms of the immediate response to the disaster, local communities generally reported that the fastest assistance was from local organizations (Table 2.2). In the medium term, issues of shelter and severe loss of income were rated of high importance (Box 2.2). However, as the country surveys in later chapter show, the degree of overall satisfaction in the aid-recipient communities varied considerably depending on local circumstances and how the delivery of assistance proceeded over time.

AID EFFECTIVENESS

It is not really possible to review the overall Asian tsunami aid effort without, first, considering the question: how can we decide whether the large assistance program was successful or not? Alternatively: what criteria should be used to reach a judgement as to whether the tsunami aid effort was effective?

To ask these questions is not to suggest that the provision of large scale humanitarian assistance following the Asian tsunami was not worthwhile. Rather, these issues need to be discussed so that the goals of the wide variety of actors involved in the relief effort can be considered and so that some criteria for judging the success of the aid effort can be suggested. Further, the issue of the effectiveness of the tsunami aid program can hardly be avoided. In recent years, the international donor community has given a great deal of emphasis to the issue of effectiveness. In numerous international meetings around the world, donors have constantly emphasized the need to define and measure the effectiveness of aid programs. Dozens of reports have been commissioned on the subject, and hundreds of studies have been published on various aspects of aid effectiveness.

Difficult, therefore, though it is to evaluate the overall effectiveness of a major aid program encompassing the activities of a very large number of actors across a number of countries, some effort to do so is needed.

Former US President Bill Clinton, in his role as UN Special Envoy for Tsunami Recovery, speaking in Washington DC in 2006, drew attention to the criteria that would form the basis for a review of NGO operations in tsunami-affected areas (Clinton 2006b: 19):

- Accountability to the beneficiaries of assistance
- Enhanced local capacity of government institutions and the NGO community in affected countries
- Ensuring high standards of professionalism in the field
- Communication and coordination among the NGO community
- Incorporating human rights principles into recovery operations.

This useful list points to various key issues which many observers argue should be used as benchmarks to evaluate the performance not only of NGOs, but of all agencies that delivered assistance during the 2004 tsunami aid program.

In addition, given the scope of the tsunami assistance effort, other aspects of the effectiveness of activities need to be considered. The usual preferred approach in trying to evaluate the effectiveness of aid is to, first, define objectives, then establish measurable performance indicators, and finally evaluate the aid activity against the agreed indicators. But this type of approach is rarely followed in the provision of humanitarian assistance following a major disaster. Rather, as noted earlier, in the initial stages the urgent focus tends to be on getting the job done. And the culture of concentrating strongly on the logistics of aid delivery, sometimes with little concern for costs, is reinforced by the involvement of military, police, and civil disaster personnel in the aid operations in the field. And once the longer-term aid effort is underway, it is difficult to coordinate program-wide approaches to issues of effectiveness.

It is, therefore, often not easy to arrive at firm judgements about the effectiveness of humanitarian aid for three reasons:

- Different actors involved in the provision of assistance may have different objectives; moreover, these objectives are not always clear.
- Measurable performance indicators are rarely established, and data collection against agreed indicators is often hard to evaluate.
- Judgements about effectiveness are often provided by donor and other assistance agencies themselves; these tend to be subjective and may be difficult to verify.

Table 2.2 Recall about service providers by affected families (first 48 hours)

	Rescue %	Burial %	Food %	Water %	Clothes %	Shelter %	Medical care %	Counselling %
Indonesia (N = 500, in the five most affected areas)[b]								
Private individual	91	88	88	93	86	87	74	78
Government	5	2	6	4	4	8	10	3
International NGO	1	1	1	1	1	1	3	4
Local NGO	2	2	2	1	2	1	1	1
Religious orgns.	1	7	2	1	7	2	13	1
Corporate sector	0	0	0	0	0	0	0	0
Total[a]	100	100	100	100	100	100	100	100
Sri Lanka (N = 800, from 98 villages)[b]								
Private individual	72	60	52	48	57	24	11	30
Government	8	11	4	9	3	17	34	6
International NGO	6	5	11	14	11	15	26	22
Local NGO	8	10	10	9	8	12	13	13
Religious orgns.	1	8	16	15	15	24	9	22
Corporate sector	4	3	5	4	3	5	4	3
Not aware	1	4	1	1	2	3	4	4
Total[a]	100	100	100	100	100	100	100	100

India (N = 1000, from 93 villages)[b]

Private individual	4	3	11	8	16	8	5	5
Government	23	40	24	40	8	32	57	26
Local village community	47	24	26	18	20	20	1	7
International NGO	0	0	2	1	5	3	12	6
Local NGO	3	2	11	10	15	9	7	19
Religious orgns.	5	5	17	12	9	11	5	15
Corporate sector	0	1	9	10	10	5	3	3
Not aware	18	25	2	2	16	12	11	20
Total[a]	100	100	100	100	100	100	100	100

Notes:
(a) Not all columns add precisely to 100% due to sampling procedures and rounding errors. For details of methodology, see the Fritz Institute report.
(b) N = number of respondents.

Source: Fritz Institute (2005).

BOX 2.2   AID DELIVERY AS SEEN BY TSUNAMI-AFFECTED COMMUNITIES

1. Aid provided during the first 48 hours was overwhelmingly local; citizens played a critical role.
In the recollections of the tsunami-affected people, the aid provided during the first 48 hours was mostly from private individuals or the local community. In Indonesia, 91 per cent of the rescue services were provided by local individuals.

2. Satisfaction with the services provided during the first 48 hours varied widely; at 60 days, satisfaction levels across countries were more similar.
There was wide variation across countries in satisfaction with the immediate rescue and relief services provided. Overall, beneficiaries in India were most satisfied with the services provided in the first 48 hours. Their counterparts in Indonesia were the least satisfied.

3. Nine months after the tsunami, life was far from normal; there had been sharp decreases in household income in all affected areas.
Across the three countries, the proportion of losses in income was greatest in Indonesia where an astounding 83 per cent lost more than 50 per cent of their income. In Sri Lanka and India, 59 per cent and 47 per cent, respectively, of those surveyed reported more than a 50 per cent drop in income.

4. Livelihood restoration programs did not get high satisfaction scores.
In all three countries, multiple programs to restore livelihoods were implemented. Overall, these programs were not well rated by beneficiaries.

5. Permanent shelter was the most significant continuing challenge.
The issue of permanent shelter continued to be mired in controversy over a considerable period. Safety and land were key issues. The great majority of affected families were still living in camps or temporary shelters nine months after the disaster. This hampered a return to normal lives and kept the disaster in the forefront of the minds of those affected.

6. Efforts to restore shelter were recognized.
Beneficiaries recognized that efforts were being made to restore shelter. Asked about the services supplied, beneficiaries expressed the greatest satisfaction with international NGOs.

7. Psychosocial support, not widely provided, was seen as a critical service.
Many aid providers supplied psychosocial support including counselling. Services provided by international NGOs tended to be rated the most highly.

8. Excellence in aid delivery was recognized.
In Indonesia, international NGOs were seen as the best aid providers. In Sri Lanka, several local NGOs were rated highly. In India, the central and state governments were seen as responsive, organized, and visible.

Source: Adapted from Fritz Institute report (2005).

Because of the nature of these difficulties it is perhaps useful to foreshadow here that even after surveying the information provided in the country chapters below, as well as the wealth of detailed material provided in other reports about the delivery of Asian tsunami aid, it will be difficult to draw specific conclusions about the overall effectiveness of the tsunami aid program. For one thing, many thousands of specific activities and projects were implemented by a very large number of individual agencies across a number of countries. Needless to say, some activities were widely acknowledged to be very effective while others ran into problems. For another thing, to some extent beauty is in the eye of the beholder. In the absence of clear criteria, and given that much of the available data is hard to sift through, different observers are likely to make different judgements.

Rather, therefore, than aiming to reach specific conclusions, it may be helpful to bear a checklist of questions in mind:

- *Delivery of assistance* Was physical aid (food, clothing, medical help, housing, livelihood assets, and in the longer-term, infrastructure) delivered in a timely and satisfactory manner?
- *Cross-cutting issues* Was appropriate attention paid to cross-cutting issues (such as peace-keeping matters, gender and age, environment, and social participation) agreed as needing priority?
- *Finance* Was the promised aid committed and disbursed in a timely, transparent way? Were financial controls satisfactory?

- *Coordination and administration*   Was the overall delivery of aid well coordinated? Was there good agreement between agencies providing assistance about the arrangements for the delivery of aid? Were the systems established to encourage regular reporting effective?
- *Non-humanitarian goals*   Were the non-humanitarian goals of actors involved in the tsunami assistance program achieved?
- *Sustainability*   Did the assistance provided contribute to the long-term sustainability of social life and economic livelihoods in the tsunami-affected communities?
- *Community satisfaction*   What did the people living within the tsunami-affected communities think about the aid programs? Were recipients of assistance generally satisfied with the results of the programs?

There are, of course, many other aspects of effectiveness which might be considered as well. However views about the answers to these questions will certainly assist in reaching a judgement about the broad effectiveness of the overall tsunami assistance program. We return to consider these issues in Chapter 7.

NOTES

1. For information on steps taken by individual countries in Asia, see the PreventionWeb website, supported by the UN ISDR at: http://www.preventionweb.net/english/countries/asia/, accessed on 15 August 2009.
2. Additional information about recent developments at the international level is at the ISDR website (2009c). The ISDR 2009 Global Assessment Report on Disaster Risk Reduction (2009a) also provides an extensive discussion of the issues. In addition, the annual World Disaster Reports issued by the IFRC contain valuable reports on disaster risk reduction policy; see, for example, IFRC 2009.
3. For a recent discussion of the Hyogo Framework of Action and of progress made in implementing the framework, see ISDR (2009a: Chapter 5).
4. In Indonesia, for example, a new Disaster Management Law was approved in 2007 which was seen as creating several 'fundamental shifts of paradigm' (Triutomo 2008: 4).
5. The ADB has discussed the establishment of a structure of this kind (Marianti 2007: 19). See also Freeman et al. (2003).
6. See the extensive discussion of difficulties of this kind in implementing policy in Indonesia in Triutomo (2008).
7. The Roman god Janus was usually depicted as having two faces looking in opposite directions. He was the god of gates, doors and beginnings and endings, and thus looked in each way at once.
8. The RAN database is at: http://rand.brr.go.id/RAND/, accessed 16 September 2009.
9. The regional Tracking Tsunami Resources and Results website is at http://tsunamitracking.org/undprcb/index.jsp?sid=1&id=1&pid=1, accessed 16 September 2009.
10. Cross-cutting issues are matters seen as affecting the effectiveness of aid across many

activities and which should therefore be mainstreamed into the delivery of assistance whenever possible.

11. There is a very substantial literature on these issues. For references to articles and reports on such issues as civil war, military activities, reconciliation, safety, and relations with dissident groups in the tsunami-affected countries, see Cosgrave et al. (2009).

12. A useful summary of the background to attempts to broker peace in Aceh in the period before the tsunami is in a special edition of *Asian Ethnicity* published in October 2004. See, especially, the survey of the issues by He and Reid (2004).

13. Illegal logging is common in Indonesia. Tacconi (2007) discusses the issues in detail. For a detailed survey of illegal logging in North Sumatra in the regions close to Aceh, see McCarthy (2007).

14. See the numerous references in Cosgrave et al. (2009) indexed under the headings of community, information, and local.

REFERENCES

ANAO (Australian Government, Australian National Audit Office) (2006), *Arrangements to Manage and Account for Aid Funds Provided under the Australia–Indonesia Partnership for Reconstruction and Development*, Report no. 50 2005–06, Canberra: Australian National Audit Office.

Aspinall, Edward (2007), *Peace without Justice? The Helsinki Peace Process in Aceh*, Geneva: Centre for Humanitarian Dialogue.

AusAID (2009), 'Investing in a safer future: a disaster risk reduction policy for the Australian Aid Program', Canberra: AusAID, http://www.ausaid.gov.au/ publications, accessed 18 August 2009.

Brusset, Emery, M. Bhatt, K. Bjornestad, J. Cosgrave, A. Davies, Y. Deshmukh, J. Haleem, S. Hidalgo, Y. Immajati, R. Jayasundere, A. Mattsson, N. Muhaimin, R. Polastro and T. Wu (2009a), *A Ripple in Development?: Long Term Perspectives on the Response to the Indian Ocean Tsunami 2004*, Stockholm: SIDA, http://www.sida.se/publications, accessed 20 August 2009.

Brusset, Emery, M. Bhatt, K. Bjornestad, J. Cosgrave, A. Davies, Y. Deshmukh, A. Ferf, J. Haleem, S. Hidalgo, Y. Immajati, R. Jayasundere, A. Mattsson, N. Muhaimin, A. Pain, R. Polastro and T. Wu (2009b), *Summary Report: A Ripple in Development? Long Term Perspectives on the Response to the Indian Ocean Tsunami 2004*, Stockholm: SIDA, http://www.sida.se/publications, accessed 20 August 2009.

Center for Nursing Advocacy (2005), 'Physician, nurse and center debate merits of New York Times Banda Aceh story', http://www.nursingadvocacy.org/ news/2005jan/20_aceh.html, accessed 10 August 2009.

Clinton, William J. (2006a), 'Key propositions for building back better', United Nations, http://ochaonline.un.org/OchaLinkClick.aspx?link=ocha&docid=100 5912, accessed on 23 August 2009.

Clinton, William J. (2006b), 'Finding our collective voice – President Clinton April 12, 2006', transcript of speech, http://www.kaisernetwork.org/health_ cast/uploaded_files/041206_interaction_clinton_transcript.pdf, accessed 15 September 2009.

Cosgrave, John (2007), *Synthesis Report: Expanded Summary. Joint Evaluation of the International Response to the Indian Ocean Tsunami*, London: Tsunami

38 *The Asian tsunami*

Evaluation Coalition, http://www.alnap.org/pool/files/Syn_Report_Sum.pdf, accessed 15 September 2009.

Cosgrave, John, E. Brusset, M. Bhatt, L. Fernandez, Y. Deshmukh, Y. Immajati, R. Jayasundere, A. Mattsson, N. Muhaimin and R. Polastro (2009), *A Ripple in Development? Document Review*, Annotated Bibliography prepared for the Joint Follow-up Evaluation of the Links between Relief, Rehabilitation and Development (LRRD) in Responses to the Indian Ocean Tsunami, Stockholm: SIDA, http://www.sida.se/publications, accessed 22 August 2009.

De Silva, D.A.M. and M.Yamao (2007), 'Effects of the tsunami on fisheries and coastal livelihood: a case study of tsunami-ravaged southern Sri Lanka', *Disasters*, **31** (4), 386–404.

Drury, A. Cooper, R.S. Olsen and D.A.Van Belle (2005), 'The politics of humanitarian aid: US foreign disaster assistance, 1964–1995', *Journal of Politics*, **67** (2), 454–73.

Freeman, Paul K., L.A. Martin, J. Linnerooth-Bayer, R. Mechler, G. Pflug, and K. Warner (2003), *Disaster Risk Management: National Systems for the Comprehensive Management of Disaster Risk and Financial Strategies for Natural Disaster Reduction*, Washington, DC: IBRD, http://idbdocs.iadb.org/wsdocs/getdocument.aspx?docnum=1441898, accessed 6 July 2009.

Fritz Institute (2005), 'Recipient perceptions of aid effectiveness: rescue, relief and rehabilitation in tsunami affected Indonesia, India and Sri Lanka', http://www.fritzinstitute.org, accessed 13 August 2009.

Fulu, Emma (2007), 'Gender, vulnerability, and the experts: responding to the Maldives tsunami', *Development and Change*, **38** (5), 843–64, http://www.ingentaconnect.com/content/bpl/dech/2007/00000038/00000005/art00003, accessed 14 July 2009.

He, Baogang and A. Reid (2004), 'Special issue editors' introduction: four approaches to the Aceh question', *Asian Ethnicity,* **5** (3), October, 293–300.

Hovanesian, Ashot and A. Cox (2007), 'ICT for tsunami recovery: best practices and lessons learned', paper presented at the East-Asia Conference, Malaysia, 2007.

IDLO and UNDP (2007), 'Perempuan Aceh di hadapan hukum setelah konflik dan tsunami berlalu: laporan case study', http://www.idlo.int/publications/17.pdf, accessed 10 September 2009.

IFRC (2009), *World Disasters Report 2009 – Focus on Early Warning, Early Action*, Geneva, Switzerland: United Nations.

International Meeting on Good Humanitarian Donorship (2003), 'Meeting conclusions', Stockholm, 16–17 June, http://www.ifrc.org/Docs/idrl/I267EN.pdf, accessed 18 July, 2009.

ISDR (2009a), *Risk and Poverty in a Changing Climate: Invest Today for a Safer Tomorrow,* 2009 Global Assessment Report on Disaster Risk Reduction, Geneva, Switzerland: United Nations.

ISDR (2009b), *Risk and Poverty in a Changing Climate: Invest Today for a Safer Tomorrow: Summary and Recommendations*, 2009 Global Assessment Report on Disaster Risk Reduction, Geneva, Switzerland: United Nations.

ISDR (2009c), 'Hyogo Framework for Action 2005–2015: building the resilience of nations and communities to disasters (HFA)', http://www.unisdr.org/eng/hfa/hfa.htm, accessed 4 August 2009.

Marianti, Ruly (2007), *What is to be Done with Disasters? A Literature Survey on Disaster Study and Response,* Jakarta: SMERU Working Paper, December.

McCarthy, John F. (2007), 'Turning in circles: district governance, illegal logging and environmental decline in Sumatra, Indonesia', in Luca Tacconi (ed.), *Illegal Logging: Law Enforcement, Livelihoods and the Timber Trade*, London: Earthscan, pp. 69–90.

Multi Donor Fund (2008), 'Investing in institutions: sustaining reconstruction and economic recovery. Four years after the tsunami', http://www.multidonorfund. org, accessed 25 August 2009.

Nowak, Barbara S. and T. Caulfield (2008), *Women and Livelihoods in Post-Tsunami India and Aceh*, Working paper no. 104, Singapore: Asia Research Institute, National University of Singapore, http://ssrn.com/paper=1317142, accessed 25 July 2009.

Oey-Gardiner, Mayling (2005), 'Women in Aceh facing human rights problems', *Jakarta Post*, 16 May.

Parker, Ronald, K. Little and S. Heuser (2007), *Development Actions and the Rising Incidence of Disasters*, Evaluation Brief 4, Washington: World Bank, http://www.worldbank.org/ieg/docs/developing_actions.pdf, accessed 20 July 2009.

Perlez, Jane (2005), 'For many tsunami survivors, battered bodies, few choices', *New York Times*, 6 January.

Rice, Robert (2007), 'Planning for the end of the construction boom in tsunami-stricken Aceh and transition to a rapidly growing sustainable economy', *Economic Papers*, **26** (3), September, 261–75.

Scheper, Elizabeth, A. Parakrama and S. Patel (2006), *Impact of the Tsunami Response on Local and National Capacities: Indonesia Country Report (Aceh and Nias)*, London: Tsunami Evaluation Coalition.

Tacconi, Luca (2007), *Illegal Logging: Law Enforcement, Livelihoods and the Timber Trade*, London: Earthscan.

Triutomo, Sugeng (2008), 'Indonesia: interim national progress report on the implementation of the Hyogo Framework for Action', http://www.prevention web.net/english/countries/asia/idn, accessed 15 July 2009.

UNEP (2007), *Environment and Reconstruction in Aceh: Two Years after the Tsunami*, Geneva: United Nations Environment Programme.

World Bank (2009), 'Aceh economic update: May 2009', http://www-wds.worldbank. org/external/default/WDSContentServer/WDSP/IB/2009/07/01/000333038_ 20090701013738/Rendered/PDF/491870NEWS0P111june091english1final.pdf, accessed 25 August 2009.

3.   The matter of money

INTRODUCTION

This chapter considers matters relating to the financial flows associated with the Asian tsunami. Some main issues concerning both the revenue and expenditure sides of the financial flows are discussed.

There is little in this chapter that will surprise those with experience in the delivery of disaster relief in developing countries. It is in the nature of large-scale disaster-related emergencies in developing countries that coordination is difficult. However, the efficient management of financial flows is a key part of any effective response. In the midst of disasters, it is often difficult to manage financial issues well. Former US president Bill Clinton in his capacity as UN Special Envoy for Tsunami Recovery summed up some of the key problems when he said (Clinton 2006: 13):

> Tracking financial flows in recovery efforts is notoriously difficult, largely because most financial reporting is voluntary and funding comes from many sources. The tsunami experience has not been different in this regard. In Thailand, Maldives, Sri Lanka, and Aceh, governments established aid management platforms to provide an online vehicle for a comprehensive inventory of projects, financial commitments, and disbursements. In general, such databases could play a crucial role in filling the longstanding gap on accurate financial tracking, but to do so, they need to come online very early in a recovery effort, enjoy wide support from all the organizations involved in the effort, and be tied more directly to the needs . . .

Against this background, the central questions addressed in this chapter are, in principle, relatively straightforward. They are:

- How much money was provided by donors and others in response to the disaster?
- How was the money used?
- What are the main lessons to be drawn about the financial aspects of the response to the tsunami?

But as we shall see, although the questions are straightforward, the answers are not. It is not easy to obtain details of what overall aid flows were promised by donors and how much was provided. While many individual agencies and NGOs provided detailed financial reports of their activities, many did not. And any discussion of the way that aid money was used must necessarily try to consider aggregate data relating to both the quantity and the quality of the activities paid for by national governments, international donors, NGOs and others. But five years after the tsunami, it remains extremely difficult to obtain a comprehensive picture of the financial flows associated with the tsunami aid effort.

THE INITIAL RESPONSE

For a range of reasons the immediate public response to the 2004 Asian tsunami, both within the affected countries and across the international community, was overwhelming. The international media provided intense coverage of the impact of the disaster and NGOs in many countries quickly launched appeals for funds to assist survivors.

The initial response of governments in some rich donor nations in the first few days after the tsunami was tentative. This caution perhaps reflected a desire to wait for detailed reports from the field to arrive before announcing large-scale aid programs. However public pressure quickly led leaders in donor countries to announce comprehensive aid packages to help tsunami survivors. The result of this combined support from both governments and the public was that in terms of the amounts of money usually raised for international disaster appeals, there was a strong response and the tsunami international assistance effort was relatively well funded.

The headline figures that are frequently mentioned as approximate totals of financial support provided by the international community in response to the tsunami disaster are in the US$13–14 billion range. Because these amounts were large when compared to the sums usually raised in response to many other international appeals, the sums attracted much comment. The generosity of donors in rich countries, and especially the public response, was widely remarked upon. Nevertheless, on closer examination, many of the financial references to 'aid' or 'assistance' are rather vague (Appendix 3A.1). It is useful, therefore, to examine the various estimates of financial flows in more detail. This needs to be done so as to put the tsunami relief effort into context and to obtain a meaningful sense of magnitudes.

Contributions: Mobilization of Funds

The first problem in evaluating the financial situation is that there is no single reliable and comprehensive source of data. Different sources provide

different estimates. Further, funds were provided through numerous different channels and through a very large number of separate accounts (Figure
3.1). The result is that it is not easy to reconcile the different estimates.
The single most carefully prepared set of overall estimates for the early
period appears to be the study by the Tsunami Evaluation Coalition (TEC)
issued in July 2006 (Flint and Goyder 2006).[1] The TEC study reported
that around US$14 billion was pledged by international donors and a
minimum of another US$3.5 billion of financial support was estimated as
forthcoming from domestic sources in the affected countries, making up a
total of around US$17.5 billion (Table 3.1).[2] However, as Flint and Goyder
observe, these figures were no more than broad estimates.[3] Really, to be
used for meaningful comparisons with international aid flows as usually
measured, they would best be adjusted in a range of ways.[4]

Information on financial flows shows that numerous donor countries
provided assistance. Almost half of the total amount was provided directly
to Indonesia (Table 3.2). There was notable support from some Asia-
Pacific regional donor countries supplemented by important flows from
European Union institutions, the United States, and European as well as
other bilateral donor nations. Other aspects of the pledges provided by the
international community included strong support from the major multilateral development banks (World Bank and Asian Development Bank)
as well as from the Islamic Development Bank.

Terms of Assistance

As far as the terms of aid were concerned, the overall figures shown in
Tables 3.1 and 3.2 need to be considered from the point of view of three
main characteristics – timing, type of funding (grants or loans), and conditionality. But an accurate overview of the funding picture in terms of these
characteristics is hard to obtain. Some part of the total funding (probably
small) was provided immediately in the form of grants with few strings
attached; a larger amount appears to have been offered with various conditions attached in a mixture of grant and loan terms over an uncertain
period.

Information about the time period for which assistance was being
offered, for example, is hard to compile. In spite of the uncertainty, what is
clear is that the time periods for which the funds were offered varied widely.
In many cases donors were prepared – if possible, and consistent with the
conditions that were attached to the provision of aid – to disburse funds
quickly. But in other cases the bulk of funding was evidently intended to
be spent over longer periods so that the immediate assistance provided
was limited. The vagueness on this matter is significant for a number of

reasons. For one thing, the immediate provision of funding is, in financial terms, more valuable than the promise of the provision of support at some distant time in the future. For another, it is helpful to have some idea of the timing of the supply of funds in order to be able to make judgements about the likely amount of additionality.

The financial terms on which assistance was offered also appear to have varied widely. Most assistance – it is hard to know precisely how much – was provided in grant form, sometimes in cash and sometimes in kind. The rest was provided in loans of varying kinds, mostly apparently as soft loans on below-market terms. In principle, it would be useful to convert these various types of loans into net ODA (official development assistance) flows to allow for more meaningful comparisons to be made between them.

Similarly, conditionalities set down by donors appear to have varied widely. In some cases, onerous procurement conditions were attached to the provision of aid. In other cases, the preferred reporting requirements set out by different donor bodies were difficult for recipient agencies to meet. And in yet other cases, donors looked for partnership commitments from national institutions which, under the emergency conditions of the day, placed a heavy load on an already overburdened local administrative system.

The overall effect of this kaleidoscope set of arrangements as far as the terms of aid is concerned is that it is very difficult to compare the bewildering variety of apples and pears of different sizes which made up the estimated total of US$14 billion of international assistance. Telford and Cosgrave (2007a: 4) observe that 'financial tracking was incapable of presenting a comprehensive, accurate and up-to-date picture of funding at any stage'. And to add to the complications, there are two further factors which need to be considered in attempting to arrive at some judgement about the total flow of aid: the size of other flows of assistance, and the question of to what extent the tsunami aid flows were really additional (that is, additional to the aid flows which donors could have been expected to provide to the tsunami-affected countries in the normal course of events)?

Other Assistance Flows

The data in Tables 3.1 and 3.2 understate the total amounts of assistance provided, probably significantly, because of lack of adequate data relating to various local contributions. First, national governments in the tsunami-affected countries provided very considerable resources towards the relief effort. A minimum estimate of the value of this assistance is set by the TEC at US$3.4 billion (Table 3.1). However, the true amount is probably

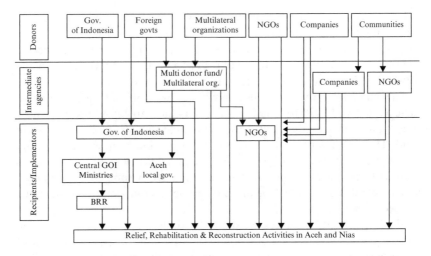

Source: Adapted from Nasution (2009).

Figure 3.1   Flow of tsunami-related aid in Indonesia

considerably more. Second, anecdotal evidence suggests that significant amounts of private remittances were sent directly, both from overseas and from within each of the countries, to families and communities affected by the tsunami. Third, and usually very important, is the value in kind of local self-help assistance provided by local communities themselves. It is usual, in many aid budgets, to estimate a value of the assistance provided in kind and to show this in the overall aid budget. A proper measure of resource flows should therefore include an estimate of the value of these local contributions.

There is no reliable way of measuring the amounts of assistance provided in these ways. However the anecdotal evidence is that the amounts were sizeable. In particular, numerous reports suggest that although local self-help assistance is often unrecorded, it is in fact immediate, large, and effective. If the individuals and community groups involved in these efforts had a stronger voice in the national and international media, their efforts would probably be far more widely recognized.

Additionality

The headline announcements of aid for tsunami-affected countries were impressive. However, to what extent were these flows genuinely *additional* in the sense that they represented assistance over and above the flows

Table 3.1   Overall estimates of tsunami funding

Source of funds		US$ million
International sources		
Governments		6481
Pledged by DAC donor governments*	5888	
Pledged by non-DAC governments	593	
Private donations		5490
Private donations to NGOs	3214	
Private donations to UN agencies	494	
Private donations to Red Cross/Crescent	1783	
Pledges by multilateral banks (loans)		2095
Private remittances		n.a.
Other private donations		n.a.
Total identifiable funds (international sources)		14067
National sources		
Affected governments (minimum estimate)		3400
Private donations in affected countries (minimum estimate)		190
Affected population		n.a.
Total funds (all identifiable sources)		17657

Note: * DAC governments are the donor governments which are represented on the OECD's Development Assistance Committee.

Source: Flint and Goyder (2006: 15).

which might otherwise have been expected to occur in the absence of the tsunami disaster? There is no easy answer to this question. It calls for information about hypothetical aid flows. Nevertheless, the question is an important one. It reminds us that at least some of the tsunami aid reflects, in effect, a diversion of aid which probably would have occurred under normal circumstances into the tsunami-affected countries. Donor countries are generally not eager to discuss such issues; recipient countries, on the other hand, are generally quite aware of them.

Extremely rough indications of additionality can be obtained by estimating the difference between, first, the likely amount of aid which might have been provided in the absence of the tsunami, and second, the likely flow of tsunami aid. Needless to say, estimates of both of these flows are

The Asian tsunami

Table 3.2   *Donor funding for tsunami by donor and recipient (US$ million)*

Donor	Regional	India	Indonesia	Maldives	Sri Lanka	Total
Asia-Pacific regional governments						
Australia	46	–	760	–	7	814
Japan	252	–	250	20	175	697
PRC	59	–	–	2	318	379
Republic of Korea	6	–	15	–	33	54
Non-regional governments						
EU/ECHO/EIB	186	–	500	18	208	912
United States	294	–	400	10	65	788
Germany	105	–	500	–	110	715
Canada	104	–	173	–	84	361
France	29	–	150	–	104	283
United Kingdom	134	–	71	–	–	205
Norway	83	–	84	–	19	186
Netherlands	43	–	100	10	25	178
Kuwait	30	–	40	10	20	100
Italy	27	–	–	–	72	99
Spain	7	–	25	–	62	95
Estonia	88	–	–	–	–	88
Switzerland	27	–	50	–	9	86
Sweden	41	–	–	–	11	51
Denmark	38	–	–	–	8	46
Subtotal of governments						6 137
ADB	–	200	386	24	157	766
World Bank	–	529	64	14	150	757
Islamic DB	–	–	446	1	–	447
IMF	–	–	–	6	158	164
IFAD	2	30	35	5	18	90
Subtotal of multilateral banks						2 224
TOTALS	1 602	759	4 049	119	1 813	8 360
%	19	9	48	1	22	100

Source: UN, Office of Special Envoy: http://www.tsunamispecialenvoy.org, accessed 15 November 2007.

highly speculative. Nevertheless, the exercise is instructive because of the light it throws on the impact of the tsunami on aid flows.

A rough estimate of the possible distribution of tsunami aid flows is shown in the second line of Table 3.3. It is assumed, for example, that 20 per cent of the US$14 billion was spent in 2005 and that another 20 per cent was spent in 2006. The resulting total expenditure flow for the seven-year period to 2011 of US$14 billion is shown in the third line. But as against this flow (which is a mixture of loans and grants and is therefore not net ODA), it needs to be borne in mind that in the *absence* of the tsunami the affected countries would have received flows of perhaps US$1.5 billion in net ODA per year or around US$10.5 billion over a seven-year period (compared with US$14 billion for the tsunami flows).

What do these rough estimates tell us about additionality? Perhaps the main thing that the data illustrate is the rough limits of minimum and maximum likely aid flows to the main tsunami-affected countries over the seven-year period 2005–11 under alternative scenarios. Under a *full-additionality scenario*, total assistance flows might be expected to reach around US$24.5 billion over the seven-year period. However, under a *no-additionality scenario*, assistance flows would only amount to around US$16 billion. The latter scenario, in turn, would imply that what might be called the 'true additionality' of tsunami aid was around US$3.5 billion. And these flows, it needs to be recalled, were apparently a mixture of loans and grants, the true value of which was rather less than the generally accepted measure of 'foreign aid' (which is net ODA).

Financial Flows

Weighing up all of these factors, it is very difficult to reach firm conclusions about the real value of the total foreign aid provided. It is certainly not clear what the value of true foreign aid (in net ODA terms) was or how much was really additional.

Some might wonder whether worrying about all of this is like counting angels on the point of a needle. Surely the main point is that generous amounts of aid were provided in response to the tsunami disaster? Surely attempts to measure the details are just accounting gimmicks? But this, precisely, is the point: *magnitudes are important*. The meaningful measurement of financial flows is needed. All actors in the public policy arena need to have a sense of relevant magnitudes. And the worrying fact is that when the commitments of donor agencies of all kinds (international, national, official, and non-government) are examined, it is very hard to know what they mean. Amartya Sen (2005) has spoken of the 'celebration of the outburst of human sympathy' in the aftermath of the tsunami. But to what extent the outburst of human sympathy was reflected in the provision of financial resources is very hard to determine.

SPENDING: USE OF FUNDS

Expenditure issues are sometimes seen as being at the dull end of aid delivery work. Dull or not, they are central to issues of effective aid delivery. And the devil is in the detail. It is in the detail of the day-to-day delivery of aid that many of the real difficulties in implementation lie. Issues of key interest in the delivery of tsunami aid relate to both quantity and quality. More specifically, it is useful to consider: how quickly was the money spent? And was the money spent well?

In addressing these questions it needs to be borne in mind that the appropriate patterns of spending vary considerably depending on the phase of the response to an emergency. In the early relief stage during the first days and weeks of a disaster management cycle (Carter 1991), major expenditures on items such as food and temporary shelter are generally appropriate. Later, the emphasis often shifts to housing and social support such as education for children. Still later, major infrastructure spending is likely to gather pace (Figures 2.1 and 4.4).

Quantity

While it is difficult to obtain an accurate picture of the mobilization of funds for tsunami assistance, it is even more difficult to track data on spending. The Tsunami Evaluation Coalition report referred to earlier provides useful information on the situation during the period up to the end of September 2005. More recent estimates for Indonesia to early 2009 are provided on the World Bank Indonesia tsunami website (World Bank 2009). TEC estimates suggest that disbursements of promised funds had reached slightly over 30 per cent of pledges at that time. But this, at best, is only indicative of spending levels. The TEC report (Flint and Goyder 2006: 16) notes that 'disbursement by a donor does not necessarily mean that the funds have been spent'. Funds are generally recorded as disbursed when they are transferred into the bank account of an implementing agency and so 'there is little information on how much has actually been spent'.

Audit reports from the US and Australia on the use of tsunami funds provide thoughtful summaries of the practical challenges in the field in implementing spending programs. These reports are a valuable supplement to the TEC information. In the case of the US, in May 2005 Congress

Table 3.3   Rough estimates of additionality, 2005–11

			2005	2006	2007	2008	2009	2010	2011	Total
Normal aid flow	(a)	$ bn	1.5	1.5	1.5	1.5	1.5	1.5	1.5	10.5
Tsunami aid flow		%	20	20	20	20	10	5	5	100
		$ bn	2.8	2.8	2.8	2.8	1.4	0.7	0.7	14.0
Additionality	(b)	Max $	2.8	2.8	2.8	2.8	1.4	0.7	0.7	14.0
	(c)	Min $	1.3	1.3	1.3	1.3	−0.1	−0.8	−0.8	3.5
Total aid (including tsunami aid)										
	(b)	Max $	4.3	4.3	4.3	4.3	2.9	2.2	2.2	24.5
	(c)	Min $	2.8	2.8	2.8	2.8	1.5	1.5	1.5	15.7

Notes:
(a)   The average net ODA flow to Indonesia and Sri Lanka combined for 2002–04 was approximately US$1.5 billion (OECD data).
(b)   *Maximum additionality* assumes that the total amount of traditional aid flows continue to be provided in addition to the tsunami aid pledges.
(c)   *Minimum additionality* assumes that all tsunami pledges are met by reducing aid which would, in the absence of the tsunami, have been provided for other activities. It is also assumed (for 2009 to 2011) that nominal aid flows are never actually reduced below normal levels.

Source: Authors' calculations.

appropriated US$908 million for relief and reconstruction. A summary of progress to early 2006 from the US Government Accountability Office (USGAO 2006) is reflected in Table 3.4. The pattern of spending in the table, which appears to be similar to patterns of spending by some other major bilateral donors, sheds useful light on the way that post-tsunami aid activities were being approached. While emergency relief funds had been spent quickly, funds earmarked for long-term reconstruction activities were being drawn down much more slowly. Out of a total of over US$430 million allocated to reconstruction work in Indonesia and Sri Lanka, more than one year after the tsunami less than 3 per cent had been expended.

In the case of the Australian assistance program, the Australian government, responding quickly to the tsunami disaster in early January 2005, announced a large A$1 billion (approximately US$800 million) contribution to a newly formed Australia–Indonesia Partnership for Reconstruction and Development (AIPRD). A report from the Australian National Audit Office in June 2006 provided a preliminary assessment of the framework established to manage the AIPRD rather than of the management of the program itself (Australian Government 2006). Nevertheless, the report canvassed some of the major issues likely to emerge in spending significant amounts of money across Indonesia.

Taken together, these two audit reports, along with many other reports about progress in spending tsunami monies, point to a range of well-known challenges.

These include the following:

- The need for proper controls, including risk management controls, over contract and tendering arrangements for the procurement of goods and services.
- The additional pressures which tsunami-related programs place on already over-burdened administrative systems in the tsunami-affected countries.
- The high probability that final costs of construction programs would exceed initial estimates by considerable amounts because of the escalation of local construction costs in tsunami-affected areas.
- Working in regions with long-standing civil conflicts.
- Coordinating activities with host governments and with non-government organizations.
- Ensuring that the focus on tsunami-related programs does not hamper other, non-tsunami, development programs.

Table 3.4   US tsunami response: summary of progress to early 2006

Item	US$ mil.	Comment
Emergency relief	327	For immediate needs; mainly completed by end 2005
Long-term reconstruction		
Indonesia	349	US$9 mil. (3%) expended as of 31 January 2006
Sri Lanka	85	US$2 mil. (2%) expended as of 31 January 2006
Other countries and regional	62	
Total long-term	496	Rising prices are expected to increase project construction costs
Other	85	
Total	908	

Source: USGAO (2006).

In addition to these challenges there was a growing reluctance, much discussed in Indonesia in recent years, on the part of public officials being prepared to approve any spending on anything whenever there were any doubts at all about the legality of doing so.[5] Given the weaknesses of the legal system in Indonesia, as well as the lack of clarity which often exists in official regulations, a highly risk-averse approach to approvals of public expenditures meant that spending plans often got badly delayed.

Against this background it is hardly surprising that spending in the first nine months after the tsunami appears to have been around 30 per cent of total planned expenditures. A little over three years later, by early 2009 according to World Bank data (World Bank 2009), disbursements in Indonesia reportedly climbed to around 62 per cent of original commitments.[6] However, overall estimates of spending do not seem to exist. Some rough estimate of the overall situation can therefore perhaps be obtained by assuming that patterns for total spending in all the tsunami-affected countries reflected spending patterns in Indonesia. Disbursements of aid in Indonesia at the end of 2007, three years after the tsunami, appear to have reached the relatively modest figure of 55 per cent of original commitments (Table 3.5). If a similar spending pattern applied to the total of around US$18 billion of original commitments by all donors in all countries, then no more than US$9.9 billion was apparently disbursed by the end of 2007.

At first glance, these figures might seem rather low. Are they unreasonably low? Did the expenditure systems perhaps fail to facilitate a timely flow of resources to tsunami-affected communities? What can be said about these issues?

On one hand, measured against some of the expectations that the early publicity about large-scale assistance programs encouraged, the rate of spending was seen by some as disappointing. Certainly there was evidence of dissatisfaction from some stakeholders. There were media reports of complaints from affected people and sometimes incidents of demonstrations. On the other hand, it is inevitable that longer term reconstruction programs such as road-building take time to implement.

To some extent, the priority to be given to immediate relief and humanitarian needs has to be balanced against the importance of longer term development programs. In terms of immediate needs, initial evaluation reports clearly pointed to problems. But in terms of longer term programs, it is hardly surprising that delays occurred for all the well-known sorts of reasons that tend to cause delays in such development programs.

Perhaps the main thing that can be said is that spending was not especially rapid. Some observers argue that too many activities took too long to get underway. Others argue that quality was more important than speed and

Table 3.5   Estimates of tsunami spending flows to end 2007

	Original commitments		Allocated (end 2007)		Disbursed (end 2007)	
	US$ bn	%	US$ bn	%	US$ bn	%
Indonesia						
Official donors	3.0	100	2.3	77	1.3	43
NGOs	2.1	100	1.9	90	1.2	57
GoI	2.6	100	2.6	100	1.7	65
Total (Indonesia)	7.7	100	6.8	88	4.2	55
All tsunami-affected countries (a)						
Official donors	7.0	100	5.3	77	3.1	43
NGOs	4.9	100	4.4	90	2.8	57
National governments	6.1	100	6.0	100	4.0	65
Total (all countries)	18.0	100	15.8	88	9.9	55

Note: (a) Data for all tsunami-affected countries is calculated by assuming that the ratios for each category of the Indonesian data are applicable to the commitments for all countries of approximately US$18 billion.

Source: Indonesia data is from ADB (2008). Data for All countries shows authors' calculations.

quantity. Whatever the different views on these issues, it is certainly true that spending systems which rely on cumbersome contract-based procurement arrangements are not suited to the fast provision of disaster assistance. If a main goal of disaster relief is to reach people quickly, revisions to the bureaucratic ways in which much relief aid is provided are needed.

Quality

Two main issues concerning quality need to be considered. These are, first, the expenditure choices that were made in the delivery of tsunami aid, and second, the quality of the process (in terms of administration, controls over procurement, and so on).

The indications are that, as is so often the case during emergency situations, the overall patterns of donor spending reflected a combination of supply side and demand side factors. On one hand, donors who were trying to respond quickly sometimes supplied goods or prepared programs too hurriedly. When this is done, mistakes can be made. One AusAID survey (Commonwealth of Australia 2007: 10) noted that

One of the important lessons from the 2004 Indian Ocean tsunami and other disasters is that it is not a good idea to donate second-hand clothing. . . . many of the second-hand clothes were culturally unacceptable . . . Relief supplies need to be appropriate to the conditions and needs of disaster survivors. That is why cash is usually the best form of donation – money can be spent quickly on the most urgently needed items purchased locally. This is quicker and cheaper than transporting goods from other countries and can also provide a much-needed boost to local retail outlets.

On the other hand, because of problems of coordination, communications, and lack of strong representation, local communities sometimes found it difficult to identify their needs effectively at short notice.

In the immediate wake of the disaster, funds appear to have been generally well spent. In Sri Lanka, for example (Jayasuriya et al. 2006: 10):

While there were hiccups and some amount of confusion in organizing relief, for a country that had not previously experienced such a disaster, Sri Lankan institutions responded reasonably well. Essential medical aid, emergency food and other relief supplies were mobilized within a day. Temporary shelter was provided to the displaced in schools, other public and religious buildings, and tents.

As against this, some observers commented on problems, including those stemming from the actions of international agencies and NGOs. For example, Batha (2005) observed that 'the vast amount of funding meant aid agencies could afford to hire their own helicopters and boats and make individual assessments and distribution arrangements rather than co-ordinate with one another and through the United Nations'.

Nevertheless, many anecdotal reports about the responses in Indonesia, Sri Lanka and Thailand concluded that while inevitable mistakes occurred, the overall delivery of emergency aid in the first stages of response to the disaster was generally effective. In the longer term, expenditure priorities shifted to relief and rehabilitation schemes such as housing and programs to support local commercial activity (provision of assets such as fishing boats, microfinance programs).

What can be said about the quality of the process? From the earliest stages of the international response to the tsunami disaster, donors indicated the quality of aid delivery was a matter of considerable concern. There are several reasons for this.

First, the quality of international aid has attracted much attention in the international donor community in recent years. Increasingly, international conferences of donors and reports sponsored by the donor community have emphasized the importance of improving the impact of aid. Indeed, the need to improve the effectiveness of aid has become something of a mantra across the international donor community. Thus checks and balances of various kinds have been introduced into many international aid programs across the world with the aim of increasing aid effectiveness. The provision of large programs of tsunami aid in Asia took place against this background of heightened international concern about quality issues.

Second, Indonesia is regarded as a corruption-prone country so the topic of controls over tsunami expenditures assumed considerable importance from a very early stage in the tsunami aid program there. Indonesian leaders quickly acknowledged the need to address this issue. Among other measures, steps were taken to introduce improved auditing controls and the *Badan Rekonstruksi dan Rehabilitasi* (BRR) was established. Similarly, in Sri Lanka the issue of proper controls over expenditures was seen as important. Significant lapses in the administration of funds were noted in an Auditor General's Department report in September 2005 (Jayasuriya et al. 2006: 52).

Despite these and other steps, some international donors remained sufficiently concerned about expenditure procedures as to be reluctant to share authority over spending programs. In some cases this reluctance, which reflects the legal and auditing requirements which donor governments have set for bilateral agencies, exacerbated problems of coordination between spending agencies in the field.

SOME OVERALL CONSIDERATIONS

A number of issues arise out of this overview of the financial issues associated with the response to the tsunami disaster in Asia.

First, there was often a lack of transparency about the arrangements (both volume and conditions) on which promised assistance was to be provided. This is true for both national and international agencies, and for official and non-government bodies. Agencies tended to report on the assistance provided in a range of ways – in different currencies, for different (or undefined) time periods, and they tend to group both grants and loans (of varying terms) together. Moreover, the definitions used by different agencies for such things as 'aid' and 'assistance' varied widely. To take just one example, the UN Office for the Coordination of Humanitarian Affairs (OCHA) made a useful effort to maintain updated information on tsunami relief aid (http://www.reliefweb.int) but was obliged to note that 'In their original pledges, donors who broke pledges down between humanitarian and reconstruction aid applied their own definitions of humanitarian aid (also called "immediate relief" or "emergency" by some donors).'

Further, the systems for recording and tracking assistance were frequently unsatisfactory. The reporting of flows was often incomplete and delayed. Important attempts were made, it should be noted, to improve the recording systems (Ramkumar 2006; Hovanesian and Cox 2007). In a determined effort to deal with the daunting problem of highly confused and unreliable financial data, the United Nations Development Programme (UNDP) supported the development of a regional Donor Assistance Database (DAD). It was hoped that the DAD would be able to provide current data about financial flows for all of the main countries affected by the tsunami.[7] In Indonesia, for example, the main agencies involved in tsunami relief were asked to register with the local office of the national coordination agency, the BRR, to set up an account on the local DAD known as RAND (Recovery Aceh-Nias Database) and to regularly update data on funds committed and disbursed (TGLL 2009: 63). As one local staff member of the United Nations put it, 'We needed something that was very transparent so anyone in the world, including mums and dads in London, could use it.'[8]

But in practice, mums and dads in London could not use the RAND. They could not really use any of the other DADs established by the UNDP either. And most other people would have found the DADs very difficult to use as well. The basic problem was that any system of this kind was dependent on the willingness and capacity of a myriad aid agencies to cooperate by regularly providing accurate financial information. This did not happen. The TGLL study summarized the outcome as follows (2009: 63)

> The database faced numerous challenges and fierce criticism. Indeed, one of the main criticisms, from the World Bank and NGOs, amongst others, was that because each agency was responsible for updating its own entries, inaccurate data or misrepresentations of activities might be included. In the beginning, only about 33 percent of organizations on RAND were updating their accounts. Data entry errors and other factors cost RAND credibility for providing a timely, accurate picture; in 2006, for example, it did not capture even half of recovery efforts in Aceh and Nias.

Even several years later, in 2009, the DADs were difficult to use and contained data that appeared to be quite unreliable.[9]

The result is that at best, only an incomplete picture of flows of tsunami aid is available. In a survey of disaster-related aid conducted in 2007, a task force established by INTOSAI (the International Organization of Supreme Audit Institutions) made the following observations (INTOSAI 2007: 6):

> Donors and recipients want trust, but want assurance, that aid that is provided is well spent in terms of regularity, efficiency and effectiveness. For this reason

information is needed on planning of aid projects, how the aid is spent, the implementation of projects, and the results that were achieved. The basis of this should be an information structure, an audit trail, that makes it possible to follow aid from source to destination and to capture the results of the aid provided. The Task Force has studied the flows of Tsunami-related aid and has come to the conclusion, as have others like the Tsunami Evaluation Coalition and the UN Board of Auditors, that such an information structure is lacking. As a result, there is no transparency and accountability in place to follow aid from source to destination. The information that is available is not complete, not up-to-date and not reliable enough to be used for planning, monitoring and auditing disaster-related aid.

And specifically, talking of the transparency of tsunami-related aid, the INTOSAI task force report said that (2007: 5):

- There is no overview of relevant stakeholders and the aid handled by them;
- There is no reliable or complete overview of aid flows in available aid coordination databases;
- There has been a loss of identity of significant portions of aid (is aid public or private?);
- There is a lack of standardisation in definitions (for example, administrative costs), and accounting and reporting standards;
- It is extremely difficult to follow aid from source to destination, due to a lack of information (e.g., on purpose, destination, projects, amounts and sector).

A second aspect of the international aid system is that raising funds is sometimes given priority over disbursement and accountability. The international aid industry is understandably concerned about the need to mobilize resources. Considerable effort therefore goes into fund-raising, including into publicizing the successful aspects of aid programs. But the industry is sometimes less successful in the more mundane tasks of spending the money well in developing countries and accounting for the expenditures. Telford and Cosgrave (2007b) summarized the situation as follows:

In the aftermath of the tsunami, media-driven competition and political considerations resulted in what was described as a donor 'beauty contest'. The problem was not the funding itself, but the mechanisms through which it took place. Official funding decisions were not made on the basis of need. Assessments were often slow, overlapping, poorly shared and imprecise. Flawed financial tracking systems were incapable of presenting a comprehensive and up-to-date picture of funding. In particular, they failed to account for the substantial contributions made by the people and the governments of the affected countries, and Muslim sources that operate outside the 'conventional' relief framework.

Indeed, many of the staff working for well-known multilateral and bilateral development agencies are officials and planners mainly involved in 'upstream' or 'wholesale' aspects of the administration of international assistance. The nuts-and-bolts tasks in the aid industry of delivering activities in the developing countries are often outsourced to service providers of various kinds – to contractors, consultants, NGOs, education and training and health providers, and so on.

These arrangements, which relate to the structure of the supply side in the global assistance industry, prompt a number of questions for the delivery of emergency aid. Are systems in place to direct spending into the right areas? Do the delivery systems at the 'retail' end of the aid industry operate effectively, especially in times of severe stress following disasters? Is there a 'missing middle' in the international development debate (between discussions of the mobilization of funds and broad aid outcomes) that reflects a need for more attention to be given to the administration and management of aid delivery on the ground?

A third issue relates to trade-offs between quantity and quality. Issues of whether there are trade-offs between the quantity and quality of spending, and if there are, what choices are appropriate, need consideration in the delivery of assistance in post-disaster programs. There are many who wish to see significant increases in the volume of international assistance. But it is also true that much attention has been given by international donors in recent years to the issue of the quality of aid. And to some extent, the differences of view between those who argue that quantity and speed are important and those who stress quality have been evident in recent discussions about post-tsunami delivery programs.

On the one hand, there were numerous comments in the media and elsewhere about delays in providing post-tsunami assistance. In some cases, there were instances of demonstrations (such as in Banda Aceh on 21 September 2006 when a crowd of people protesting against delays in the provision of housing gathered outside government offices). It would seem, at least from anecdotal evidence, that affected local communities in tsunami-affected areas tended to favour more rapid disbursement of funds where possible.

On the other hand, many international observers emphasized quality. This approach was implicit in the 'build back better' motto which attracted considerable support from international agencies in the delivery of post-tsunami aid programs. Reflecting these views, Brusset et al. (2006: ii) argued that:

> Although the recovery period has taken time to move into high gear, there are many reasons for proceeding slowly, perhaps the most important being to *get*

it right. The Government of Indonesia, leading the process, will ultimately be
judged by its own people less for slowness and caution than on the quality and
sustainability of final outcomes . . .

In a similar vein, Paul O'Callaghan, Executive Director of the Australian
peak NGO group Australian Council for International Development
(ACFID) (media statement, 30 March 2006) said that:

> It would be a mistake to rush projects and build shoddy structures simply to
> demonstrate rapid progress. We have aimed to 'build back better' through
> close consultation with local communities. The reconstruction of Darwin [in
> Australia] after Cyclone Tracy [in 1974] took over six years. For this more
> complex disaster, the process requires governments and international agencies
> to remain committed for a very long period in order to produce the necessary
> quality of results.

It would seem that there are some significant differences of emphasis
about the issue of the priority to be given to quantity and quality, not least
between local communities on the one hand (the consumers) and international providers of assistance on the other (the producers).

A fourth issue which received much attention in the delivery of post-
tsunami aid programs was the targeting of assistance. The effective targeting of aid is a subset of the broader issue of the quality of development
assistance. In Sri Lanka, for example, Jayasuriya et al. (2006: 47) noted
that 'The selection of beneficiaries for housing grants has caused dissatisfaction in some places', and in both Sri Lanka and Indonesia there were
numerous problems reported with the provision of assets such as housing
and fishing boats.

Dissatisfaction on the part of recipients is easy to understand.
However it is also true that the effective targeting of government programs in developing countries, even during normal times when agencies
are not operating under emergency conditions, is often difficult. One
recent survey from India (Srivastava 2005: 72) concluded that 'poverty
targeting in India has achieved some modest success but in general
the picture is highly disappointing . . .' A survey of Indonesian programs (Perdana and Maxwell 2005: 125) observed that 'the targeting
of poverty alleviation programs in Indonesia has been a difficult and
frustrating process'.

Perhaps the best that can be hoped for under emergency conditions in
developing countries is a second-best approach to targeting. In such situations to aim for the best can be the enemy of the good. The use of a combination of techniques designed, in broad terms, to encourage improved
targeting might achieve an acceptable outcome. A broad brush approach

which mainly relies on the provision of basic supplies and housing, combined with the supply of appropriate social goods (elementary health support and education) along with grants and food-for-work programs might indeed be the most appropriate way to ensure that the largest amount of assistance reaches those who most need it.

Finally, the way in which aid money is spent following disasters needs close consideration. Traditionally, a great deal of post-disaster aid in developing countries has been given in kind in one form or another – as food and fuel, clothing, shelter, materials, health and education support, and through post-emergency development projects such as roads and agricultural development programs.

However assistance does not need to be provided in this way. Far more aid than is currently provided could be disbursed in the form of cash or cash-based forms of aid such as vouchers or through cash for work (CFW) programs (Harvey 2007). Indeed, a considerable variety of cash-based forms of aid were used by various assistance agencies in Aceh. The list of measures included the following (Kelaher and Dollery 2008: 121):

- Cash for work and cash for food programs;
- Asset replacement through cash grants and vouchers;
- Cash for non-food items (household utensils, work tools, hygiene kits, clothing, drugs, and health equipment);
- Cash for materials for communities and livelihood activities;
- Cash grants for families hosting displaced persons; and
- Indonesian government social welfare assistance which included US$0.40 (approx.) per day per person, direct cash assistance of US$10 per person per month, and other forms of support for the poor.

As this list shows, cash-based forms of aid can be provided for a wide range of purposes and can be tailored by policy-makers to provide quite specific incentives.

In fact, it is donors themselves who often insist on providing aid in kind. And from one point of view, this traditional attachment to the provision of aid in kind reflects a reluctance to relax bureaucratic controls over the delivery of programs, as Harvey notes (2007: 1):

> Obstacles to the use of appropriate cash are partly institutional in the sense that some donors continue to tie assistance to food aid . . . Reluctance to use cash is also a function of the individual attitudes of aid providers, and the sense that cash is threatening because it implies handing over power from the agency to the beneficiary.

The international literature relating to public policy issues is full of examples of the advantages, in appropriate conditions, of cash-based forms of assistance. And within rich countries, a large proportion of the transfers that governments provide to citizens is in the form of cash. Indeed, following disasters in rich countries, it is common for governments to make quite large amounts of assistance available to affected populations in the form of cash. This prompts the question of whether or not more disaster assistance in developing countries should be provided through cash-based forms of aid.

A survey by Harvey (2006) which provides a useful review of the role of cash transfers in emergencies notes two main findings. The first is that cash and voucher approaches remain largely underutilized. The second is that there is increasing experience in the use of cash and voucher programs which suggests that these approaches are useful. Post-tsunami experience in Aceh supports these conclusions (Kelaher and Dollery 2008; Doocy et al. 2006). Harvey summarized the findings of Doocy et al. as follows (2006: 275):

> For the majority of CFW participants and their households, cash for work was the only source of household income . . . The CFW program empowered displaced populations to return to their communities . . . Other reported psychosocial benefits indicated giving communities an opportunity to work together. *Perhaps the most striking features of the programme were its scale and speed.* The programme began on 7 January 2005, just two weeks after the tsunami, was implemented in 60 villages, and at its peak had nearly 18,000 participants and was disbursing over USD 1 million per month. [Emphasis added]

Further, by their very nature, programs of this kind which create jobs tend to be self-targeting on lower income groups. The average daily rate for unskilled labour in the Mercy Corps program in Aceh was set at approximately US$3 per day while the average reported monthly income for households included in the scheme was around US$300 (of which over 90 per cent was attributed to the CFW activities).

A further advantage of cash-based programs is that, properly designed, they work to rebuild the independence of communities devastated by disasters. The UN Special Envoy for Tsunami Recovery, Bill Clinton, drew attention to this aspect of cash-based programs in a 'lessons learned' report that he issued at the end of his period as UN Envoy (Clinton 2006: 5):

> A greater reliance on direct cash transfers to households has also been a positive feature of the tsunami effort, helping to empower local communities and families. Shortly after the tsunami, hundreds of thousands of people were involved

in cash-for-work projects, clearing rubble, repairing small infrastructure, or cleaning paddy fields. The majority of houses under construction in Sri Lanka are being managed through an owner-built scheme under which beneficiaries receive cash installments to rebuild their own houses.

Emphasizing the importance of empowering local communities to take on tasks of local rebuilding, Clinton suggested that 'More resources should be directed to cash-for-work programs, owner-build housing schemes, microfinance, and other approaches that put resources directly into survivors' hands to chart their own path to recovery.'

It is true that there are pros and cons in disbursing post-emergency assistance in cash-based forms. However, the indications are that the use of cash-based delivery programs warrants more attention than the matter has so far received.

CONCLUSION

This chapter has considered matters relating to the financial flows associated with the Asian tsunami. Some main issues on both the revenue and expenditure sides of the financial flows have been discussed. It has proved extremely difficult to obtain satisfactory data on the overall flows of finances associated with the tsunami relief operation. However, it needs to be noted that the problems of obtaining reliable information relate more to issues of coordination and difficulties of administration rather than to matters of deliberate mismanagement or malfeasance. INTOSAI summarized the situation as follows (INTOSAI 2007: 7–8):

> Currently organizations involved in the humanitarian aid sector have to report to various stakeholders with different reporting requirements regarding accountability and have to provide a level of assurance to their accountability organizations (for instance an unqualified opinion by an external auditor). . . . Due to complexities in the accountability and transparency of disaster-related aid flows, it is often unclear which organisation is accountable to whom, and for what. The identity of Tsunami-related funds is blurred and sometimes even lost, due to the mixing of public and private funds, and the splitting of accumulated funds. This creates difficulties for the overview of aid flows and blurs accountability and audit responsibilities.

In short, the performance of the international donor community sometimes fell below the standards of financial reporting generally expected in the delivery of international aid (Telford and Cosgrave 2007a). But to no small degree, quite serious difficulties of international coordination contributed greatly to these problems. The issues surrounding the difficulties of coordinating tsunami assistance are taken up again in Chapter 7.

NOTES

1. For a more recent view, see the thoughtful discussion in Masyrafah and McKeon (2008).
2. For reasons which the text makes clear, unless otherwise specified, all financial references in this chapter should be regarded as approximate.
3. See also the detailed supporting notes to the Flint and Goyder study, in *Overall Funding Flows* (German et al. 2006).
4. A careful set of adjustments to the data would provide information on the following: (a) flows by donor and recipient country; (b) terms of aid (time period covered by the funding, form of aid by grants and loans including conditions of loan terms, and conditionalities); (c) national and local contributions as well as international contributions; (d) an estimate of net additionality; and (e) other contributions not covered by these flows, including military contributions, resources provided in kind, and private remittances.
5. A similar set of issues attracted comment during the response to the earthquake in Yogyakarta in May 2006.
6. The World Bank data for 2009 are for Indonesia but may perhaps be taken as a proxy for overall patterns of spending including spending in other countries.
7. According to the comprehensive User Manual for the Regional DAD, the DAD is 'a powerful tool for tracking and analysing aid flows' and is a 'centralized system for tracking aid flows to the entire region affected'.
8. UNORC Aid Coordination Advisor, quoted in TGLL (2009: 63).
9. The website is at http://tsunamitracking.org/undprcb/.

REFERENCES

ADB (2008), *Indonesia: Aceh-Nias Rehabilitation and Reconstruction*, Progress Report, Project no 39127, June.
Australian Government, Australian National Audit Office (2006), *Arrangements to Manage and Account for Aid Funds Provided under the Australia-Indonesia Partnership for Reconstruction and Development*, Canberra: Australian National Audit Office.
Batha, Emma (2005), 'Post-tsunami chaos wastes aid', Reuters Foundation, AlertNet, 5 October 2005, http://www.alertnet.org/thefacts/reliefresources/112849687980.htm, accessed 31 October 2009.
Brusset, Emery, W. Pramana, A. Davies, Y. Deshmukh, S.B. Pedersen, R. Davies and T. Vaux (2006), *Evaluation of the Linkage of Relief, Rehabilitation and Development (LRRD) Regarding Interventions in Connection with the Tsunami Disaster in December 2004: Indonesia Case Study*, Report prepared by Channel Research for SIDA, March, Ohain, Belgium.
Carter, W. Nick (1991), *Disaster Management: A Disaster Manager's Handbook*, Manila: ADB.
Clinton, William J. (2006), *Key Propositions for Building Back Better*, United Nations: Office of the UN Secretary General's Special Envoy for Tsunami Recovery,

http://ochaonline.un.org/OchaLinkClick.aspx?link=ocha&docid=1005912, accessed 4 September 2009.

Commonwealth of Australia, AusAID (2007), *Relief in Sight: Australia's International Disaster Response in Pictures*, Canberra.

Doocy, Shannon, M. Gabriel, S. Collins, C. Robinson and P. Stevenson (2006), 'Implementing cash for work programmes in post-tsunami Aceh: experiences and lessons learned', *Disasters*, **30** (3), 277–96.

Flint, Michael and H. Goyder (2006), *Funding the Tsunami Response: A Synthesis of Findings*, London: Tsunami Evaluation Coalition.

German, Tony, J. Randel, T. Mowjee and L. Baker (2006), *Overall Funding Flows*, Background Paper prepared for the Tsunami Evaluation Coalition, Somerset, UK: Development Initiatives.

Harvey, Paul (2006), 'Editorial: mini special issue on cash transfers', *Disasters*, **30** (3), 273–76.

Harvey, Paul (2007), *Cash-Based Responses in Emergencies*, HPG Report 24, January, London: ODI.

Hovanesian, Ashot and A. Cox (2007), 'ICT for tsunami recovery: best practices and lessons learned', paper presented at the East-Asia Conference, Malaysia, 2007.

INTOSAI (2007), *Activity Report of the INTOSAI Task Force on Accountability for and Audit of Disaster-Related Aid*, memo submitted to the XIXth INCOSAI Meeting 2007, Mexico City, Mexico, November, www.intosai.org/blueline/upload/15ie.pdf, accessed 10 September 2009.

Jayasuriya, Sisira, P. Steele and D. Weerakoon (2006), *Post-Tsunami Recovery: Issues and Challenges in Sri Lanka*, ADB Institute Research Paper 71, January.

Kelaher, David and B. Dollery (2008), 'Cash and in-kind food aid transfers: the case of tsunami emergency aid in Banda Aceh', *International Review of Public Administration*, **13** (2), 117–28.

Lampman, J. (2005), 'Much has been given, much still to be done', *Christian Science Monitor*, 21 November.

Masyrafah, Harry and J.M.J.A. McKeon (2008), *Post-Tsunami Aid Effectiveness in Aceh: Proliferation and Coordination in Reconstruction*, Wolfensohn Center for Development Working Paper 6, Washington: The Brookings Institution, http://www.brookings.edu/~/media/Files/rc/papers/2008/11_aceh_aid_masyrafah/11_aceh_aid_masyrafah.pdf, accessed 26 September 2009.

McCawley, Peter (2006), 'Aid versus trade: Some considerations', *Australian Economic Review*, **39** (1), 89–95.

Nasution, Anwar (2009), 'The auditing of tsunami disaster relief funds in Aceh and Nias between 2004–2009', PowerPoint presentation at the International Public Sector Convention 2009, March, Sydney, http://www.bpk.go.id/web/files/2009/03/tsunami-warna-revised-13-03-091.pdf, accessed 9 September 2009.

Oddone, R. (2005), 'How dodgy accounting on donors' budgets continues to dilute aid', *Financial Times*, 5 September, p. 12.

OECD, DAC (2001), 'Is it ODA?', May, http://www.oecd.org/dataoecd/2/21/34086975.pdf, 15 January 2009.

Perdana, Ari A. and J. Maxwell (2005), 'Poverty targeting in Indonesia', in John Weiss (ed.), *Poverty Targeting in Asia*, Cheltenham, UK and Northampton, MA, USA: Edward Elgar and the Asian Development Bank Institute.

Ramkumar, Vivek (2006), 'Analyzing the UN tsunami relief fund expenditure tracking database: can the UN be more transparent?', The International Budget Project, www.internationalbudget.org, accessed 26 June 2008.

Sen, Amartya (2005), 'Ethics, development and disaster', keynote address at the IDB, 11 January 2005, www.iadb.org/ethics, accessed 5 November 2006.

Srivastava, Pradeep (2005), 'Poverty targeting in India', in John Weiss (ed.), *Poverty Targeting in Asia*, Cheltenham, UK and Northampton, MA, USA: Edward Elgar and the Asian Development Bank Institute, pp. 34–78.

Telford, John and J. Cosgrave (2007a), 'The international humanitarian system and the 2004 Indian Ocean earthquake and tsunamis', *Disasters*, **31** (1), 1–28.

Telford, John and J. Cosgrave (2007b), 'Tsunami exposes flaws in the international humanitarian response system', *id21*, ODI blog, www.id21.org/id21ext/s10cjt1g1.html, accessed 15 September 2009.

TGLL (Tsunami Global Lessons Learned Project) (2009), *The Tsunami Legacy: Innovations, Breakthroughs and Change*, TGLL Project Steering Committee, http://www.reliefweb.int/rw/rwb.nsf/db900sid/MUMA-7RF7PQ?OpenDocument, accessed 26 August 2009.

USGAO (2006), *Foreign Assistance: USAID Has Begun Tsunami Reconstruction in Indonesia and Sri Lanka, but Key Projects May Exceed Initial Cost and Schedule Estimates*, Report to Congressional Committees, GAO-06-488, April, Washington DC.

World Bank (2009), 'Reconstruction progress', tsunami website included on the Indonesia country website, http://go.worldbank.org/TE61DUE9G0, accessed 17 September 2009.

APPENDIX 3A.1   WHAT IS 'AID'?

Like many other economic magnitudes, 'aid' may be defined in various ways. And, like many other economic magnitudes, the term is often used in a vague way.

A useful place to start is the internationally accepted definition of net official development assistance (net ODA) agreed to by OECD member countries (OECD 2001).[1] In an effort to encourage some uniformity in the way in which financial terms are used in the global aid industry, donor countries have agreed on a careful definition of ODA. But despite the attempts of the OECD's Development Assistance Committee to encourage more accuracy and transparency in the reporting of aid terms, there is still much vagueness in both official reporting of aid flows and public policy discussion of the issues, including magnitudes. This vagueness is the source of much confusion (McCawley 2006).

Official Reporting

There are various reasons for the vagueness. One is the considerable confusion that surrounds many references to financial flows. Terminology used in the international aid industry is often vague about such key matters as differences between net and gross flows, loans and grants, the financial and other conditions on which loans are provided, commitments and disbursements, and the time period during which an announced program will be implemented. Clearly, the real value of assistance programs varies greatly depending on the conditions under which funding or other assistance is provided. An untied grant for an agreed development purpose, for example, would normally have a net ODA value equal or close to 100 per cent while a loan of the same amount provided on market terms would normally not be classified as ODA at all (OECD, DAC 2001).

Despite the fact that the conditions on which funds are provided are crucial in assessing the real value of aid, bilateral and multilateral development agencies are often vague about these matters. Press announcements are frequently issued referring in general terms to levels of 'assistance' or 'support', or perhaps to 'total project value'. In fact, announcements of this kind usually provide very little useful information about the level of net ODA transfers. But the differences between the various magnitudes which may be described as 'assistance' can be very substantial indeed. In this context, it is instructive to consider the difference between four magnitudes frequently referred to when discussing project activities in developing countries:

- total project costs
- loan approvals
- loan disbursements, and
- net transfers.

Differences between these magnitudes can be very substantial indeed. Depending on circumstances, a relatively large project in a developing country (say, amounting to US$1000 million) 'supported' by international donors might involve only very small net transfers. To complicate the picture further, none of these magnitudes refers to net ODA.

There are other considerations that frequently make it difficult to form meaningful judgements about the size of aid flows. One is timing; official announcements often indicate that programs will be implemented over a period of time (three or four years is quite common). This means that it is often difficult to know how much will be spent in any particular year, or indeed even when the programs will be regarded as having begun! Another is that it is not uncommon for the same program to be announced on a number of occasions. This practice leads to the risk of double-counting in media reporting about aid programs. The upshot of factors such as these is quite unsatisfactory. The inevitable result is that there is often considerable vagueness and even confusion across the international community about the size of aid programs (Oddone 2005).

Media Coverage

A second and quite different reason why many people think that international aid programs are much larger than they are is the language used in media reports about aid. Media reports often tend to use extravagant language to describe aid programs. Aid is said to be 'huge', 'massive', or is described as 'largesse' which is 'poured' into recipient countries. Governments in developing countries are said to be 'rewarded' with aid, or to have aid 'showered' upon them. Other reports talk of borrowing countries having aid 'pumped in', or of being 'flooded' with aid. Recipient countries are said to have aid 'heaped' upon them with the result that they are 'awash' with funds.

Reinforcing the impression that aid flows are large are statements from political leaders in both donor countries and recipient countries. In donor countries, leaders often describe national aid programs as 'generous', while leaders in recipient countries often also find it useful for various reasons to imply that volumes are significant. It is, in fact, hard to know what to make of the frequent suggestions that donor nations are generous because of the highly subjective nature of judgements about what sort of actions might be described as 'generous'. For example, an article in the *Christian Science Monitor* about charitable contributions in the United States in the period following the tsunami reported that 'Americans have given generously in 2005, reaching into their pockets . . . to respond to the Asian tsunami and the Gulf Coast hurricane' (Lampman 2005). However, the article went on to note that out of the estimated total level of charitable contributions in the United States in 2005 of US$250 billion (which was well over double the level of net ODA from all OECD countries to all developing countries at the time), only 2 per cent, or around US$5 billion, was typically provided to international aid. The great bulk of US charitable giving is spent within the United States.

Against this background of confused aid statistics and extravagant media coverage, it is not surprising that surveys of opinion in donor countries indicate that many people think that aid flows are large. The truth is that compared with many other areas of public expenditure, the international aid programs of OECD countries are quite modest, especially when compared with the extremely ambitious objectives ('Save the planet' and 'Make poverty history') often set for these programs.

NOTE

1. Data relating to ODA flows (including definitions of relevant concepts) is provided by the Development Assistance Committee of the OECD at www.oecd.org/dac.

4. Indonesia: the first two years after the tsunami[1]

INTRODUCTION

Indonesia, the country worst hit by the December 2004 tsunami, is located in the 'Ring of Fire' which consists of volcanic arcs and oceanic trenches partly encircling the Pacific Basin. The Basin sits between the Indo-Australian and Eurasian plates, making it a zone of frequent volcanic eruptions and earthquakes. Historically, several of the natural disasters that have occurred in Indonesia have been among the worst in the world. The Tambora and Krakatoa eruptions in 1815 and 1883 were among the largest eruptions in history. Further, the contour and climate of the archipelago increase the likelihood of other deadly natural disasters such as cyclones, droughts, and floods. From 1907 to mid-2006 there were 338 natural disasters in Indonesia – an average of around three to four disasters per year.[2] On average, approximately 700 people died, 1200 were injured, 5200 became homeless, and 64 000 people were affected per event.[3] Indonesia is considered to be among the five countries that most frequently experience deadly natural disasters – the others being the US, the People's Republic of China, India, and the Philippines. Recent data suggests that the frequency of these deadly events may be increasing in these countries (Figure 4.1).

In terms of human fatalities the tsunami on 26 December 2004 was the worst natural disaster in Indonesian history. Most people in Aceh and North Sumatra and other nearby parts of Indonesia felt the tremor caused by a massive earthquake measuring 9.0 on the Richter scale that occurred beneath the seabed about 300 kilometres off the west of Sumatra around 8 am local time. Shortly after, a great tsunami hit the northern and western parts of Aceh and North Sumatra as well as other smaller islands such as Nias and Simeulue. Twenty-metre waves struck Banda Aceh, the provincial capital city of the province of Aceh, at a tremendous speed of around 800 kilometres per hour. In some places waves swept over seven kilometres inland. Waves as high as 12 metres hit the towns of Meulaboh, Calang, and Lamno in western Aceh and in some places up to about 10 kilometres from the coastline were submerged (Soehaimi et al. 2005). The official

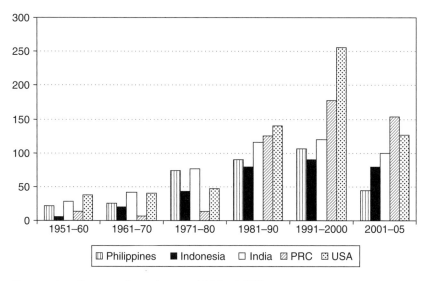

Source: http://www.em-dat.net/, accessed 3 March 2007.

Figure 4.1   *Frequency of natural disasters in the five countries most prone to natural disasters, 1951–2005*

death toll (including missing) in Aceh and Nias was close to 167000. More than 500000 persons were displaced. Official reports also listed widespread destruction, including the loss of over 110000 houses, 3000 kilometres of roads, 14 seaports, 11 airports and air strips, 120 arterial bridges, 2000 school buildings, and eight hospitals, among much other damage (BRR and International Partners 2005; BRR 2006).

On 28 March 2005, while Aceh was still coping with the first emergency, another major earthquake devastated the western part of Sumatra. The epicentre of this earthquake, 8.7 on the Richter scale, was located to the north of Nias – halfway between Simeulue and the Nias islands (Figure 4.2). Although the government never declared this to be a national disaster, for an island as small and poor as Nias the impact was overwhelming. Over 800 people died and 6300 were injured. In the capital city of Gunung Sitoli around 70 per cent of the buildings collapsed. There was widespread fear and it was estimated that over 15000 people fled the island. The earthquake disrupted the livelihood of the entire population of Nias, most of whom are farmers and fishermen (*Kompas*, 29 March 2005; Aceh Media Center, 5 May 2005; BPS Kabupaten Nias 2005).

This chapter aims to evaluate the rehabilitation process in Aceh and Nias as at the end of 2006, two years after the tsunami. The evaluation

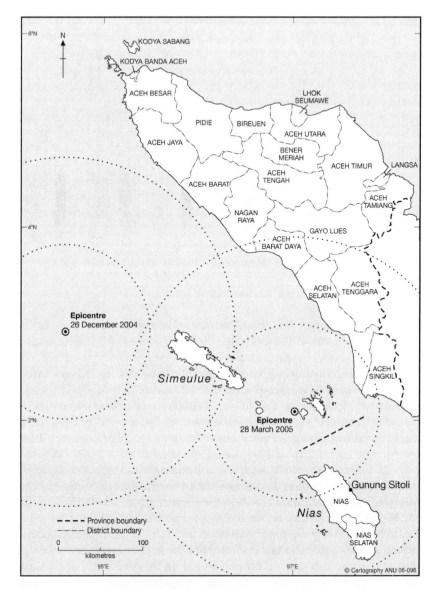

Figure 4.2   Aceh, Nias and the epicentres of the earthquakes

sets out to assess progress and to identify the challenges of redevelopment. With this goal in mind, three main tasks were undertaken. First, a survey of the data sources on the impact of the disasters in Aceh and Nias and on the progress of reconstruction was conducted. Second, data from the census (*Sensus Penduduk Aceh dan Nias* or SPAN 2005) carried out by the Indonesian Central Statistics Agency (*Badan Pusat Statistik* or BPS) in Aceh and Nias in September 2005 was analysed to obtain a picture of the impact at household level (see BPS, Bappenas et al. 2005a; 2005b, hereafter cited as SPAN 2005).[4] Third, interviews with national government officials in Jakarta, local government officials, officials at the *Badan Rekonstruksi dan Rehabilitasi* (BRR) reconstruction agency, contractors, and many others were arranged. Most of the interviews took place in January, May, and June 2006. A triangulation procedure was applied to draw inferences from these interviews (Patton 2002).[5]

This chapter is structured as follows. Following this introduction, background material is provided on the socio-economic and political situation in Aceh and Nias before the disasters. In particular, information is provided about political conflicts and the Aceh freedom movement. The next section summarizes the impact of the December 2004 tsunami in Aceh and the March 2005 earthquake in Nias. This section is followed by a discussion of the emergency relief stage. Three main issues need to be elaborated upon concerning the foundations of the recovery:

- the Master Plan,
- the establishment of the reconstruction and rehabilitation agency (BRR), and
- the peace agreement between the Government of Indonesia (GoI) and the Free Aceh Movement (GAM).

Then progress in various areas – land titling, housing, livelihood arrangements, school and health services, and infrastructure – to the end of 2006 is described. It is noted that progress towards meeting goals was slow and that at that stage huge challenges remained. Issues relating to managing expectations, coordination and commitments, budget realization, and the exit strategy of the BRR are also discussed. Finally, some conclusions are set out.

ACEH AND NIAS BEFORE THE DISASTERS

There are significant differences between the socio-economic and political structures in Aceh and on the island of Nias. Aceh is a much larger and more heterogeneous region than Nias. Aceh is a province while Nias is only a small region of the province of North Sumatra (Figure 4.2). Although the majority of the population in Aceh work in the agricultural sector, the economy of Aceh has been dominated for decades by the oil and gas industry. In contrast, Nias has a predominantly semi-subsistence

Table 4.1　GDP with and without oil and gas, Aceh, 2000–04 (billion rupiah)

Year	GDP (with oil & gas) (Rp bn)	GDP (without oil & gas) (Rp bn)	Growth (with oil & gas) (%)	Growth (without oil & gas) (%)
2000	35883	19259	–	–
2001	32565	19136	−9.3	−0.6
2002	39961	20426	22.7	6.9
2003	42239	21204	5.7	3.7
2004	39664	21778	−6.1	2.7

Note:　Based on 2000 constant prices. 2004 data are preliminary figures.

Source:　Bappeda Aceh (2005).

economy. In the period before the tsunami, Aceh had experienced three decades of serious political conflict while there had not been any serious political turmoil in Nias.

Economic Conditions in Aceh

The regional GDP of the province of Aceh in 2003 was approximately US$4.5 billion, about 2 per cent of the GDP of Indonesia. While the economy of Aceh had generally benefited from the regional oil and gas industry, in 2004 the local energy sector contracted somewhat, contributing to negative growth in the province (Table 4.1). The agriculture sector, which made up around 32 per cent of regional GDP, also plays a key role in the local economy. Agriculture absorbs almost 50 per cent of labour in Aceh. Other major sectors of employment are trade (21 per cent) and public services (18 per cent) (Bappeda Aceh 2005).

In the early 2000s Aceh's exports to other parts of Indonesia were small, around 8 per cent of regional output. About 26 per cent of Aceh's output was exported abroad and 66 per cent was consumed within the province. Imports from other parts of Indonesia and from abroad were a small part, about 6 per cent and 4 per cent, respectively, of the total material inputs needed for Aceh's productive sectors (Athukorala and Resosudarmo 2005). Regional inflation (as measured in the provincial capital of Banda Aceh) was moderate in the period just before the tsunami (Figure 4.3).

Aceh's population was around 4.1 million in 2003. Although on paper Acehnese GDP per capita (almost US$1100) was among the highest in Indonesia because of the statistical boost to measured production

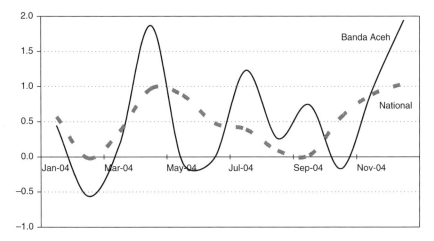

Source: Bappeda Aceh (2005).

Figure 4.3   Monthly rates of inflation (%), Banda Aceh, prior to December 2004 earthquake and tsunami

provided by the oil and gas sector, in fact many local areas in Aceh did not receive noticeable benefits from the enclave energy sector and were quite underdeveloped. Indeed, before the tsunami, the Indonesian Ministry for the Development of Least Developed Regions classified eleven districts in Aceh (around half of the total in the province) as 'least developed districts'. In 2003 it was estimated that the percentage of poor people in Aceh was almost 30 per cent compared to the Indonesia-wide figure of around 17 per cent. Aceh was among the five provinces with the highest percentage of poor people (BPS 2005). The long-term socio-political conflict was widely believed to be one of the major causes for the lack of development in the province (Soesastro and Ace 2005).

The Indonesian national decentralization program which became effective in 2001 brought dramatic changes to public revenue and expenditure patterns in Aceh. Regional government spending in 2004 was double that of 1999. However, the bulk of the expenditure was still for routine administrative expenses such as salaries and building maintenance (World Bank 2003 and 2006b; Bappeda Aceh 2005).

Economic Conditions in Nias

With a population of about 700000 people, the island of Nias is considered to be one of the poorest regions in the province of North Sumatra.

There is not much trade between Nias and other parts of North Sumatra. Its contribution to the provincial economy of North Sumatra is very small. Per capita income was estimated at about US$340 per annum in 2004. The share of the population living below the poverty line in 2002 was 31 per cent, roughly twice North Sumatra's level of 16 per cent or the Indonesia-wide figure that year of 18 per cent. Further, compared to the regions in the North Sumatra province and nationally, recorded human development levels were low and signs of progress were also very slow. Close to half of the household heads in Nias had only elementary schooling. About one-third of children from 7 to 18 years of age did not attend school in 2002. Despite the availability of health centres throughout the island, lack of access to satisfactory basic health services was still widespread because of inadequate services and poor infrastructure (BPS Kabupaten Nias 2005).

Lack of infrastructure is commonly cited as one of the main reasons for the economic backwardness of Nias. Poor infrastructure limits mobility across the island and isolates villages from markets, leading to low levels of economic development. In 2004 the local Nias economy was still mainly reliant on agriculture and trade services, accounting for almost 37 and 35 per cent, respectively, of the total regional GDP. Trade services in Nias, however, are largely limited to activities conducted in the informal sector. As in other backward regions of Indonesia, the role of local government in the small formal sector of the economy was quite high. In 2004, total local government expenditure was around Rp200 billion (a little over US$20 million), approximately 10 per cent of the Nias GDP (BPS Kabupaten Nias 2005).

Conflict and Freedom Movements in Aceh

Socio-political conflict between the Free Aceh Movement (GAM) and the Indonesian government began in the mid-1970s. Conflict escalated in the five years prior to the 2004 tsunami, destroying or damaging about 900 schools, causing a dramatic decline in school attendance, and displacing over 100 000 people. Meanwhile, health care became less accessible because people were afraid to visit medical centres for security reasons (Soesastro and Ace 2005; World Bank 2005). Another significant impact was the drop in the number of economic establishments and in the quality of infrastructure in the region. The total number of firms declined from around 7600 in 2001 to only around 1200 by 2004. Many roads were not properly maintained and people were often afraid to travel outside of their towns and villages, particularly at night (Bappeda Aceh 2005).

The basic causes of the separatist movement can be found in the history of the relationship between the people of Aceh and the central authorities in Jakarta. During the Dutch colonial period the region was never formally annexed. Consequently, during the early years of Indonesian independence in the late 1940s there was a strong feeling in some quarters of Aceh that the region should not be automatically incorporated into the new state of Indonesia and that, certainly, the Acehnese people should have been consulted as to whether they wanted to join with Indonesia or to form an independent state. Twenty years later, the centralized mode of government during Soeharto's 'New Order' government strengthened this sentiment among some Acehnese, particularly when the central government signed contracts with foreign companies for the mining of natural resources in Aceh without consultation with the people of Aceh. Much local resentment was generated when the Acehnese realized that most of the income from the oil and gas activities in the region flowed to the central government rather than into local coffers.

The armed struggle waged by the GAM guerrilla movement escalated in the 1980s when they allegedly received support from overseas groups. The Government of Indonesia responded with repressive measures and placed the region under Operational Military status. This led to an increase in local conflict, causing deaths and a rise in the number of internally displaced persons. During the military operations, both GAM and the Indonesian government accused each other of violating human rights. The military operation officially ended in 1996. However, the military presence in the region was not reduced, even after President Soeharto stepped down from office in 1998. In fact the military presence is thought to have increased in the early 2000s during the Megawati Sukarnoputri administration (World Bank 2006b).

THE IMPACTS

This section reviews the impact of both disasters – the December 2004 tsunami in Aceh and the March 2005 earthquake in Nias.

Human Loss and Displacement

Within days of the December 2004 tsunami, international news reports led the world to expect huge losses in Aceh. Nevertheless, it was several months before the world knew of the real extent of the death toll and the numbers missing, and of the continuing plight of internally displaced persons (IDPs) in Aceh. Indeed, different agencies provided different numbers. The official death toll in Aceh was estimated at close to 167 000 by the Department of Social Affairs in mid-March 2005, and the number displaced was put at 811000, of whom 920 were in hospitals while approximately 477000 were living in refugee camps. Several organizations reported that children, women, and the elderly accounted for more than two-thirds of the tsunami victims (see also Athukorala and Resosudarmo 2005). This meant that the demographic structure of many villages and towns hit by the tsunami had changed dramatically. By 1 June 2005, the Secretary General of the United Nations, Kofi Annan, described the Aceh tsunami as 'the largest natural disaster the organisation has had to respond to on behalf of the world community, in the 60 years of our existence' (UN Press Release SG/SM/9666 IHA/978, 6 January 2005).

In contrast, Nias did not suffer greatly as a result of the tsunami. The March earthquake resulted in a high local death toll which was, however, small in total compared to that in Aceh. The official BRR report stated that 850 people had been killed and 6000 injured (BRR Nias 2005).

As noted earlier, in response to the need for accurate demographic data after the disaster, BPS conducted the Aceh-Nias population census (SPAN 2005) in September 2005 (Table 4.2). The earthquakes and tsunami displaced a total of almost 900000 people. In September 2005, almost 260000 people still held IDP status. The districts of Aceh Jaya, Aceh Barat, Aceh Besar, and the city of Banda Aceh suffered most from the tsunami (Table 4.3). Although it is impossible to determine the exact numbers more precisely, these estimates seem to provide a reasonably accurate picture of the overall impact in terms of the numbers of people killed and missing. The impact of the earthquakes and tsunami was certainly concentrated in these areas.

It is important to note that the relatively high percentage of IDPs on Simeulue Island was not preceded by a high death toll. Only seven deaths were recorded on the island despite the fact that Simeulue is situated only about 100 kilometres from the epicentre of the March earthquake. The island was indeed severely hit by the December tsunami: approximately 5500 houses were destroyed and hundreds of people were injured (*Kompas*, 1 April 2005). There are two probable explanations for the relatively small number of fatalities. First, the coastal ecosystem – the coral reef, sea grass, and mangrove forests – softened the force of the giant waves. Second, local customs and traditions on the island include important information about the warning signs of a tsunami: according to local tradition a tsunami is always preceded by the retreat of the sea, knowledge that has been transferred from one generation to another.

Indeed, the retreat of the sea did occur on the morning of 26 December 2004. Local inhabitants who recognized the signs of an impending tsunami ran to the closest hills shouting '*smong . . . smong . . . smong*' (tsunami in

Table 4.2 Population and internally displaced persons (IDPs), Aceh and Nias, 2005

Region & sub-region	Population in Sept. 2005	IDP in early 2005	% IDP	Still IDP in Sept. 2005	No longer IDP by Sept. 2005	% IDP in Sept. 2005
Aceh province	4031589	508671	13	209822	298849	5
Aceh Jaya	60660	34198	56	27755	6443	46
Simeulue	78389	56606	72	15498	41108	20
Aceh Barat	150450	47660	32	28018	19642	19
Aceh Besar	296541	67554	23	46998	20556	16
Banda Aceh	177881	92589	52	24210	68379	14
Sabang	28597	7122	25	2061	5061	7
Nagan Raya	123743	11828	10	6314	5514	5
Aceh Singkil	148277	28040	19	7106	20934	5
Pidie	474359	42876	9	19906	22970	4
Bireuen	351835	34647	10	10032	24615	3
Aceh Selatan	191539	19366	10	4547	14819	2
All other areas	1949318	66185	3	17377	48808	1
Nias region	712075	387102	54	47055	340047	7
TOTAL	4743664	895773	19	256877	638896	5

Source: BPS et al. (2005a, 2005b).

the local language). Others took up the warning, running to the hills while contributing to the chorus of '*smong . . . smong . . . smong*'. This simple procedure proved to be very effective in Simeulue when the tsunami struck (Wetlands International – Indonesia Programme 2005; *Kompas*, 1 April 2005). Sadly, in other areas of Aceh and North Sumatra such simple traditional mitigation procedures imbedded in local cultures had never existed or had been long forgotten. The experience in Simeulue suggests it is important to develop programs strengthening local knowledge about natural disasters. One way of doing so would be to introduce special training courses on natural disasters into the national elementary education system across Indonesia.

SPAN 2005 also provided information on the impact of the disaster on personal livelihoods and the daily lives of affected people (Table 4.4). Almost 265000 people in Aceh and over 85000 in Nias lost their sources of income; over 190000 people in Aceh and almost 62000 in Nias lost their houses; and around 391000 people in Aceh and 539000 in Nias suffered damage to their houses.

Table 4.3   *Estimated number of people killed and missing in Aceh and Nias, December 2004 and March 2005 tsunami and earthquake disasters*

	No. of people killed	No. of people missing
Aceh Province		
Aceh Barat	10 874	2 911
Aceh Barat Daya	3	n.a.
Aceh Besar	92 166	15 176
Aceh Jaya	16 797	77
Aceh Selatan	1 566	1 086
Aceh Singkil	22	4
Aceh Tamiang	n.a.	n.a.
Aceh Tengah	n.a.	n.a.
Aceh Tenggara	n.a.	n.a.
Aceh Timur	52	n.a.
Aceh Utara	2 098	218
Banda Aceh	n.a.	15 394
Bener Meriah	n.a.	n.a.
Bireuen	461	58
Gayo Lues	n.a.	n.a.
Langsa	n.a.	n.a.
Lhokseumawe	189	11
Nagan Raya	1 077	865
Pidie	4 401	877
Sabang	25	108
Simuelue	44	1
Nias Region		
Nias	784	18
Nias Selatan	177	n.a.

Note: n.a. indicates data not available.

Source: Satkorlak Report (10–16 October 2005).

Physical Impacts

The immediate physical impacts of the December tsunami in Aceh and the March earthquake in Nias were tremendous. The tsunami wiped out practically all physical objects in many parts of Aceh's western and northern coastal areas, flattening hundreds of thousands of houses, infrastructure of all kinds, and many other facilities (Table 4.5).

Table 4.4 Impact on livelihood and daily life situation following December 2004 and March 2005 tsunami and earthquake disasters, Aceh and Nias

Type of impact	Aceh	% of population	Nias	% of pop.
House damaged	391 316	10	538 816	76
Loss of primary source of income	264 650	7	85 462	12
Loss of house	191 353	5	61 588	9
Loss of household members	106 480	3	3 097	. . .
Mental illness	62 794	2	18 849	3
Disabled	6 639	. . .	2 457	. . .
Other impacts	279 877	7	109 331	15

Source: Authors' calculation from SPAN (2005).

While the disasters in Aceh and Nias wrought similar types of devastation on local people, there was an important difference as to the causes. In Aceh, a great wave smashed buildings, cars, trees, people, and everything else in its path. Most of those who were able to climb up trees or onto roofs or those in higher storey premises, survived. In Nias, the earthquake preceding the December tsunami did not do much damage and caused few deaths. But things were quite different in March. The March earthquake in Nias destroyed numerous buildings. The fact that the March earthquake occurred when most people were asleep added to the toll because when the earthquake struck, houses collapsed and many sleeping occupants were buried. In addition, the typical construction of houses in urban areas in Nias also added to the fatalities. As is the case in other towns in Indonesia, typical urban houses in Nias are made of bricks that have usually replaced previous wooden structures. The foundations are usually not sufficiently strong for a brick structure because compliance with building codes is mostly lax. Worse, some homeowners add a second storey imposing additional strains on the inadequate foundations. This non-compliance with building codes is the main reason why four out of five houses in Nias were damaged (BRR Nias 2005).

In many cases in poorer areas of Aceh and Nias, the heavy physical damage to infrastructure (such as fallen bridges) was apparently due to the low quality of the structures or insufficient maintenance rather than to the severity of the natural disasters. In rural areas, lack of proper maintenance

Table 4.5   Housing damage assessment following December 2004 and March 2005 tsunami and earthquake disasters, Aceh and Nias

Region & sub-region	Total houses	Mild	Severe	Destroyed	Total damage	% damaged in total
Aceh province	865744	66597	26760	14670	99738	12
Simeulue	17315	6573	4214	31	10818	63
Banda Aceh	35443	7011	2509	94	10202	29
Aceh Barat	31252	4692	2298	2125	8033	26
Nagan Raya	29169	5236	1640	2278	7299	25
Aceh Singkil	31442	5972	1564	7	7650	24
Aceh Selatan	41445	5117	1475	24	6635	16
Aceh Jaya	11539	733	438	32	1716	15
Bireuen	74564	7623	2426	5	10379	14
Aceh Barat Daya	24685	2068	855	149	2976	12
Aceh Utara	106581	8273	2068	1449	11764	11
Sabang	6721	443	194	4	695	10
Aceh Besar	56104	2701	1904	157	5559	10
Lhokseumawe	32824	1901	526	5	2452	8
Pidie	108948	4353	1729	129	6690	6
All other areas	257712	3901	2920	8181	6870	3
Nias region	131217	57378	37090	10070	104538	80
TOTAL	996961	123975	63850	24740	204276	21

Source: Authors' calculation from SPAN (2005).

probably contributed to the destruction of schools or health facility buildings. In December 2005, the BRR announced its initial estimates of physical damage in Aceh and Nias caused by the natural disasters. In April 2006, the BRR corrected its estimates of damages, particularly regarding damages in Nias (the corrected estimates are shown in Table 4.6).

Economic Impacts

The World Bank's assessment of the total damage caused by the Aceh tsunami was US$4.45 billion, almost equal to Aceh's GDP in 2003.[6] Of this total, 60 per cent was estimated to be physical damage and 40 per cent was from losses of income flows through the economy. Almost 80 per cent of total damage and losses was borne by the private sector while

Table 4.6 *BRR estimate of destruction in Aceh and Nias, December 2004 and March 2005, and progress towards reconstruction, 2005–06*

	Destruction	Progress	
		by December 2005	by December 2006
Housing	80–110 000 houses in Aceh and 13–14 000 in Nias	16 000 new houses	57 000 new houses and 15 000 transitional shelters
Infrastructure	3000 km of roads	235 km of roads restored (and major road projects underway)	over 1200 km of roads in Aceh and 300 km in Nias built/restored
	14 seaports	5 major ports being built	All ports operational; 11 ferry terminals and harbours in Aceh and 3 in Nias built/under development
	11 airports/ airstrips		all airports operational: 5 airports and 1 airstrip in Aceh and 2 in Nias built/under development
	120 arterial bridges and 1500 minor bridges	35 arterial bridges rebuilt	121 bridges in Aceh and 37 in Nias repaired
Education	2000 school buildings	335 new schools built	623 new schools in Aceh and 124 in Nias built
	2500 teachers	more than 1000 new teachers trained	5100 teachers in Aceh and 285 in Nias trained
Health	8 hospitals and 114 health centres	38 hospitals and health centres rebuilt (and 51 more under reconstruction)	305 health facilities in Aceh and 19 in Nias
Fisheries	around 5000 fishing boats	3122 boats replaced	4420 fishing vessels replaced
	20 000 ha of fish ponds	5000 ha of fish ponds repaired	6800 ha of fishponds rehabilitated
Agriculture	60 000 farmers displaced	40 000 farmers assisted to return	68% of male and 45% of female labour force are working in rural areas

Table 4.6   (continued)

	Destruction	Progress	
		by December 2005	by December 2006
Agriculture (*cont.*) Enterprises	70 000 ha of agricultural land more than 100 000 persons lost livelihoods in small business	13 000 ha of farmland restored 7000 workers given skills training (and over 120 000 benefited from cash-for-work schemes)	50 000 ha of farmland restored 69% of male and 36% of female labour force actively engaged in urban areas

Source: BRR and International Partners (2005); BRR and Partners (2006).

the rest was borne by the public sector (World Bank 2005). The Institute for Economic and Social Research (LPEM) at the Faculty of Economics, University of Indonesia, estimated the total damage in Aceh to be slightly higher than the World Bank's estimate at US\$4.6 billion (LPEM 2005). The World Bank also estimated the damage of the March earthquake in Nias to be around US\$392 million. Therefore, after adjusting for predicted inflation, the World Bank put the expected cost of repairing the damage caused by the two disasters at around US\$5.8 billion (BRR and International Partners 2005).

According to the World Bank, Aceh's GDP in 2005 could contract by 7–28 per cent of the 2004 level (World Bank 2005). LPEM (2005) arrived at a slightly lower estimate than the World Bank's upper estimate (22 per cent). The destruction in the province of North Sumatra was mainly concentrated in Nias, the poorest district in the province and one whose contribution to the overall regional economy is rather small. In Nias, the island economy was predicted to contract by around 20 per cent (BRR and International Partners 2005).

The oil and gas industry in Aceh escaped the tsunami virtually unharmed. The most seriously affected sector in terms of both the number of casualties and capital destroyed was agriculture, particularly fisheries (Soesastro and Ace 2005).

According to information gathered by the Ministry of Marine Affairs and Fisheries, by mid-January 2005 approximately 55 000 fishers and aquaculture workers were confirmed dead (approximately one-half of the total number of fishers in Aceh) and around 14 000 were still missing. The Food and Agriculture Organization of the United Nations (FAO) reported that 40–60 per cent of coastal aquaculture ponds along coastal Aceh and between 36 000 and 48 000 hectares of brackish-water aquaculture ponds (which mainly produced shrimp and milkfish) were seriously damaged. It is estimated that about 65–70 per cent of the small-scale fishing fleet and associated gear was destroyed in Aceh (FAO 2005a).

In Aceh about 30 000 hectares of rice fields – around 10 per cent of the area under rice cultivation in the province – were badly affected. Soil salinity problems were the main concern. Fortunately, because of humid conditions, salt-polluted arable land was cleaned by rainfall and by irrigation water relatively quickly. A survey carried out by FAO in early 2005 indicated that salt deposited in more than two-thirds of the affected agricultural land was leached out within a few months allowing planting to resume in April and May 2005. It was estimated that only 9000 hectares could no longer be used for farming (*China View*, 31 March 2005; FAO 2005b).

The impact of the decline in Aceh's GDP on Indonesia's overall economic performance was small. Both the World Bank and the LPEM estimated that Indonesia's GDP growth in 2005 was expected to be no more than around half a per cent less than the pre-tsunami growth forecast (World Bank 2005; LPEM 2005). An immediate sharp increase in poverty was probably the single most serious economic problem caused by the tsunami. In 2004, the Indonesian Central Bureau of Statistics calculated that almost 30 per cent of people in Aceh were living below the poverty line. At the time, LPEM predicted that this figure could grow to around 50 per cent.

THE IMMEDIATE RESPONSE

Rescue and Relief

In the first couple of days after the tsunami, little information was received by the outside world so initial rescue operations were relatively limited and slow. In this early stage, local people had to depend on their own resources to survive for some days before Indonesian government agencies responded. Soon after, when the outside world began to realize what had happened, international responses started to get underway. During this first week, the Indonesian military – which had come under some criticism for their military operations in Aceh – provided crucial assistance in conducting rescue and relief operations and in helping to cope with the large number of dead.

By the beginning of the second week, the numbers of domestic and international aid organizations arriving in Aceh increased significantly.

Although there was some lack of coordination between these organizations, the fact that they were able to provide relief for the tsunami victims
was much more important. In the third week, the number of international
organizations arriving in Aceh continued to rise – around 250 domestic
and international organizations sent workers to Aceh. Countless others
provided other types of assistance (Sen and Steer 2005; Indrawati 2005).
The media also played a key role by attracting domestic and international
support.

By mid-February 2005, the UN Office for the Coordination of
Humanitarian Affairs (OCHA) recorded that total pledges and commitments from over thirty countries and various organizations had reached
approximately US$800 million (OCHA 2005). Around 2.3 million people
were directly affected by the disaster so the aid contribution for rescue and
relief activities per person was about US$350. The norm in previous inter-
national fundraising attempts in the face of natural disasters in developing
countries has been a mere US$40 per person (*Economist*, 5 February 2005;
Athukorala and Resosudarmo 2005).

The Indonesian central government also responded quickly by announcing at the end of December 2004 that the government would release
approximately US$5 million to support relief activities. The government
also announced that it would support operations in three phases: (1) emergency rescue and relief operations, (2) rehabilitation and reconstruction
of basic socioeconomic infrastructure and restoration of law and order,
and (3) reconstruction of the economy and government system. The first
phase was completed by April 2005. The second phase began around April
2005 and was expected to last for around two years. The third phase was
expected to take around three to five more years (BRR and International
Partners 2005).[7]

The relief efforts conducted by both domestic and international organizations provided great physical and financial assistance. It should also
be noted, however, that local people were obliged to depend on their
own resources during the first couple of days after the disaster. This
fact underlines the importance of establishing strong and resilient local
communities.

Funding

The international focus on victims of the Aceh tsunami as well as the Nias
earthquake continued well beyond the initial relief period. The Paris Club
of creditor nations at its meeting in Paris on 12 January 2005 declared
a moratorium on the foreign debt of the tsunami-hit countries. Some
key players in the international aid community, including World Bank

President James Wolfensohn, suggested that debt write-offs would be preferable to debt deferral. However this proposal was not agreed to on the grounds that it might raise moral hazard issues: countries absolved of debt might be tempted to borrow excessively in the future in the expectation that they would eventually be bailed out if, for some reason, they had difficulties in meeting repayments. The IMF and World Bank officially endorsed the moratorium and the major international credit-rating agencies agreed that they would not regard deferral of debt service payments as a negative factor in their risk assessments and credit ratings. Subsequently, the IMF and the World Bank also announced considerable debt relief for the affected countries, particularly the Maldives, Sri Lanka, and Indonesia (Soesastro and Ace 2005; *Economist*, 5 February 2005).

Members of the Consultative Group on Indonesia (CGI) at a meeting convened hurriedly on 19–20 January 2005 agreed to contribute US$1.7 billion in 2005 for the reconstruction of Aceh. Of this amount, US$1.2 billion was promised in the form of grants and the remaining US$0.5 billion was pledged as soft loans at zero or near-zero interest rates. Of the US$1.2 billion in grants, only US$0.2 billion was to be distributed through the Indonesian government. The rest was to be distributed through non-government organizations (NGOs) (Soesastro and Ace 2005).

In February 2005, the Asian Development Bank (ADB) set up a US$600 million Asian Tsunami Fund to provide grants for emergency technical assistance and reconstruction projects. Indonesia was to receive half of the grant, divided into US$290 million for the Earthquake and Tsunami Emergency Support Project (ETESP) and US$10 million as the ADB's contribution to the Multi Donor Fund (MDF) for Aceh-Nias. The ETESP was intended to support disaster management, reconstruction and rehabilitation in affected areas of Aceh and North Sumatra. The sectoral targets of the grant included agriculture, fisheries, micro and small enterprises, health, education, water supply, irrigation, housing, power, roads, and spatial planning (ADB 2006).

Commitments from various countries, organizations, and private individuals to support the reconstruction effort were considered generous. For example, Australia agreed to provide financial support amounting to about A$1 billion. A$500 million was expected to be in the form of grants and A$500 million in soft loans over the period 2005–10. According to records maintained by the BRR, 78 countries, 30 organizations, and many individual donors pledged support (both grants and soft loans) of around US$6.1 billion in total by November 2005. The total amount given through direct private contributions was quite large; according to some estimates, this amounted to US$2.5 billion out of the total donor pledges. In some cases, such as in the United Kingdom, United States, and

Italy, private contributions exceeded government contributions by a wide margin (BRR and International Partners 2005).

A multi-donor trust fund for Aceh-Nias, the MDF, was established by the Indonesian government in early 2005. The main goal of this fund was to attract and pool bilateral and other resources so as to ensure a coordinated approach to the support of rehabilitation activities in Aceh and Nias.[8] Contributions were also expected from the private sector, foundations, and NGOs. The fund was designed to support two types of activities (MDF 2005):

1. New projects or new components of existing projects, including the co-financing of existing or new projects supported by multilateral agencies or other financiers.
2. Assistance for government programs that were part of the rehabilitation and reconstruction efforts.

By January 2006 about 66 per cent of the US$530 million pledges had been formalized in the form of a contribution agreement and the MDF had received US$229 million in cash. Disbursements had been made to seven projects amounting to US$79 million. These projects included land titling, rural and urban community recovery, housing and settlements, waste management, and technical assistance to the BRR. By December 2006 the amount provided to the fund had reached US$655 million with pledges from fifteen donors (Table 4.7). About 77 per cent of these pledges had been formalized in the form of contribution agreements and approximately US$480 million had been allocated to 17 projects in four sectors: recovery of communities, infrastructure and transport, capacity building and governance, and sustainable management of the environment. Disbursement to these projects had reached around US$170 million (http://www.multidonorfund.org/).

The Indonesian government also provided large-scale support for reconstruction in Aceh and Nias. The 2005 government budget allocation for reconstruction in Aceh (which included some of the funding received from international agencies) was approximately US$880 million (*Kompas*, 27 August 2005) and in 2006 was approximately US$960 million. Over five years, the total government budget for Aceh's reconstruction, including government loans, was expected to be around US$3–4 billion (*Tempo Interactive*, 27 March 2005).

Table 4.8 shows the composition of funding commitments according to the BRR, for rehabilitation and reconstruction activities until 2009. This total amount of over US$9 billion, which is much larger than the initial estimate of damages and losses, reflected an intention to 'build

Table 4.7   List of pledges through multi donor fund (MDF) as at December 2006

	Pledges (US$ million)
European Commission	253
Netherlands	174
United Kingdom	72
World Bank	25
Sweden	20
Denmark	18
Norway	18
Germany	14
Canada	11
Belgium	10
Finland	10
Asian Development Bank	10
United States of America	10
New Zealand	9
Ireland	1
Total Contributions	655

Source: http://www.multidonorfund.org/, accessed 18 May 2007.

Table 4.8   2005 composition of funding commitments for rehabilitation and reconstruction to 2009

	US$ billion
Domestic sources through the government budget	3.0
Foreign governments	3.6
Private sector and NGOs	2.5
Total	9.1

back better' in Aceh and Nias. By the end of 2005, around US$4.4 billion had been allocated to specific projects (BRR and International Partners 2005).

FOUNDATIONS FOR RECOVERY

As noted earlier, the Indonesian government responded to the disasters in three main phases: emergency rescue and relief; rehabilitation and restoration of law and order; and longer-term reconstruction of the economy and government systems. Because of the difficult economic and political conditions of Aceh and the sheer magnitude of the destruction of its infrastructure, the first phase of crisis management took much longer than expected.

There were three main concerns regarding the activities in the rehabilitation phase. The first was the need to coordinate the activities conducted by the very large number of official and other agencies active in the field. The Indonesian government appointed the national planning agency, Bappenas, as the central agency for developing recovery planning for the tsunami-affected areas. The main challenge for Bappenas was to develop a master plan that satisfied all of the main institutions working in the province. For a considerable time, dialogue between Bappenas on the one hand, and local governments in the region on the other, was rather limited. Lacking direct involvement in much of the planning process, many local governments felt that they had been excluded from the reconstruction process by the central government. As a result, local governments had drawn up programs that in some cases were incompatible with Bappenas plans. At times, this led to duplication of activities and the inefficient utilization of funds.

There were also cases of poor coordination of activities between NGOs and Bappenas. Many NGOs resisted accepting plans that were drawn up exclusively by Bappenas. Indeed, several groupings of NGOs prepared their own reconstruction programs for Aceh although it was not clear how they intended to relate these plans to those of Bappenas or local governments.

In these difficult circumstances the Indonesian government decided to establish an entirely new agency to coordinate recovery activities. However local governments, communities, and private sector firms as well as NGOs were not very keen on this approach. They were worried that this new agency would add an additional layer of bureaucracy to the problems of working in Aceh. They were also concerned that construction work would be tendered in Jakarta and would be won by large construction companies with good connections to high-ranking officers in the central government and that the implementation of these activities would be conducted without proper attention to the needs of local people. Local communities and NGOs pressed for a more decentralized approach (Athukorala and Resosudarmo 2005).

A second concern related to security conditions in Aceh. The three decades of conflict between the GAM and the Indonesian government had held back development and had severely limited the flow of news out of Aceh, to other parts of Indonesia as well as to the rest of the world. For example, it was not until 28 December 2004 – two days after the tsunami

– that most of Indonesia and the rest of the world knew how badly the tsunami had hit Aceh. In contrast, news of the scale of the disaster in Sri Lanka and Thailand reached the international media almost immediately. Poor roads and telecommunications also made it difficult to provide speedy assistance to many villages along the coast of Aceh. Additionally, there were worries that the ongoing political conflict would hinder reconstruction operations.

A third concern was to ensure that commitments pledged by international donors would materialize in a timely way. For various reasons beyond the control of Indonesian officials, there was a risk that some of the commitments would never translate into actual aid flows. It is also true, however, that there were limitations on Indonesia's ability to absorb aid quickly. For these and other reasons, it soon became clear that it was necessary for Indonesian officials and local NGOs to work effectively with donors to minimize mismatches between donors' interests, on the one hand, and local reconstruction priorities on the other (Athukorala and Resosudarmo 2005).

The Master Plan

The central government seemed to understand the need for more effective coordination with local governments and NGOs as well as for a more decentralized approach to the reconstruction effort. From March 2005 onwards, Bappenas conducted intensive consultations with community and political leaders in the affected areas as well as with NGOs and donors. Syiah Kuala University in Banda Aceh was given assistance to organize input from local communities into the consultation process while central and local government line agencies also provided expertise. Donors were encouraged to contribute suggestions. The Master Plan that resulted was comprehensive and the central government helpfully recognized that no one plan could address every issue likely to arise in the rehabilitation process.[9]

Nevertheless, despite the extensive consultations, many local communities and NGOs reacted negatively to the Master Plan. Many local communities felt that their aspirations had not been properly reflected. In response, as a conciliatory gesture only a couple of days after his inauguration in April 2005, the new Head of the BRR, Dr Kuntoro, agreed that many aspects had not been adequately dealt with. He indicated that the BRR would not follow the Master Plan to the letter and that rather, it would be used as a reference document in a flexible way (*Kompas*, 3 May 2005). The local Head of the BRR in Nias also agreed that the Master Plan was not necessarily a suitable strategy for redevelopment in Nias (*Kompas*,

19 August 2005). It was therefore soon agreed that an evolutionary approach would be adopted and that there would not be any single rigid 'blueprint approach' to the process of reconstruction (Indrawati 2005; World Bank 2005). For example, under the new approach, communities were to be provided with opportunities to participate in decision-making about where, how, and by whom houses and other buildings were to be reconstructed. The central government would concentrate on the provision of principal infrastructure facilities.

Earlier plans that had outlined regulations for tough zoning, mandatory setbacks from the sea, relocation of local markets, and so on, were set aside. Leaders in Jakarta committed themselves to ensuring that local people in Aceh and Nias were involved in making decisions about such matters (Sen and Steer 2005). In this way, disagreements between the central government on the one hand, and local governments and communities on the other, were kept to a minimum. If the reconstruction process in Aceh ultimately turns out to be successful over the long term there is a strong likelihood that this pattern of strong collaboration between stakeholders will be adopted as the blueprint for regional development in other parts of Indonesia.

The Aceh-Nias Rehabilitation and Reconstruction Agency (BRR)

The central government preferred to set up a special Aceh-Nias Rehabilitation and Reconstruction Agency as a one-stop shop for the coordination of all agencies and donors in Aceh and Nias. There was no strong objection from local governments, communities, NGOs, and international donors to this decision. There were two main reasons for this. First, the central government had shown that it was willing to collaborate with local stakeholders as well as donors in developing the Master Plan and to be flexible in implementing the plan. Second, the person appointed to head the BRR, as well as the deputies, had a reputation for being 'clean' and capable.

In April 2005 the government embarked on the second phase of recovery operations. On 16 April 2005, the government established the *Badan Rekonstruksi dan Rehabilitasi* (BRR) Aceh-Nias, with the stated mission of restoring livelihoods and strengthening communities in Aceh and Nias by overseeing a coordinated, community-driven reconstruction and development program. Initially, the BRR was established as a coordinating rather than executive agency to operate for a four-year period. It was based in Banda Aceh, with a branch office in Nias and a representative office in Jakarta. Operationally, the BRR comprised three bodies: the Executive Agency (*Badan Pelaksana* or Bapel), the high-level Advisory

Board (*Badan Pengarah*), and the Supervisory Board (*Badan Pengawas*). At the end of 2005, the BRR received an additional mandate to build around 120 000 houses in Aceh and Nias starting in 2006. With this mandate, the BRR to some extent took over responsibilities earlier given to the Ministry of Public Works (*Tempo Interaktif*, 26 December 2005).

The Executive Agency (Bapel), commonly referred to by the term BRR, was the body responsible for managing the reconstruction and rehabilitation activities. The BRR had four main offices and several regional offices. This structure was much leaner than in the initial period of its establishment. The BRR had an Advisory Board chaired by the Coordinating Minister for Political and Security Affairs. This board consisted of 17 representatives from central and regional governments, religious and *adat* (local custom) institutions, and other participants from civil society. It was responsible for ensuring that the aspirations of agencies and groups that they represented were reflected in the BRR's operational planning. The Supervisory Board, meanwhile, consisted of nine members appointed by the President. It was made up of community representatives and technical advisers, including representatives of donor organizations. This board was responsible for ensuring that the reconstruction and rehabilitation activities were carried out effectively in a manner corresponding with the needs of local people (Kuncoro and Resosudarmo 2006).

Peace Agreement

One of the few unexpected benefits of the bitter wind brought by the tsunami was a new willingness among political disputing parties in Aceh to cease military hostilities, and later to begin negotiations. The Government of Indonesia and the GAM understood that a peace treaty was an essential part of a successful reconstruction process in Aceh. A series of talks was conducted to bring about the process.

Facilitated by the former President of Finland, Martti Ahtisaari, GAM and Indonesian government officials commenced talks in February 2005 and signed an official peace agreement just six months later on 15 August 2005. The agreement, set out in a Memorandum of Understanding (MoU) signed in Helsinki, provided for the cessation of all hostilities between the Government of Indonesia and the GAM. Key points of the agreement included the following (World Bank 2006a):

- The Government of Indonesia and GAM would cease all hostilities; to this end, the Government of Indonesia would withdraw non-local military and police forces from Aceh by the end of 2005.

- GAM would decommission all arms, demobilize its 3000 troops, and surrender 840 weapons.
- The Government of Indonesia would facilitate the establishment of Aceh-based political parties.
- Aceh would be governed under a new special law and would be entitled to 70 per cent of revenues from its natural resources.
- GAM members and political prisoners would be granted amnesty.
- A human rights court and a truth and reconciliation commission would be established.
- An Aceh Monitoring Mission (AMM) would be established by the EU and ASEAN.

Following the agreement, GAM surrendered all weapons and the Government of Indonesia withdrew all non-local military and police by the end of 2005. The EU and ASEAN oversaw the disarmament process by establishing the Aceh Monitoring Mission. A presidential decree was later issued granting amnesty to GAM members in exile in other countries and about 1400 GAM members were released unconditionally from jails. The Government of Indonesia agreed to facilitate the formation of a local political party, which would participate in the election of local regional government representatives (World Bank 2006a, 2006b).

To reintegrate ex-GAM personnel into the community, the Indonesian government agreed to provide assistance in both cash and kind. Each ex-combatant and released prisoner was to receive Rp5 million support (around US$500) in the form of cash and in kind from the Indonesian government. It was estimated that around 3000 ex-GAM combatants and 1400 political prisoners would receive this support.

At the implementation stage, the planned package for former combatants was changed due to difficulties in providing rigorous proof of eligibility. Hence, the Government of Indonesia distributed three rounds of Rp1 million per person (around US$100) of livelihood assistance as a form of minimum social security.

In reality, as reported by the World Bank, the actual amount received by each former GAM member was much less, often only around Rp170 000–260 000 (US$18–30). This is because ex-GAM leaders included orphans and widows in their calculation of who should receive support, resulting in a greater number of people claiming assistance. The process of allocating the amount of money involved local people and was relatively transparent so that in general this approach was accepted without trouble (World Bank 2006a).

The peace agreement, nevertheless, had several immediate side effects. It refuelled efforts to form new provinces in Aceh by sub-dividing Aceh into several separate provinces. Since early 2000 various groups had aspired to form new provinces within Aceh. The two most favoured new provinces were Aceh Leuser Antara (consisting of Aceh Tengah, Aceh Tenggara, Aceh Singkil, Gayo Lues, and Bener Meriah districts) and Aceh Barat Selatan (consisting of Aceh Barat, Aceh Selatan, Simeulue, Aceh Barat Daya, Aceh Jaya, and Nagan Raya districts). The symbolic declaration of these two new provinces was made by several local government officers, local parliament members, and informal leaders in these eleven districts before thousands of supporters in Jakarta on 4 December 2005 (*Kompas*, 6 December 2005 and 14 August 2006).

The central government, however, was ambivalent about these plans to establish new provinces. Law 32 of 2004 on Regional Government allowed for the formation of new administrative units, although, in practice, the exact mechanism involved was not clear. In various interviews officials from the Ministry of Home Affairs said that consideration of the division of current Aceh into new provinces still had a long way to go. The provincial government of Aceh also maintained an ambivalent position delaying recommendations to the central government for the formation of the new provinces. Moreover, the ex-GAM activists who supported the Helsinki MoU were also opposed to the division of Aceh into several provinces because the Helsinki MoU states that the borders of Aceh correspond to those of 1 July 1956, and as such constitute the current province of Aceh. This reluctance may also be seen as a way for ex-GAM activists to maintain useful bargaining power.

On 11 December 2006, almost two years after the tsunami, for the first time in Indonesian history the Acehnese people voted to directly elect their own governor and district/municipality heads. The election process was widely judged as successful. There were no major conflicts, the division of Aceh did not become an issue, and the participation rate was very high. Interestingly, a prominent ex-GAM member, Irwandi Yusuf, won the election to be Governor of Aceh from 2007 to 2012. The success of this election and the fact that an ex-GAM member was able to win the election were promising signs that the peace agreement might eventually lead to a truly peaceful and democratic environment in Aceh.

REHABILITATION, RECONSTRUCTION AND RECOVERY

The BRR commenced operations in May 2005 and began to implement the agreed plans for rebuilding housing, infrastructure, and livelihoods. The BRR followed the sequence of emergency and recovery activities shown

Level of activity

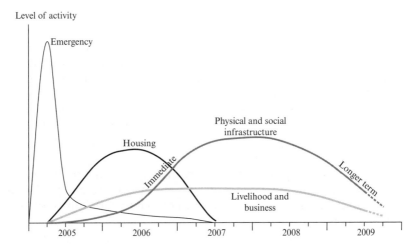

Source: BRR and International Partners (2005).

Figure 4.4   Sequencing emergency and recovery

in Figure 4.4. The plan was that the intensive relief operations that began
in early 2005 would be wound down by mid-2005 and formally ended in
mid-2007. The main priority in the early period was to be house building.
House building activities were expected to peak at the end of 2006 and be
completed by the end of 2007. The second priority in the early period was
rebuilding livelihoods. Rebuilding infrastructure would take longer – only
limited activity was expected until 2006, but the activity was then expected
to intensify rapidly and become the main priority from mid-2006 onwards.
The process of rebuilding livelihoods and infrastructure was expected to
be mostly complete by the end of 2009.

Land Titles

Significantly, the tsunami changed much of the physical landscape in some
parts of Aceh. Not only were houses destroyed but worse, in many places
boundaries and reference marks of land simply disappeared. Although
regarded as less tragic than losing family members, the loss of land is one
of the greatest blows that can befall an Acehnese family. For many people,
land is their most valuable physical asset. In many cases, the legal documents
of ownership were lost after the disaster. The changes the tsunami made
to the contours of the landscape in some places further complicated claims
of land ownership. There was also a risk of land-grabbing. In urban areas
land-grabbing was more likely to affect the more vulnerable groups: women,

children, and orphans. Because of all these concerns, tsunami survivors were sometimes seen installing markers on land where they believed their house had stood. In contrast, problems with land titles were much less serious in Nias. The earthquake in Nias caused houses to collapse but proprietary landmarks were unchanged. Where difficulties for individuals were concerned, land title problems in Nias were limited to the loss of legal documents.

Looking to the future, the protection of land rights is a high priority. Land rights provide the foundation for spatial planning, compensation, and long-term economic development. Indeed, already there have been some important cases where reconstruction activities have been delayed because people in the affected area were not satisfied with the arrangements under which ownership rights to land had been assigned for construction activities.

In response to this serious problem of land ownership, a US$28.5 million Multi-Donor Fund project for the Reconstruction of the Aceh Land Administration System (RALAS) was launched in August 2005. RALAS had two major components: first, the reconstruction of property rights and the issuance of land titles, and second, the reconstruction of a land administration office in Aceh. The project, executed by the National Land Administration Agency (*Badan Pertanahan Nasional* or BPN), was designed to identify land ownership and to issue land titles through establishing a community land inventory, recovering land records, and establishing a land database. The original aim was to issue around 600 000 land titles by the time the project finished in 2008. In the event, by 2009 somewhat less than half of this target was achieved (http://www.multi donorfund.org/).

Project implementation was expected to take place in several stages. First, community land mapping would be arranged, facilitated with the support of NGOs. After that, a team from BPN would arrange adjudication procedures that measured the land parcels and validated ownership and boundary demarcations. BPN would then issue public notifications of adjudication, and provided there were no objections, BPN would subsequently issue the land titles. Under the RALAS project all services were to be provided free of charge.

The first supervision team fielded in November 2005 observed that progress had been slow. The team noted that there had been delays on the part of the Indonesian Ministry of Finance in signing regulations for the waiver of taxes and other charges relating to the issuance of land titles. However the supervision team remained optimistic that the 2006 targets would still be met. The team also noted that the first component of RALAS was more advanced than the second. By end of 2006, about 17 400 land titles had been signed and 134 300 land parcels had been measured

Table 4.9   Location of internally displaced persons (IDP) and ex-IDP as at September 2005, Aceh and Nias

As at September 2005	Aceh	Nias
Still internally displaced families	48 181	8 729
No longer internally displaced and:	66 721	62 585
* Already obtained a house	7 147	5 003
* Still not obtained house so they:	59 574	57 582
* Return to old house	41 882	40 485
* Contract and rent	8 541	1 670
* Stay with family/relative	6 433	6 532
* Stay in an official house	5 262	724

Source: Authors' own calculation using data from SPAN (2005).

(BRR and Partners, 2006). This was certainly an achievement, demonstrating that local communities can effectively resolve such problems at grass roots level (UNORC 2006).

Housing

Major housing rehabilitation, resettlement of displaced people, and restoration of basic utilities only began in mid-May 2005. According to SPAN 2005 data, around 66 700 displaced families (almost 300 000 IDPs) in Aceh and around 62 600 (around 340 000 IDPs) in Nias had returned to their areas by September 2005 (Table 4.9).

However in Aceh only around 7000 families (who were no longer considered internally displaced) and around 5000 families in Nias had received new houses by this time. Most of the others (around 59 000 families in Aceh and 57 000 families in Nias) returned to their old properties even though their houses had not yet been renovated or rebuilt. For these people the first priority was to reclaim their properties and then wait until it was their turn for their houses to be rebuilt or renovated. Many families had to rent houses or stay with relatives.

During the second half of 2005 building activity gathered pace. The BRR estimated that by October 2005 around 10 000 houses had been built, by December around 16 000, by April 2006 around 42 000, and by December 2006 around 57 000 had been completed. However, although activity accelerated in 2006, the number of houses completed was expected to be well behind the BRR target of 90 000–100 000 houses completed by the end of 2006.

Table 4.10   Rough estimates of costs of labour and housing materials in Aceh and Nias, 2004–06

	Cost	End 2004	Mid-2005	Early 2006	Oct 2006	Change (%)
Aceh						
Labour	Rp 000/day	30	40	50	50	67
Wood	Rp million/m³	1.0	1.5	1.9	2.2	120
Cement	Rp 000/50 kg	20	26	34	37	85
Sand	Rp 000/3 m³	150	300	300	300	100
Red Brick	Rp each	250	580	700	700	180
Wall Paint	Rp 000/25 kg	66	75	90	110	67
Wood Paint	Rp 000/litre	22	27	32	34	55
Nias						
Labour	Rp 000/day	40	40	50	50	25
Wood	Rp million/m³	1.2	1.6	1.8	2.0	67
Cement	Rp 000/50 kg	22	27	34.5	37	66
Sand	Rp 000/3 m³	150	150	300	300	100
Red Brick	Rp each	400	600	700	1 000	150
Wall Paint	Rp 000/25 kg	90	90	125	135	50
Wood Paint	Rp 000/litre	22	25	25	38	73

Note: Change in the percentage increase in prices is from end 2004 to Oct 2006.

Source: Authors' own market survey.

The total estimated budget committed by donors and the Government of Indonesia for housing was almost US$976 million. Initially the BRR estimated that the cost of building a 36 square-metre house was around US$3000. Meanwhile, compensation to rehabilitate damaged houses varied, but for planning purposes the upper limit was also set at US$3000. With this figure in mind, it was estimated that the total committed funding for housing would be enough to build or rehabilitate around 200 000 houses (BRR and International Partners 2005).

However there were significant cost escalations. By the end of 2005 it was reported that the cost of building a new 36 square-metre house had increased to around US$5000 (BRR and International Partners 2005). Table 4.10 illustrates the significant increases in building costs compared to the situation before the disasters. Consequently, by early 2006, the BRR revised their estimate of the cost of a new 36 square-metre house to around US$4000 (BRR and International Partners 2005).[10]

Why did construction costs rise after the tsunami? The issue of cost increases is an important one because reports from other places in the world hit by more recent disasters (Pakistan, the US following Hurricane Katrina, and even in Yogyakarta in Indonesia after the earthquake in 2006) indicate that sharp cost increases in disaster zones are not unusual. But unusual or not, it is important to establish whether the cost increases reflected plausible economic factors or, instead, unacceptable profiteering. Looking at the components of construction costs in an effort to find answers, it is notable that increases in labour costs in Aceh and Nias were not as markedly high as the increase in prices in some other material inputs. It seems, therefore, that the supply of labour was apparently more elastic than the supply of materials. One likely reason for this is that the peace agreement in Aceh quickly led to an improvement in the security situation in the region. Hence, workers from elsewhere in Indonesia were apparently willing to move to Aceh for only small premiums over their existing wages. In addition, North Sumatra, adjacent to Aceh, is a relatively labour-abundant region; it became the main source of outside labour for reconstruction in Aceh. Nias, on the other hand, never had a serious security problem. The main issue affecting the supply of labour there was the ease of transportation to the island after the reconstruction began. It appears that the reconstruction efforts attracted outside labourers to take up work in Nias.

At first glance, a large increase in the price of timber is surprising given that Indonesia, and Sumatra in particular, is well endowed with forest resources. The BRR estimated that the housing reconstruction activities would need about 1.5 million cubic metres of timber. Many observers estimated that this amount could easily be supplied from normal domestic timber production supplemented by drawing on seized illegal timber stocks held by the Indonesian government as well as small amounts of imported timber and supplies provided by donor countries. However, it is now thought that the significant increases in timber prices were probably related to difficulties in accessing the stocks of seized illegal timbers and in using imported and donated timbers. Further, from the outset there was a consensus among the BRR, donors and NGOs that reconstruction activities in Aceh and Nias would only use legal timber, and where possible would only use timber available locally or from elsewhere in Indonesia (*Jawa Post*, 27 December 2006). This attitude introduced legal and administrative bottlenecks that restricted the supply of timber in the short-run. Moreover, the legal status of the stocks of seized illegal timbers needed to be clarified before the timber could be released for use in Aceh. Similarly, criteria establishing the amount of timber that could be imported and the guidelines for the use of timber provided by donor countries needed to be established. Reflecting general concerns about these issues, there has been a call for serious efforts from the government to legalize the use of illegal timbers so that they could be utilized immediately. The matter was not as straightforward as it might seem since there were valid concerns that the legalization of illegal timber might encourage further illegal logging because of the possibility of legalizing this product.

It may seem surprising that the supply of other building material inputs has not been more elastic. Construction activities in other parts of the country since the 1997–98 Asian economic crisis were relatively sluggish compared to the situation before the 1997 crisis and it is likely that there was excess capacity in other regions. But even if inputs for house reconstruction can be accessed relatively easily elsewhere in Indonesia, it takes time to physically move materials and for labourers to arrive. There were, therefore, practical constraints on the rate at which housing could be supplied. Realistically, the upper limit of housing construction achievable was probably significantly lower than the original BRR target of 90 000–100 000 houses by the end of 2006.

Livelihoods

Efforts to rehabilitate livelihoods involved several activities. First, steps were taken to restore the agriculture and fishery sectors through revitalizing agricultural and plantation land, rebuilding ports, and replacing lost fishing boats. Second, microfinance, other forms of cheap credit, and assistance were made available for small and medium enterprises. Third, employment programs such as cash-for-work and training programs were developed (BRR and International Partners 2005).

By December 2006 the BRR reported that approximately 50 000 hectares of agricultural land had been restored (around 70 per cent of the total area damaged). In the fishery sector about 4400 boats had been replaced and around 6800 hectares of fish ponds had been repaired (approximately 30 per cent of the total area of fish ponds damaged) (Table 4.6).

The information available on how many livelihood activities needed to be rehabilitated and created, however, is not very clear. Table 4.4 indicates that more than 260 000 people in Aceh and 85 000 in Nias lost their sources of income. But it is also important to note that unemployment and poverty were serious problems in Aceh and Nias before the disasters.

SPAN 2005 data indicates that in September 2005 around 46 per cent of the population in Aceh above the age of ten was engaged in some form of employment while around 10 per cent was unemployed (Table 4.11). Of those who worked, around 49 per cent were self-employed (Table 4.12) which is common in the informal sectors. Approximately 14 per cent in Aceh of those who were working were unpaid workers, most likely family members involved in family businesses. Around 15 per cent of IDPs and

The Asian tsunami

Table 4.11   Employment activity of the population aged 10 years and over as at September 2005, Aceh and Nias ('000 people)[1]

	Still IDP* by Sept. 05	Ex-IDP	Total for IDP and ex-IDP	Never been IDP	Total
Aceh:					
Employed	65	98	163	1277	1440
%	39	41	40	47	46
Seeking work[†]	18	17	35	148	183
%	11	7	9	5	6
Available for work[†]	14	11	25	112	136
%	8	5	6	4	4
In school or taking care of children	68	112	180	1162	1342
%	41	47	44	43	43
No answer	2	3	5	24	28
Total Aceh	166	241	407	2723	3130
%	100	100	100	100	100
Nias:					
Employed	20	152	171	156	327
%	57	62	61	66	63
Seeking work[†]	3	11	14	8	22
%	8	4	5	3	4
Available for work[†]	1	6	7	4	11
%	3	2	2	2	2
In school or taking care of children	11	78	89	69	158
%	32	32	32	29	31
No answer	. . .	. . .	. . .	. . .	. . .
Total Nias	34	245	281	237	518
%	100	100	100	100	100

Notes:
[1]   During the week prior to the survey.
*   IDP = internally displaced person.
[†]   The description 'seeking work' refers to people who report that they are actively looking for work. The description 'available for work' refers to people (sometimes referred to as 'discouraged workers') who are not actively seeking work but who report that they would be available to work if jobs were available.

Source: Authors' calculation from SPAN (2005).

Table 4.12 *Occupational status of the population aged 10 years and over as at September 2005, Aceh and Nias ('000 people)*[1]

	Still IDP* by Sept. 05	Ex-IDP	Total among IDP & Ex-IDP	Never been IDP	Total
Aceh:					
Self-employed with no assistant	34	48	82	621	702
%	52	49	50	49	49
Self-employed with temporary or unpaid labour assistant	3	5	8	141	149
%	5	5	5	11	10
Employer	6	6	12	45	56
%	9	6	7	4	4
Employee	18	31	49	264	313
%	28	32	30	21	22
Unpaid worker	3	6	9	188	197
%	4	7	6	15	14
No answer	1	2	3	19	22
Total Aceh	65	98	163	1277	1440
%	100	100	100	100	100
Nias:					
Self-employed with no assistant	12	81	93	90	183
%	60	54	54	58	56
Self-employed with temporary or unpaid labour assistant	2	17	19	17	36
%	9	11	11	11	11
Employer	. . .	1	1	1	2
%	1	1	1	1	1
Employee	1	11	13	9	22
%	7	8	7	6	7
Unpaid worker	4	39	43	37	80
%	21	26	25	24	24
No answer	. . .	2	3	3	5
Total Nias	20	152	171	156	327
%	100	100	100	100	100

Note:
[1]   During the week prior to the survey.
*   IDP = internally displaced person.

Source: Authors' calculation from SPAN (2005).

ex-IDPs were unable to find any employment, suggesting that reconstruction activities in the early post-disaster period were not able to generate employment for significant numbers.

Overall, around 300 000 jobs in Aceh and around 30 000 in Nias needed to be created, certainly a challenging task. By April 2006, the BRR reported that around 148 000 people had received some skill training to enable them to re-enter the job market and that more than 41 000 farmers had been assisted to return to their fields (BRR 2006). By December 2006, the BRR claimed that around 69 per cent of the male and 36 per cent of the female labour force in urban areas as well as around 68 per cent of the male and 45 per cent of the female labour force in rural areas of both Aceh and Nias was actively engaged in some form of work (BRR and Partners 2006). Nevertheless, reliable data on how many of the people who were unemployed in mid-2005 actually obtained some form of employment is not available.

School and Health Services

In the aftermath of the disasters around 2000 school buildings needed to be rebuilt and approximately 2500 teaching positions needed to be refilled (Table 4.6). It should be noted that there was a serious shortage of teachers in Aceh even before the tsunami. By December 2006, the BRR reported that around 750 school buildings had been built and approximately 5400 teaching positions had been filled. In other words, in terms of school buildings, only around 40 per cent of the target had been reached but the number of teachers now exceeded pre-tsunami levels, thus partially alleviating the teacher shortage (BRR and Partners 2006).

In rebuilding the education system in Aceh and Nias, besides taking into account the damage caused by the disasters it is important to understand local needs. Table 4.13 shows the numbers of children and young adults who had never been to school and those who had dropped out. Around 23 000 young persons aged 7 to 24 years in Aceh and around 31 000 in Nias had never been to school. Table 4.14, furthermore, shows that among those who had left education, around 50 000 in Aceh and 30 000 in Nias had not obtained any elementary education degree. Thus, considering the low elementary school attainments and the low attainments at higher educational levels, even if the elementary schools and teacher numbers were restored to pre-disaster levels they would still fall well below those needed to rebuild a better Aceh and Nias.

In the health sector, by December 2006 324 hospitals and health centres had been rebuilt. This far exceeded the number of hospitals and health services damaged by the earthquakes and tsunami. It should be

Table 4.13   *Educational status of the population aged 7–24 years, Aceh and Nias, 2005 ('000 people)*

Age	Never attended school	Not in school any more	In school	No answer	Total
Aceh					
7–12	12	14	514	2	542
%	2	3	95	. . .	100
13–15	2	34	238	1	275
%	1	12	87	. . .	100
16–18	2	98	169	2	271
%	1	36	62	1	100
19–24	6	370	8	4	389
%	2	95	2	1	100
Total	23	516	929	9	1477
%	1	35	63	1	100
Nias					
7–12	9	5	105	. . .	118
%	7	4	89	. . .	100
13–15	4	11	37	. . .	52
%	8	21	71	. . .	100
16–18	6	24	23	. . .	53
%	11	45	44	. . .	100
19–24	12	59	8	. . .	79
%	15	75	10	. . .	100
Total	31	99	173	. . .	302
%	10	33	57	. . .	100

Source: Authors' calculation from SPAN (2005).

said that health facilities before the disasters were in a state of neglect and the need for health facilities has substantially increased in the aftermath. Approximately 63 000 people in Aceh and Nias suffered some mental problems following the disasters. Although reconstruction activities were underway, the risk of communicable disease outbreaks remained high. Looking at household sources of drinking water and sanitation facilities (Tables 4.15 and 4.16), it can be seen that access to piped water in Aceh and Nias had been very limited and relatively few households had septic tanks.[11] Moreover, many people were still living in shelters. With the majority of people in Aceh depending mainly on wells for drinking water, it was important to monitor the water quality of these wells.

The Asian tsunami

Table 4.14   *Educational status of children and young adults no longer in education, Aceh and Nias, 2005 ('000 people)*

Age	Not graduated from elementary School	Graduated from elementary school	Graduated from secondary school	Graduated from high school	Graduated from university	No answer	Total
Aceh							
7–12	10	5				. . .	14
%	67	32				1	100
13–15	8	21	5			. . .	34
%	23	61	16			. . .	100
16–18	11	37	36	14		. . .	98
%	11	38	37	14		. . .	100
19–24	22	103	105	127	13	1	370
%	6	28	28	34	4	. . .	100
Total	50	165	146	141	13	1	516
%	10	32	28	27	3	. . .	100
Nias							
7–12	4	1				. . .	5
%	82	18				. . .	100
13–15	5	5	1			. . .	11
%	45	50	5			. . .	100
16–18	7	11	5	1		. . .	24
%	30	45	20	5		. . .	100
19–24	14	22	12	10	1	. . .	59
%	24	38	20	17	1	. . .	100
Total	30	39	17	11	1	. . .	99
%	30	40	17	12	1	. . .	100

Source: Authors' calculation from SPAN (2005).

Infrastructure

Towards the end of 2005 USAID signed an MoU with the Ministry of Public Works to reconstruct 240 kilometres of road from Banda Aceh to Meulaboh. Phase 1 of the project (80 km – connecting Banda Aceh to Lamno) was expected to be completed by August 2006. Phase 2 of the project, the remaining 160 kilometres, was expected to take another two or more years. Meanwhile, the Japan International Cooperation Agency agreed to rehabilitate the existing 122 kilometre road from Calang to Meulaboh (BRR and Partners 2006).

Moreover, the Asian Development Bank agreed to finance the rehabilitation of another main route, a 490 kilometre road connecting Banda

Table 4.15   Main household sources of drinking water as at September 2005, Aceh and Nias ('000 households)

	Still IDP by Sept. 05	Ex-IDP	Total for IDP and Ex-IDP	Never been IDP	Total
Aceh					
Piped water	2	14	16	75	91
%	12	22	20	10	11
Pump/well	9	36	44	556	600
%	63	54	55	72	70
Spring	2	4	6	103	109
%	12	6	7	13	12
Bottled water	1	7	7	10	17
%	4	10	9	1	2
Other	1	6	7	34	41
%	9	8	9	4	5
Total	14	67	80	778	859
%	100	100	100	100	100
Nias					
Piped water	. . .	3	3	1	4
%	. . .	5	5	1	3
Pump/well	1	22	24	19	42
%	40	36	36	31	34
Spring	1	33	34	31	65
%	51	52	52	52	52
Bottled water	. . .	. . .	. . .	6	6
%	. . .	. . .	. . .	9	5
Other	. . .	4	4	4	8
%	. . .	7	7	7	6
Total	3	63	65	60	125
%	100	100	100	100	100

Source: Authors' calculation from SPAN (2005).

Aceh with North Sumatra. Overall, the total road length needing to be rehabilitated or built in Aceh following the disaster was around 3000 kilometres (Table 4.6). Nias, naturally, did not need as many roads as Aceh (BRR and International Partners 2005).

Besides roads, the BRR also indicated that 14 seaports, 11 airports and air strips, 120 arterial bridges, and around 1500 minor bridges needed to be rebuilt (Table 4.6). Compared with progress in other sectors, infrastructure reconstruction was relatively slow. The BRR reported that

Table 4.16   Household sanitation facilities as at September 2005, Aceh and Nias ('000 households)

	Still IDP by Sept. 05	Ex-IDP	Total for IDP and Ex-IDP	Never been IDP	Total
Aceh					
Toilet with septic tank	4	28	32	221	253
%	31	42	40	28	29
Toilet without septic tank	1	7	8	125	134
%	10	11	11	16	16
Pond/river	3	9	12	186	198
%	20	14	15	24	23
Directly on cesspool	1	5	6	117	123
%	9	8	8	15	14
Yard/bushes/forest	3	13	16	104	120
%	21	19	19	14	14
Other	1	4	5	25	31
%	9	6	7	3	4
Total	14	67	80	778	859
%	100	100	100	100	100
Nias					
Toilet with septic tank	...	4	4	3	7
%	...	6	6	5	5
Toilet without septic tank	1	15	16	15	31
%	24	24	24	25	25
Pond/river	...	11	12	9	21
%	...	18	18	15	17
Directly on cesspool	...	11	11	11	23
%	...	17	17	19	18
Yard/bushes/forest	1	11	11	10	22
%	24	18	18	17	17
Other	...	11	11	11	22
%	...	17	17	19	18
Total	3	63	65	60	125
%	100	100	100	100	100

Source: Authors' calculation from SPAN (2005).

around 1200 kilometres of roads in Aceh and 300 kilometres in Nias had been built or repaired as at December 2006. Further, 14 ferry terminals and harbours, 8 airports and airstrips, and 158 bridges had been restored (BRR and Partners 2006). The types of problems which caused slow progress in this area can be illustrated by an example. The construction of the road from Banda Aceh to Meulaboh experienced serious delays. Issues concerning land acquisition and poor weather were mentioned as the main reasons for the delay (USAID 2006). As far as land acquisition was concerned, significant differences emerged between the kind of road that local people wanted and what USAID wanted to build. USAID planned to build a highway with seven-metre carriageways and two-metre shoulders. Locals, however, not only feared speeding traffic but also wanted to be able to sell snacks and tea from stalls along the roadside (*New York Times*, 9 October 2006). The dilemma was an interesting one. While, as noted earlier, the Indonesian government had been willing to set aside the Master Plan and follow a more bottom-up approach by taking into account local voices, some donors seemed to be committed to a top-down approach.

CHALLENGES

At the end of 2006 there were four main challenges facing the reconstruction and rehabilitation process. The first arose from the unrealistically high community expectations generated by the various statements and pledges from government leaders, NGOs, donors, and others. Local communities had come to expect not only to have their houses rebuilt and their livelihoods restored but also to participate in reconstruction activities. It was hoped that expectations could be managed by focusing on reasonable targets although the BRR's operational approach did not yet provide for this.

The BRR's budget realization for the 2005 and 2006 fiscal years was quite low. This was the second challenge faced in the reconstruction process. The third challenge related to issues of coordination and commitment. As a coordinating agency, the BRR needed to establish smooth coordination arrangements with local governments and donor agencies. The relationship with local governments was pivotal to spending monies effectively while the relationship with donor agencies was vital to ensure that aid commitments were implemented efficiently. Finally, there was the challenge of establishing a viable exit strategy for the BRR. The mandate of the BRR extended until 2009. By then it was expected that the BRR would have arranged the transfer of the whole redevelopment process to local governments. There was, therefore, a challenge for both the BRR and local governments in handling the transition processes well.

The following sections elaborate on these four challenges.

Managing Expectations

The ambitious plans for reconstruction and rehabilitation in Aceh and Nias created high expectations. During the initial emergency stage, local inhabitants witnessed the arrival of large-scale support from both government and non-governmental organizations alike. Figure 4.4 indicates a peak of activity in the early stage which was much more intensive than the more sustained work carried out later in the recovery stage. But as the diagram shows, there was a risk of a lull in activity when the emergency stage scaled back to a lower intensity because there was no guarantee that the housing recovery stage would kick in quickly. A lull of this kind did indeed occur and was seen by many people as reflecting inactivity on the part of the BRR. A 'slow start', which is the term some observers used in referring to the first year of BRR operations, was a polite judgement compared to the views expressed by others who cynically translated BRR as *baru rapat-rapat* (just hold meetings).

For the Acehnese in general and the people of Nias in particular, the disasters aroused expectations of significant improvements at the local level. Development in these areas had long lagged behind development elsewhere in Indonesia. People in these regions felt marginalized and isolated from the national development process, economically as well as politically – in Aceh because of the long socio-political conflict, and in Nias because of the separation from Sumatra and the remoteness of the island.

The establishment of the BRR in 2005 led to considerable excitement among the local populace in Nias. Many people imagined that they would take part in the reconstruction process following the plans set out by the agency. Who would the BRR recruit if not locals who know the region well? It has to be acknowledged that in Indonesia the sentiment of *putera daerah* (local people) was still important in isolated areas. Local people were therefore very disappointed to find that their involvement in the administration of the BRR in Nias was quite limited.

In the case of Nias, the irony is that for non-locals, an assignment to Nias was generally regarded as a punishment rather than a promotion. In the first six months of the operation of the BRR branch in Nias, only one out of twelve heads of BRR working units lived on the island. This problem was remedied in early 2006 when the heads of BRR working units were instructed to live in Nias.

Local businesses and contractors in Aceh and Nias were also excited by the prospect of involvement in BRR projects. Most local contractors, however, were disappointed to find that in practice they were unable to participate in the construction projects. The reason for this, they reported, was that the procurement procedures and requirements set down by the BRR for redevelopment construction were so complicated that local contractors were effectively excluded from participating.

Finally, the BRR's target of building around 92 000 houses in Aceh and Nias during 2006 – which, added to those built in 2005, amounted to a target of around 108 000 houses in total by the end of 2006 – raised special expectations. Although restoration of the housing stock was justifiably seen as the main priority, the feasibility of this target was questionable from the start, even allowing for the fact that the size of the new homes was expected to be small (only 36 square metres). Typically, the number of new homes constructed nationwide in Indonesia was only around 60 000 per annum. In the absence of any decline in house construction elsewhere, the BRR target implied an increase of roughly 150 per cent in the output of the national housing construction industry, a very ambitious target.

Even with the relatively modest rate of construction achieved in 2005 in Aceh and Nias, wages in the construction industry and the price of building materials increased during the year at levels higher than elsewhere in Indonesia (BRR and International Partners 2005). Adhering closely to such an ambitious target thus ran the risk of encouraging the lowering of construction standards, and this implied that the much-publicized opportunity to 'build back better' would be missed. Moreover, the heavy additional demand for timber, if not carefully managed, threatened to hasten deforestation in Aceh and other parts of Indonesia.[12]

Nevertheless, BRR officials declared themselves confident of meeting the housing targets and mentioned the following considerations in support of their optimism. First, after a delay of some months in its establishment, the agency had generally been able to demonstrate leadership in the reconstruction effort and hence had been able to encourage major participants to focus their efforts on housing. Second, the BRR was able to modify the Master Plan stipulations, where appropriate, after consultations with local communities. This pragmatic approach worked to overcome a number of conflicts between the perceived interests of local communities and the constraints of the Master Plan on housing programs. Third, most problems of land identification had been solved through the RALAS project. Fourth, the central government and the GAM agreed to end their thirty years of conflict on 15 August 2005. The result was that the general level of safety in Aceh improved greatly allowing reconstruction activities to be conducted in a conducive environment. Fifth, the BRR's special new authority, which allowed for the implementation of housing projects through direct contracting, helped to offset delays in other government agencies responsible for building houses, such as the Ministry of Public Works. Finally, funds for reconstruction activities began to flow smoothly (Kuncoro and Resosudarmo 2006). In spite of this optimism by the BRR, however, it should be noted that, judging by the number of houses built by November 2006, it seemed highly unlikely at the time that the housing target would be achieved. Delays in reaching targets, in turn, risked weakening the credibility of the BRR as a reliable reconstruction partner in the region.

There was a quite widespread view that the BRR should put more emphasis on the quality of reconstruction – that is, maintaining house construction as its main priority but without committing itself to ambitious numerical targets – while meanwhile ensuring that all those waiting to receive new housing were properly accommodated in comfortable temporary living conditions. Arguably, there should also have been stronger emphasis on supporting the restoration of livelihood activities through provision of suitable fishing boats, support for farming activities (such as the provision of seeds), repair of the relevant infrastructure, and so on (Kuncoro and Resosudarmo 2006).

BRR Spending

As at September 2006, spending by the BRR had lagged well behind budget (Table 4.17). Underexpenditure of this kind threatened to lead to widespread dissatisfaction among local people. The inability of the BRR to achieve its reconstruction targets was reflected in the planned budget for BRR operations. Indeed, for the 2005 budget, the BRR's fiscal year was extended up to 2006. Thus, during January–September 2006, there were two fiscal budgets running.

However, even after the extension of the fiscal year, the level of budget spending was still very low. Out of Rp4 trillion (around US$410 million) allocated in the 2005 budget for the BRR, only 63 per cent was spent. Moreover, the higher spending areas appear to have been on administrative activities related to offices, planning, and programming.

There was a sharp increase in the BRR budget for 2006.[13] The main reason for this was that, beginning in 2006, the BRR received an additional mandate to implement housing construction in an effort to speed up activity in this sector following the earlier disappointing performance. The agency was provided with additional funding of Rp4 trillion (around US$430 million in this case) to build up to 40000 houses during the year. Mainly because of this initiative, the budgeted expenditure for the BRR in 2006 was set at around Rp10 trillion (around US$1 billion), an increase

Table 4.17 *BRR's budget realization, as at 30 September 2006 (old format)*

	2005 Budget Plan (Rp billion)	% of realization by 12/2005	% of realization by 04/2006	% of realization by 09/2006	2006 Budget Plan (Rp billion)	% of realization by 09/2006
Total budget (US$ million approx.)	3967 (410)	10	63	63	9618 (1050)	18
By sectoral specification						
Planning and programming	90	0	73	73	176	22
Institutional	770	4	47	46	1063	14
Housing, infrastructure, and land use coordination	1619	10	67	68	5613	17
Economic and business empowerment	546	5	73	73	1065	23
Religious, social, and cultural	271	3	55	55	358	30
Health and education	480	30	56	56	1115	17
Secretariat, Nias branch, finance, and communication	191	26	82	83	228	26
By types of expenditures						
Personnel	372	47	82	n.a.	269	n.a.
Equipment	744	7	53	n.a.	1461	n.a.
Capital	2147	5	54	n.a.	5602	n.a.
Social support	704	12	89	n.a.	2286	n.a.

Source: BRR website, http://www.e-aceh-nias.org/home/, accessed 15 May 2007.

of over 150 per cent of its budget for 2005. It was not clear, however, that this approach would be successful. As a new agency lacking experience in managing large-scale construction projects at the time, it was uncertain whether the BRR would able to implement this daunting new task more successfully than the other organizations involved. Moreover, this major additional spending program risked further constraining the capacity of the BRR to coordinate other reconstruction programs. Perhaps of greatest concern at the time however was whether, having such a large budget, the BRR could avoid the taint of mismanagement. There was expected to be considerable local pressure on its officials to engage in corrupt behaviour. It was realized that if they succumbed to this pressure, the ability of the BRR to continue to lead the reconstruction effort would quickly diminish.

Data up to 30 September 2006 suggest that expenditure outcomes throughout the financial year remained well behind target (Table 4.17). While a slow start in 2005 was perhaps understandable, the continued underspending raised concerns about the ability of the BRR to deliver on the promises that had been made. Nine months into 2006 only about 18 per cent of the budget had been spent. The challenge for the BRR in the remaining months therefore was important.

What can be said about these problems? First, from the point of view of the local people, the spending delays were most unfortunate. In 2005 alone, actual spending reportedly lagged behind planned expenditures by about Rp2.8 trillion (around US$290 million), the bulk of which reflected underspending in the areas of housing, infrastructure, and land use coordination. One widely mentioned reason for spending delays was said to be the BRR's commitment to careful management of project procurement activities. This explanation, however, was not well received at the local level. What the locals knew was that they had not received the things that were promised to them by the BRR. People still living in barracks felt that they should have been able to move into permanent housing, and fishers and farmers felt that their operations should, by this stage, have returned to normal. Second, this continuing underexpenditure begged the question of whether the BRR would be able to execute planned budgets into the future.

What were the policy options? First, the BRR could perhaps have tried to speed up spending in the last three months of the fiscal year 2006. The danger was that quality would be compromised for the sake of quantity. Worse, the emphasis on careful project procurement might be compromised. Alternatively, the BRR could have asked for a technical extension of the 2006 budget into the next year. However, the Indonesian government would have been unlikely to agree to this because it would be

*Table 4.18   BRR's budget realization, as at 28 December 2006 (new
format)*

	2005 Budget Plan (Rp billion)	% of realization by 12/2006	2006 Budget Plan (Rp billion)	% of realization by 12/2006
Total budget	3967	63	10553	74
(US$ million approx.)	(410)		(1150)	
By sectoral specification				
Finance and planning	57	77	72	82
Institutional and human resources	770	47	1028	53
Infrastructure, environment, and maintenance	1244	61	2416	87
Housing and settlement	408	82	4355	75
Economic and business	546	73	843	70
Religious, social, and cultural	213	57	277	82
Health, education, and women's participation	538	55	1143	64
Secretariat	191	83	390	65

Source: BRR website, http://www.e-aceh-nias.org/home/, accessed 15 May 2007.

reluctant to accept the idea that budget extensions were a normal way of
doing business.

The BRR seems to have preferred the first option. In the last three
months of 2006, the BRR spent around 60 per cent of its total budget of
Rp10.55 trillion for 2006 (Table 4.18). In order to speed up spending the
BRR explored the idea of decentralizing expenditure authority to local
BRR offices across Aceh and Nias. For example, starting in April 2006
the BRR experimented with the idea of placing a liaison officer at the
local level by creating joint secretariats with local governments in Nias.
The secretariats were given a wide range of duties including coordinating activities carried out by stakeholders, sharing information on the
progress of recovery activities, involving local governments in the recovery process, and assisting local governments with the management capacity to be professional lead agencies for development activities. Additional

liaison officers were appointed in seven or more regional offices by the end of 2006.

This innovation seems to have helped to accelerate the housing and infrastructure development program. It was hoped that more decisions would be made at the local level under this approach. In 2005 some 90 per cent of BRR staff members were in Banda Aceh. However it was planned that the proportion of staff in the central Banda Aceh office would go down to just 50 per cent by 2008. By gradually shifting the decision-making and management to district and local town authorities across Aceh and Nias, it was expected that the BRR's role would be reduced mainly to monitoring, countering corruption, problem solving, gap filling, and donor relations.

But another option that perhaps should have been given more consideration – which is also a very effective form of decentralization – was the establishment of a much larger program of direct cash transfers. If this approach had been adopted, households would have received cash and would have been able to organize building and rehabilitating their houses themselves.

The international donor community, too, had naturally been important in all of these activities. But unfortunately little public information was readily available regarding the expenditure programs of donors. There were no comprehensive reports easily available at the time on how much the international donor community had spent. It would have been particularly interesting to know how much had been spent on the ground in Indonesia and how much, in contrast, donors had spent on their own administrative activities. In the future, more accountability on the part of donors is clearly needed.

Coordination and Commitments

Developing effective coordination within the BRR, between the BRR and local governments, as well as between the BRR and other organizations was a continuing challenge.

The three key structures within the BRR itself were the Executive Agency, the Advisory Board, and the Supervisory Board. The question of how these three bodies might interact efficiently so that the BRR as a whole could be effective had been a major issue ever since the establishment of the BRR in early 2005.

Since the early days of the BRR, the Executive Agency had shown flexibility, choosing to follow the Bappenas Master Plan when practical but being ready to modify it when necessary. However the definition of 'practical' was not clear. There was no agreement on this matter between the Executive Agency, the Advisory Board, and the Supervisory Board. There was a perception that the Executive Agency could do whatever it wanted, even though the Advisory and Supervisory Boards may have had different views. Even within the Executive Agency itself there was no clear guidance on this for staff. The result was a lack of consistency in operations. Some directors followed the stipulations of the Master Plan – even when doing so was problematic – on the grounds that abandoning the Plan would be tantamount to ignoring the law because it was embodied in a presidential decree (Kuncoro and Resosudarmo 2006).

Thus by the end of 2006, there was a growing view that the role of the Supervisory and Advisory Boards needed to be strengthened. There were also some calls to reevaluate the original Master Plan with the aim of removing the parts that created problems, simplifying others, and strengthening those that were important – particularly those relating to land use planning. The hope was that a revised version of the Plan might then provide guidance that would be followed both by the BRR and by all other institutions contributing to the reconstruction effort (Kuncoro and Resosudarmo 2006).

BRR coordination with local governments was rather weak in this early period. Initially, local governments expected that the BRR would help them implement local priorities. However, the local governments lacked comprehensive rehabilitation plans so the BRR devised its own plan and spent considerable time in 2005 establishing offices and learning about local problems. This approach did not work very well. Local governments felt that they already had sufficient knowledge about local concerns and were furious over what they regarded as a late start by the BRR. The weak coordination between the BRR and local governments should not be attributed to a lack of commitment. There were many meetings and discussions. However, the different organizations just did not relate to each other very well. As noted in the publication of BRR and International Partners (2005):

> [m]ost meetings, ostensibly for coordination, achieved little more than information-sharing rather than strategic planning [and] . . . agency leaders were so busy on their own programs that they were frustrated when they attended a meeting that wasn't useful . . . [so that] they were likely to send junior staff in future, so reinforcing the information rather than strategy content.

The result was that local Bappeda *kabupaten* (district) and *kota* (municipality) agencies did not align their 2006 regional budgets with the BRR's 2006 plan. Indeed, many regional governments complained that they did not know what the BRR planned to do in their regions.

The BRR also struggled to develop relations with other agencies involved in the Aceh-Nias reconstruction activities although, in

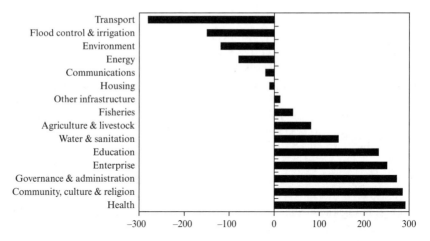

Source: BRR and International Partners (2005); Kuncoro and Resosudarmo (2006).

Figure 4.5 *Gaps between funding and minimum requirements*
(US$ million)

general, the BRR was able to take the lead in management. The struggle was evident in several areas. First, there were significant imbalances within the various components of the rehabilitation effort between the minimum requirements and the available funds. Figure 4.5 shows the difference between total current commitments of funding by government and donors in each sector and the minimum funding requirements. It can be seen that funding far in excess of actual needs was allocated to areas such as health, culture and religion, governance and administration, enterprise rehabilitation, education, and water and sanitation, while energy supply, the environment, flood control and irrigation works, and transport were significantly under-funded. The BRR, therefore, had trouble in persuading donors to reallocate funding from excessively funded to under-funded sectors. Another example of the BRR's limited ability to coordinate the recovery effort was that several of the NGOs involved were not able to deliver the outcomes they had promised, particularly in relation to housing construction and provision of income earning opportunities.

Second, it was not clear that the BRR had the ability to ensure that commitments by international and domestic donors would materialize in a timely manner. Some commitments appeared likely to not translate into actual fund flows for various reasons beyond Indonesia's control. Indonesia's capacity to absorb aid was also an important factor. It was clearly vital that the BRR aimed to maintain effective communication with donors and engaged donors in developing activities so as to minimize any mismatches between donors' interests and reconstruction priorities.

Exit Strategy

It is important that reconstruction programs following a natural disaster should fit into broader programs of economic development for the affected regions. The plan was for the mandate of the BRR to end in 2009. The question of the BRR's exit strategy was therefore a matter of some interest. Figure 4.4 suggested to some that the agency should start phasing out its activities by mid-2008. For housing, the target was to finish rebuilding by mid-2007. The dotted lines at the far right of Figure 4.4 suggested that the BRR would plan to leave certain activities for other agencies. Indeed, the expectation was that at the end of its term, the BRR would hand over the resources it had been using to local governments (at both the provincial and district or municipality levels), which would be expected to continue reconstruction and development activities.

Sustainability, then, was an issue that needed to be considered. First was the sustainability of the development process initiated by the BRR. In its operations, the BRR introduced procedures and practices that appeared in some cases to be different from the operational procedures currently in use by local governments. It was important, therefore, that the BRR's governance systems could be implemented by local governments while at the same time allowing for different local values and cultures. During the period to end-2009 when the BRR was expected to cease operations, the BRR and local governments needed to plan to work together to find governance systems that, given the local context and capability, were workable and acceptable to local people. Second, the BRR initially acted as a focal point for various budgetary matters including the coordination of funds from donor agencies. In many instances, the BRR matched local needs with possible funding from both national and international donor agencies. This task required understanding and sensitivity to local needs on the one hand, and on the other called for effective networking and good diplomatic skills to liaise with donors and upper level governments. It was expected that as 2009 approached, the BRR would increasingly share its knowledge and information about financial networks with local governments.

The issue of an exit strategy certainly emphasized the need for close communication between the BRR and local governments across Aceh and Nias.

CONCLUSION

This chapter has discussed progress in the reconstruction and rehabilitation of Aceh and Nias in the first two years following the greatest natural disaster in recorded Indonesian history. On the economic front, the December 2004 earthquakes and tsunami severely affected the livelihood of hundreds and thousands of people in the region. Furthermore, despite large-scale reconstruction activities, in the two years following the disaster many people were unable to find jobs. Moreover, the region was also affected by relatively high inflation partly caused by the reconstruction process itself.

Notably, the various stakeholders in the reconstruction process were virtually unanimous in claiming that progress had been too slow. Many reconstruction plan targets were not met in the first two years and it appeared likely that achievements would continue to tend to fall short of targets. Budget expenditures had fallen well behind targets as well, even though a four-month extension of the 2005 fiscal year was agreed to with the aim of providing leeway in implementing activities. Late realization and non-realization of the 2006 budget were no less worrying – a mere 18 per cent of spending had taken place up to the end of September 2006.

Several observations may be made about this slow progress. Effective coordination among agencies, both domestic and foreign, is essential. Ideally, the BRR as a coordinating agency needed to operate in close collaboration with local people, local governments, and donor agencies. When there was inadequate consultation and coordination, reconstruction programs tended to be delayed, parties involved lacked a sense of ownership towards the various activities, and the risk that different agencies would operate at cross-purposes increased. A second issue related to the overall financing needs of reconstruction. It became increasingly apparent that in the longer term, unanticipated and large cost increases in reconstruction activities were likely to produce a funding gap that would need to be met one way or another if reconstruction work was to be completed.

In one respect at least, the awful natural disasters brought some benefits to the conflict-ridden region of Aceh. Three decades of political and military conflict before the tsunami had caused widespread suffering in the province. Peace talks had commenced before the tsunami but progress had been slow. The natural calamity put sharply renewed pressure on the parties to the peace negotiations to reach early agreements on key issues so that reconstruction activities could proceed smoothly. In short, suddenly the great majority of people in the region were united in their demand that there be peace.

But looking back over the experience in Aceh in the first two years after the disaster, the nagging question remains: how can Indonesia best prepare to cope with natural disasters in the future? It seems clear that in a developing country such as Indonesia, disaster management should start with local society, at the local level. In this context there are two main lessons to learn. First, it is important to improve local early warning systems across the nation and to increase awareness of the local indications that a natural disaster might be about to occur. Indeed, as noted above, local knowledge of some of these indications currently exists among some traditional community groups in Indonesia. As a country prone to natural disasters, Indonesia should acknowledge the great importance of disseminating such traditional knowledge throughout the country by, for example, including the topic of natural disasters in the national curriculum beginning at the elementary school level (*Kompas*, 12 October 2006). Second, it is important to note that community self-reliance is vital in a society facing severe natural disasters, especially during the critical first hours following a disaster. It is inevitable that outside help will take time to arrive, especially in remote areas. Indeed, by the time that news of the disaster has been reported on the national, and especially the international media, it is often the case that many of the injured have already died. And, of course, international agencies also need to improve their ability to respond much faster and much more efficiently to disasters in developing countries.

As a last observation, it should be emphasized that reconstruction after a natural disaster poses numerous difficult challenges. Close coordination between all of the agents involved is essential, as is a peaceful socio-political environment and active community involvement in program implementation. Further, it is important that there are no false promises of assistance so that local people have realistic expectations about the speed of reconstruction work. Targets should be realistic, significant cost increases must be expected and budgeted for, and plans should reflect a sensible approach to the sequencing of programs. In particular, from the very beginning, rebuilding economic livelihoods and housing reconstruction should be seen as top priorities. Strategies must be developed to ensure that there is efficient coordination among different agencies, that commitments of assistance from both domestic and international organizations are fulfilled, and that those agencies are accountable for the promises that they have made. Finally, reconstruction agencies should set out clear exit strategies to allow for a smooth transfer of activities into the hands of local governments and organizations at the end of the reconstruction period.

NOTES

1. Suahasil Nazara and Budy P. Resosudarmo were primarily responsible for this chapter which draws on Nazara and Resosudarmo (2007).
2. This is based on records maintained by the World Health Organization's Center for Research on the Epidemiology of Disasters at the Université Catholique de Louvain, Brussels. To be included in this WHO database of natural disasters, a disaster should fulfil at least one of the following criteria: (1) ten or more people reported killed, (2) 100 people reported affected, (3) a call for international assistance, or (4) a declaration of a state of emergency.
3. See http://www.em-dat.net
4. The census was conducted by BPS, Bappenas, and UNFPA (with the help of the international donor agencies CIDA, AusAID, and NZAID) in response to the need for accurate demographic data after the disasters in Aceh and Nias. BPS, the main agency conducting the field survey, must be congratulated on this achievement for several reasons. First, the census was prepared very quickly. By comparison, for example, preparations for the 2010 Indonesian National Census were already being made in 2006. Second, the challenges involved in conducting a population census in the post-disaster area of Aceh and in the remote areas of Nias were enormous. These included security challenges in several conflict regions of Aceh. Third, BPS was able to include all people in Aceh and Nias in the census. The actual work, in the form of instrument finalization, started in June 2005, and the census date as the reference for the data was set as 15 September 2005. In addition to collecting demographic data at the time of the reference date, the census also collected data on internally displaced persons (IDPs) defined as persons that, due to a natural disaster, had to leave their usual dwelling. These IDPs could be located in tents, ruined houses, or other family houses.
5. In a triangular procedure, any information obtained from an interview is used only when reconfirmed by at least two other respondents.
6. The World Bank's estimate was based on a standard assessment technique developed by the United Nations Economic Commission for Latin America and the Caribbean (ECLAC, 2003).
7. In effect, the third phase was completed in April 2009. The mandate of the BRR formally ended, as scheduled, in April 2009. Ongoing functions were transferred to the provincial and other regional authorities in Aceh.
8. The MDF is co-chaired by the BRR, the European Commission (EC) as the largest donor, and the World Bank as the Trustee. The steering committee of this fund comprises the Government of Indonesia, contributors, civil society, and other international NGOs and the UN. The broad representation of the steering committee was expected to allow the MDF to act as a donor coordination mechanism and a forum for dialogue on recovery policy between the Government of Indonesia and the international community.
9. The Master Plan was released through the President Regulation (*Perpres*) No. 34/2005 in April 2005. The main book, which was effectively an extended summary of the whole study, comprised 129 pages. The sectoral information which is the detailed version of the Master Plan comprised twelve books totalling 1400 pages.
10. BRR might predict that the cost per house only temporarily increased and so the average cost per house in 2006 would be around US$4000.
11. In Aceh only around 30 per cent of households had toilets with septic tanks. In Nias the percentage was even lower; i.e., around 6 per cent. Thus a large proportion of households used toilets without septic tanks or use a pond or river as their toilet.
12. This issue caused considerable controversy. Some local environmental groups argued that reconstruction activities in Aceh contributed to faster deforestation. See Sijabat (2007).
13. Table 4.16 shows the old format of BRR's budget, while Table 4.17 presents the new format and an additional budget of around Rp1 trillion in 2006.

REFERENCES

ADB (Asian Development Bank) (2006), 'Progress report Indonesia: Aceh-Nias rehabilitation and reconstruction', http://www.asiandevbank.org/Documents/PAs/INO/31153-INO-PA.pdf, accessed 12 November 2006.

Athukorala, Prema-chandra and B.P. Resosudarmo (2005), 'The Indian Ocean tsunami: economic impact, disaster management and lessons', *Asian Economic Papers*, **4** (1), 1–39.

Bappeda Aceh (2005), *Pembangunan Propinsi Aceh Pasca Bencana Alam*, Banda Aceh: Bappeda Propinsi Aceh.

BPS (Badan Pusat Statistik) (2005), *Statistik Indonesia 2005*, Jakarta: BPS.

BPS, Bappenas, UNFPA, CIDA, AusAID, and NZAid (2005a), *Penduduk and Kependudukan Aceh Pasca Gempa dan Tsunami: Hasil Sensus Penduduk Nanggroe Aceh Darussalam 2005*, Jakarta: BPS.

BPS, Bappenas, UNFPA, CIDA, AusAID, and NZAid (2005b), *Penduduk and Kependudukan Nias Pasca Gempa dan Tsunami: Hasil Sensus Penduduk Nias 2005*, Jakarta: BPS.

BPS Kabupaten Nias (2005), *Kabupaten Nias dalam Angka 2004*, Gunungsitoli: BPS Kabupaten Nias.

BRR (Badan Rehabilitasi dan Rekonstruksi Aceh-Nias) (2006), *Membangun Tanah Harapan: Laporan Kegiatan Satu Tahun Badan Pelaksana Rehabilitasi dan Rekonstruksi Nanggroe Aceh Darussalam dan Nias April 2006*, Banda Aceh: BRR.

BRR and International Partners (2005), *Aceh and Nias One Year after the Tsunami: The Recovery Effort and Way Forward*, Jakarta: BRR.

BRR Nias (2005), 'Nias Island: rebuilding a better future', Presentation at the Nias Stakeholders' Meeting, Gunungsitoli, Nias, December 2005.

BRR and Partners (2006), *Aceh and Nias. Two Years after the Tsunami*, Banda Aceh: BRR.

ECLAC (United Nations Economic Commission for Latin America and the Caribbean) (2003), *Handbook for the Evaluation of the Socioeconomic and Environmental Impact of Disaster (LC/MEX/G.5)*, Santiago: ECLAC.

FAO (Food and Agriculture Organization of the United Nations) (2005a), 'Impact of the tsunami on fisheries, aquaculture and coastal lives', FTP.FAO.org/FI/Document/tsunami, accessed 11 October 2006.

FAO (2005b), 'Soil salinity problems are limited in tsunami affected countries. Planting could resume in many areas, but farmers are still facing other constraints', http://www.fao.org/tsunami/stories/, accessed 11 October 2006.

Indrawati, Sri Mulyani (2005), 'Toward recovery: lessons from Indonesian case in managing natural disaster crisis'. Keynote speech at the 7th IRSA International Conference on Natural Disasters' Impact and Challenges for Recovery, Jakarta, 3–4 August.

Kuncoro, Ari and B. Resosudarmo (2006), 'Survey of recent developments', *Bulletin of Indonesian Economic Studies*, **42** (1), 7–31.

LPEM (Institute for Economics and Social Research) (2005), 'Perhitungan Kebutuhan Dana Pembangunan kembali Aceh', LPEM Internal Report, Jakarta.

MDF (Multi Donor Fund) (2005), *One Year Report: Results, Challenges, and Opportunities*, Jakarta: Multi Donor Fund for Aceh and Nias.

Nazara, Suahasil and B.P. Resosudarmo (2007), *Aceh-Nias Reconstruction and Rehabilitation: Progress and Challenges at the End of 2006,* ADBI Discussion Paper no 70, June, http://www.adbi.org/discussion-paper/2007/06/29/2288.aceh nias.reconstruction.rehabilitation/, accessed 10 October 2009.

OCHA (Office for the Coordination of Humanitarian Affairs) (2005), 'Indian Ocean – earthquake/tsunami – December 2004: list of commitments/contributions and pledges as of 21 February 2005', http://www.reliefweb.int/rw/fts.nsf/doc105?OpenForm&emid=TS-2004-000147-LKA, accessed 25 October 2005.

Patton, Michael Quinn (2002), *Qualitative Evaluation and Research Methods, 3rd edn,* Thousand Oaks, CA: Sage.

Sen, Kunal and L. Steer (2005), 'Survey of recent developments', *Bulletin of Indonesian Economic Studies,* **41** (3), 279–304.

Sijabat, Ridwan Max (2007), 'International agencies furthering Aceh deforestation: greenomics', *Jakarta Post,* 11 May.

Soehaimi, A., E.K. Kertapati, Surono, Supartoyo and J.H. Setiawan (2005), 'Gempa Bumi dan Tsunami NAD-SUMUT 26 Desember 2004', paper presented in the GeoSeminar, 14 January, Pusat Penelitian and Pengembangan Geologi, Bandung.

Soesastro, Hadi and R. Ace (2005), 'Survey of recent developments', *Bulletin of Indonesia Economic Studies,* **41** (1), 5–34.

SPAN (2005): see BPS, Bappenas et al. 2005a, 2005b.

UNORC (2006), 'Humanitarian and recovery update: Aceh and Nias, May 2006', Jakarta: Office of the UN Resident/Humanitarian Coordinator in Indonesia.

USAID (2006), 'Audit of USAID/Indonesia's Banda Aceh-Lamno Road reconstruction activities under its tsunami recovery and reconstruction program', Audit Report no 5-497-06-003-p, Jakarta: USAID.

Wetlands International – Indonesia Programme (2005), 'Tsunami of Aceh and North Sumatra 26 December 2004', http://www.wetlands.or.id/, accessed 30 March 2005.

World Bank (2003), 'Decentralizing Indonesia: a regional public expenditure review', Report no. 26191–IND, Poverty Reduction and Economic Management Unit, East Asia and Pacific Region.

World Bank (2005), *Indonesia. Preliminary Damage and Loss Assessment: The December 26, 2004 Natural Disaster,* Jakarta: World Bank.

World Bank (2006a), *GAM Reintegration Needs Assessment,* Jakarta: World Bank.

World Bank (2006b), *Aceh Public Expenditure Analysis: Spending for Reconstruction and Poverty Reduction,* Jakarta: World Bank.

5. Sri Lanka[1]

The earthquake that caused the tsunami on 26 December 2004 occurred at 6:59 am Sri Lanka time with the first large wave hitting the east coast at 8:35 am. Within a very short time over 36 000 people were dead (this total includes the 5644 who remain classified as 'missing'), and several hundred thousand had been displaced. Massive damage was also inflicted on thousands of houses and other buildings, railways, bridges, communication networks, and other infrastructure and capital assets.

Although Sri Lanka had experienced periodic droughts, floods, landslides, and the occasional cyclone, in recorded history it had never experienced a tsunami, or indeed any other type of natural disaster of this scale and magnitude.[2] Although the country was completely unprepared for a disaster of this scale, the relief effort that got underway almost immediately – initially organized by local communities, followed by the government and international agencies – was able to feed, clothe, and shelter survivors; provide the injured with medical attention; and ensure that the thousands of bodies were cremated or buried, avoiding any disease outbreaks. The initial response is generally agreed to have been a success despite the understandable confusion which accompanied this effort at times.

However, as an earlier study of this issue discussed (Jayasuriya, Steele and Weerakoon 2006), it became clear as the reconstruction and rehabilitation phase proceeded that moving from the immediate relief effort to addressing the massive reconstruction tasks posed a different set of challenges that was in many ways more complex. The tsunami had come at a time of deterioration of the macroeconomic environment: GDP growth was slowing from the second quarter, inflationary pressure had been persistently building from the middle of 2004, fiscal and external current account deficits were growing, and the currency was rapidly depreciating.

As explained in the earlier report, the tsunami – paradoxically – brought a measure of stability to the economy which had been straining under growing macroeconomic imbalances. For Sri Lanka, as for other affected countries that were ready to accept external assistance, the promised international assistance appeared to be more than adequate to cover the full costs of immediate relief and reconstruction and produced an almost euphoric (though transient) national mood. In particular, it provided an

unanticipated source of foreign capital inflows for the relief and reconstruction effort and enabled the country to avoid the slide towards a currency crisis. Not only did the additional influx of foreign capital allow Sri
Lanka to maintain a fairly healthy balance of payments (BOP) during
2005–06, but relief and reconstruction-related expenditures also boosted
GDP growth to a healthy annual average of 6.7 per cent over the same
period.

While the tsunami diverted attention away from the growing structural
imbalances in the economy, the imbalances were not eliminated. As the
reconstruction and rehabilitation phase proceeded – albeit at a slower pace
than initially anticipated – issues regarding the effectiveness with which
resources were mobilized, the effectiveness of delivering assistance and its
coordination, and the gaps opening up in financing reconstruction and its
implications for macroeconomic policy management, took centre stage.

This chapter surveys the relief and reconstruction effort, with the focus
on the first two years. Other issues, in particular the renewal of armed
conflict which culminated in the defeat of the LTTE (Liberation Tigers
of Tamil Eelam) by the government forces in 2009, took precedence in Sri
Lanka's political and economic agenda. While the reconstruction activities in the South and Southwest proceeded rapidly and were successfully
completed, progress in the East and Northeast, particularly in contested
areas, was badly affected. In 2008, the World Bank (2008) described the
inequitable distribution of tsunami aid and reconstruction efforts, pointing out that the 'South and the West have received more aid than the
North and the East. In fact, in some Southern districts, more houses have
been rebuilt than were damaged by the tsunami.' Hence, overall progress
in house construction was heavily skewed towards the South and the West:
'while 90 per cent of the fully-damaged units in the South and the West
have been reconstructed, only 57 per cent of the units in the North and
the East have been completed' (p. 17). At the end of 2008, reconstruction
activities were basically completed in the South and the West but in the
North and the East, unfinished tasks remained.

IMPACT OF THE TSUNAMI

The final death toll was estimated at around 36 000. Initial estimates
of those displaced put the number at around 800 000. By mid-2005 this
number had come down to around 516 000 as some of the displaced found
alternative accommodation with friends and relatives. Damage to buildings and physical infrastructure was massive. Tens of thousands of houses
were damaged or destroyed, many hotels were severely damaged, and six

---

BOX 5.1   IMMEDIATE IMPACT

Killed/missing persons: 35 322
Injured persons: 21 441
Internally displaced persons: 516 150
Widowed, orphaned, affected elderly and disabled persons: 40 000
Lost livelihoods: 150 000 (75 per cent of the total fishing fleet)
Value of lost assets: US$900 million
Houses destroyed: 89 000
Schools destroyed or damaged: 183
Schools used as camps for IDPs: 446
Schoolchildren affected: 200 000
Health facilities destroyed or damaged: 102
Tourism infrastructure damaged:

   Large hotels: 53 out of 242
   Small hotels: 248
   Related small enterprises: 210

Cultivated arable land affected by salinity: 23 449 acres

Note: IDP = internally displaced person.

Source: GOSL (2006).

---

hotels were completely washed away. Close to 200 schools were destroyed or sustained serious damage. Several hospitals, telecommunication networks, and the coastal railway network were also damaged.

The geographic impact of the tsunami was uneven. Much of the coastal belt of the Northern, Eastern and Southern Provinces and some parts of the Western Province was severely damaged. The Eastern Province was particularly hard hit, accounting for nearly half of total deaths and displaced persons as well as numbers of houses damaged (Table 5.1). The severity of the tsunami disaster in the Northern and Eastern Provinces compounded problems arising from two decades of conflict between the Government of Sri Lanka (GOSL) and the LTTE. The majority of an estimated 360 000 conflict-related internally displaced people lived in these two provinces. From the very early stages, there were concerns about how assistance could be channelled to LTTE-controlled areas. However, basic relief supplies did manage to get through to affected people during the early phases of the relief effort.

Table 5.1   Key human and asset loss by district/province

District/Province	No of deaths[a]	No of displaced[a]	No of damaged houses[b]
Galle	4214	128077	12781
Matara	1342	13305	7464
Hambantota	4500	17723	4084
Southern Province	10056	159105	24329
Colombo	79	31239	5984
Gampaha	6	1449	675
Kalutara	256	27713	6124
Western Province	341	60401	12783
Ampara	10440	75238	24438
Batticaloa	2840	61912	17948
Trincomalee	1078	81643	8074
Eastern Province	14358	218793	50460
Jaffna	2640	39907	5109
Mullaitivu	3000	22557	5556
Killinochchi	500	1603	288
Northern Province	6140	64067	10953
Total	30895	502366	98525

Notes: [a] As of January 2005; [b] as of October 2005.

Source: Department of Census and Statistics (DCS).

The preliminary assessment of damages completed by end-January 2005 through a joint effort of the Asian Development Bank (ADB), the Japan Bank for International Cooperation (JBIC), and the World Bank (WB) (2005) estimated that Sri Lanka had suffered asset damages of around US$1 billion (4.5 per cent of GDP), and estimated that the medium-term financing needs (including immediate relief) would be around US$1.5–1.6 billion (7.5 per cent of GDP). The largest financing needs were in the housing sector (Table 5.2).[3] The destruction of private assets was substantial (US$700 million), in addition to public infrastructure and other assets. Loss of current output in the fisheries and tourism sectors – which were severely affected – was estimated at US$200 million and US$130 million, respectively. Key industrial, agricultural, and metropolitan centres were relatively unaffected and the damage to capital assets was primarily to the tourism and fisheries sectors, each of which contributes only around 1.5–2 per cent of GDP.

Table 5.2   Estimates of losses and needs assessment on reconstruction and rebuilding (US$ million)

	ADB/JBIC/WB[a]		GOSL	
	Losses	Needs	Feb. 05[b]	May 05[c, d]
Housing	306–341	437–487	400	400
Roads	60	200	210	353
Water and sanitation	42	117	190	205
Railways	15	130	77	–
Education	26	45	90	170
Health	60	84	100	100
Agriculture	3	4	10	10
Fisheries	97	118	250	200
Tourism	250	130	58	–
Power	10	67–77	–	115
Environment	10	18	30	30
Microfinance	–	–	150	157
Other	90	180	239	424
Total (US$ bn)	0.9–1.0	1.5–1.6	1.8	2.2

Sources: [a]ADB, JBIC and WB (2005); [b]GOSL (2005d); [c]GOSL (2005c); [d]MFP (2005), Budget Speech 2006 (December 2005).

These aggregate figures for financing needs were quite close to the government's own estimate of US$1.8 billion presented in February 2005, though there were some important differences at the sector level damage estimates (GOSL 2005d). Subsequently, the GOSL firmed up the country's total investment needs to be US$2.2 billion (GOSL 2005c).[4] Some of the differences between these estimates reflected the government's more ambitious longer-term plans while the donor assessment was largely geared to restoring the pre-tsunami situation. In line with the regional variation in the extent of damages incurred, the largest financing needs were identified in the East (45 per cent), followed by the South (26 per cent), North (19 per cent), and West (10 per cent).

IMMEDIATE RESPONSE

In the immediate aftermath of the tsunami, the Ministry of Public Security, Law and Order set up an operations centre, the Centre for National Operations (CNO), to handle the response, and the Secretary to the Ministry was appointed as the Commissioner General of Essential Services to oversee the coordination of government agencies involved in rescue and relief. Three task forces were set up to address specific aspects of the relief effort: the Task Force for Rescue and Relief (TAFRER); the Task Force for Logistics, Law and Order (TAFLOL); and the Task Force for Rebuilding the Nation (TAFREN).

While there were hiccups and confusion in organizing the relief, for a country that had not previously experienced such a disaster, Sri Lankan institutions responded reasonably well. Essential medical aid, emergency food, and other relief supplies were mobilized within a day. Temporary shelter for the displaced was provided in schools, other public and religious buildings, and tents. Communities and groups cooperated across barriers that had divided them for decades. Public and private sector organizations cooperated and organized relief efforts at many levels. Sri Lanka's past investments in public health paid off in this emergency: the broad-based public health system and community awareness of basic sanitary and hygienic practices ensured that there were no disease outbreaks.

Once the immediate relief and rehabilitation measures for provision of food, shelter, clothing, clean water, and sanitary and medical facilities to affected families had been provided, it was necessary to address community needs to cope with the trauma and start rebuilding lives. The initial provision of cash grants to meet immediate needs included (i) compensation to the value of SLRs (Sri Lanka Rupees) 15000 (US$150) for victims towards funeral expenses; (ii) payment of SLRs375 (US$3.75) in cash and rations for each member of the family unit per week; and (iii) a payment of SLRs2500 (US$25) towards basic kitchen equipment. These initial measures were largely successful, though there were some problems with lack of coordination.[5] Overall, the emergency relief was quite successful in meeting the immediate needs of the affected people.[6]

SHORT-TERM ECONOMIC IMPACT

The tsunami struck at a time when the Sri Lankan macro economy was already under pressure on several fronts, reigniting fears of a slide into the kind of crisis that was seen in 2001 when the economy contracted by 1.5 per cent (Table 5.3). On the policy front, there was considerable unease within the business and investor community about the direction of economic policy under the new government elected in April 2004. Its program, with the stated goal of 'growth with equity', and a strong emphasis on rural economic development, was viewed by sections of the business and investor community as being populist and interventionist.

Table 5.3 Selected macroeconomic indicators: 2001–06

	Unit	2001	2002	2003	2004	2005	2006
GDP	US$ billion	15.1	16.4	18.2	19.4	23.2	26.0
GDP growth	%	−1.5	4.0	6.0	5.4	6.0	7.4
Agriculture	%	−3.4	2.5	1.6	−0.3	1.5	4.7
Industry	%	−2.1	1.0	5.5	5.2	8.3	7.2
Services	%	−0.5	6.1	7.9	7.6	6.4	8.3
Investment	% of GDP	22	21	22	25	26	29
Savings	% of GDP	16	14	16	16	17	17
External sector							
Exports	US$ billion	4.8	4.7	5.1	5.8	6.3	6.8
Imports	US$ billion	6.0	6.1	6.7	8.0	8.9	10.2
Trade balance	% of GDP	−7.3	−8.5	−8.4	−11.2	−10.7	−12.5
Current a/c balance	% of GDP	−1.4	−1.4	−0.4	−3.2	−2.8	−4.9
FDI	% of GDP	0.5	1.1	0.9	1.1	1.0	1.7
Official reserves	US$ billion	1.3	1.7	2.3	2.2	2.7	2.8
Tourist arrivals	'000 persons	336.8	393.2	500.6	566.2	549.3	559.6
Tourist earnings	US$ million	202	250	340	408	356	410

Table 5.3 (continued)

	Unit	2001	2002	2003	2004	2005	2006
Fiscal variables							
Govt. expenditure	% of GDP	27	25	24	23	25	25
Govt. revenue	% of GDP	17	16	16	15	16	17
Fiscal balance	% of GDP	−11	−9	−8	−8	−9	−8
Govt. debt	% of GDP	103	105	106	105	94	93
Prices and money							
Rate of inflation	%	14.2	9.6	6.3	7.6	11.6	13.7
Interest rate[a]	%	13.7	9.9	7.2	7.6	10.4	13.0
Broad money (M2)	% change	13.6	13.4	15.3	19.6	19.1	17.8
Exchange rate	Rs/$	93.2	96.7	96.7	104.6	102.1	107.7
ASPI[b]	1985=100	621	815	1062	1507	1922	2722

Notes: [a] 2-month Treasury bill rate; [b] All share price index.

Source: Central Bank of Sri Lanka, *Annual Report*, various issues.

Economic growth began to slow from the second quarter of 2004 and ended the year with a growth rate of 5.4 per cent. While the election-related uncertainties and the ensuing policy vacuum no doubt contributed to the slowdown in economic activity, some policy weaknesses and the slow pace of reforms contributed to the lacklustre performance. The most visible, and potentially the most destabilizing manifestation of weakening macro-economic management in 2004 was a persistent build up of inflationary pressure from the mid-year onwards. Inflationary pressure was fuelled on multiple fronts, not least by the conduct of an expansionary fiscal policy driven by increased subsidies and transfers.

Domestic imbalances were exacerbated by a ballooning oil import bill which saw the current account deficit on BOP widening to over 3.3 per cent of GDP in 2004 (from 0.4 per cent in 2003). This was accompanied by a deceleration of capital inflows, with long-term inflows to the government (consisting primarily of foreign concessional loans) declining by US$130 million in 2004. Foreign borrowings by the commercial banking sector increased significantly in 2004 raising the country's foreign private debt exposure. The currency depreciated by 8.5 per cent against the US dollar despite efforts to bolster the exchange rate, which contributed to the decline in Sri Lanka's gross official reserves from US$2.3 billion at the beginning of 2004 to US$1.9 billion by November.

These domestic and external developments led to an acceleration of inflation from mid-2004, and real interest rates turned negative. Symptoms of a bubble economy began to emerge: a sharp increase in credit growth in excess of 20 per cent and a boom in the Colombo stock market unsupported by major indicators of economic fundamentals. The peace process between the GOSL and the LTTE appeared to have stalled, and with privatization initiatives shelved concerns over the government's ability to reduce the fiscal deficit began to increase. Markets started to get jittery with the growing realization that fundamental imbalances in the economy were intensifying. Though the external payments situation improved marginally in December 2004, rupee depreciation again gathered pace. On 17 December 2004, the currency fell to an historical low of SLRs105 against the US dollar.

Against this backdrop, the immediate negative impact on output as measured by the GDP figure was expected to be fairly limited, ranging from a 0.5 to a 0.7 per cent reduction in 2005 GDP. The relatively small impact on GDP appeared somewhat surprising given the extent of human and asset losses. This was not only owing to the fact that only a relatively small sector of the economy was affected, but also because GDP captures only the annualized flow of damages to the stock of asset damages, and spending on relief efforts was expected to have an immediate positive effect on current GDP. After 2005, the overall impact of reconstruction efforts certainly helped boost the GDP growth rate.

REHABILITATION, RECONSTRUCTION AND RECOVERY PHASE

Recovery Targets and Actual Progress

The government planned the reconstruction and rehabilitation phase to be spread over three to five years (GOSL 2005c). Nevertheless, there were pronouncements at the political level that all permanent housing needs would be met within a year. Over time, it has become clear that these were optimistic pledges. In fact, housing needs, for example, had not been met fully even by the end of 2006, while reconstruction of damaged schools and hospitals, and rehabilitation of roads, bridges, and the like was likely to take longer than envisaged.

Infrastructure

A total of 182 schools and 222 health institutions were affected by the tsunami. Targets in the education and health sectors included the reconstruction and renovation of 183 schools, four universities, seven Vocational Training Authorities, 444 internally displaced person (IDP) schools (schools used as refugee camps), and the reconstruction and renovation of 102 health institutions.

The pace of recovery, particularly of larger scale infrastructure projects, was slow with an estimated 50 per cent of construction projects yet to start by end-2006 (GOSL 2006). By end-2006, 57 per cent of damaged schools were estimated to be in various stages of construction with only 10 per cent of projects completed and handed over (GOSL 2006). Similarly, in the health sector only 55 of a total of 102 damaged buildings had been completed at the end of two years (Table 5.4).

The bulk of infrastructure damage was to roads and railways (Table 5.5). A total length of approximately 800 kilometres of national road network and 1500 kilometres of provincial and local government roads was damaged. The railway infrastructure on a 160-kilometre stretch along the tsunami-affected coastline was also severely damaged. The target date for completion of road and bridge reconstruction was set as 2009. As we shall discuss below, this target date proved difficult to meet because of serious capacity constraints and cost escalations. The government itself recognized that the construction industry did not have the necessary

Table 5.4   Progress in education and health infrastructure

	Education	Health
No. affected	183	102
Without donors	11	–
Completed	18	55
In progress	105	–
Not commenced	49	–

Source: GOSL (2006).

Table 5.5   Progress in infrastructure

	Damage	Progress 2006
Water and sanitation		130 projects planned. Donor commitment for 96 projects
Roads	Rehabilitation of 1172 km of roads	2 projects under way. 8 in tendering process.
Bridges	25 major bridges	4 commenced construction; 10 in tendering process.

Source: RADA (2006).

contractors, equipment, or skilled workforce for such a major reconstruction effort (GOSL 2005a).

In addition to the rehabilitation of damaged infrastructure, new demands for infrastructure services were created by relocated communities. As described in detail later, a significant proportion of relocated households was found to have inadequate access to water, roads, pre-schools, and health clinics, and was worse off than before.

Housing

The immediate requirement in housing was to provide 'transitional' shelters. A total of around 57 000 transitional shelter units were estimated to be needed to accommodate 50 per cent of the 500 000 internally displaced (GOSL 2005a). The remainder of the displaced were assumed to have received shelter from friends, relatives, and others. Progress on providing transitional shelters, by and large, was fairly good; by end-2005 over 56 000 units had been completed.[7]

The total number of displaced persons as of January 2005 was estimated at 98 525 (Table 5.6) of whom 56 000 were in government camps

Table 5.6   Post-tsunami numbers of displaced persons in transitional shelters

	Jan 2005	Dec 2005	June 2006[a]	Dec 2006
Government camps	56 000	53 000	42 196	17 083
Private homes	42 525	32 525	32 367	–
Total	98 525	85 525	74 563	17 083

Note: [a] Post-housing policy revision.

Source: RADA (2006).

(transitional shelter). The rest were with families/friends (RADA, 2006). By end-December 2005 the numbers of displaced had dropped to 85 525, of whom 53 000 were in transitional shelters. This figure was estimated at around 40 000 by end-2006.

There were significant revisions regarding housing policy. An initial declaration by the government of a buffer zone between land and sea of 100 metres on the south and southwest coast and 200 metres on the north and east coast of the country led to the initiation of two types of housing programs: (i) donor-built housing reconstruction and (ii) home owner-driven housing reconstruction. No reconstruction of houses (partially or fully damaged) was to be allowed within the buffer zone. Thus, all affected households within the demarcated buffer zone were to be provided with a house built with donor assistance on land allocated by the state while allowing them to retain ownership of the original land. Households were not required to demonstrate ownership of the land to qualify for such assistance.

For those whose damaged houses were deemed to be outside the designated buffer zone, the government agreed to provide grants and loans for households to re-build at the same location. In order to qualify for the entitlement, households were required to prove ownership of the land. The criteria set down in terms of financing such reconstruction included an assessment of damages on a points basis where a house deemed to be more than 40 per cent damaged would qualify for a grant of SLRs250 000 (US$2500) in four instalments, based on progress. A grant of SLRs100 000 (US$1000) was made available to rebuild a house deemed to be less than 40 per cent damaged, disbursed in two stages.

Predictably, the buffer zone became a politically controversial issue from the very outset. Limits were set in a fairly arbitrary manner, not taking into account topographical and other relevant features of the land that would affect hazard risk. There was also dissatisfaction that the rules were not to be applied across all building units, with tourist enterprises being permitted to rebuild within the designated zone. Many of the tsunami-affected fishers, for example, argued the need to retain land close to the sea to sustain their livelihoods.

Two household surveys of the tsunami-affected families were carried out by the Institute of Policy Studies of Sri Lanka (IPS) in 2005 and 2006. The first survey was carried out in April 2005 (IPS-TS 2005) covering 622 households in six affected districts. The second survey of the same households was carried out in July 2006 (IPS-TS 2006).[8] The IPS Tsunami Survey (IPS-TS) 2006 results showed that about 60 per cent of surveyed households thought that the government's original buffer zone rule was a 'good idea'. Data at the Grama Niladari Division (GND)[9] level agreed with this finding; almost all Grama Niladaris (GNs) (village level government officers) interviewed agreed that the government's original buffer zone policy was 'good'. Paradoxically, they were also happy with the relaxation of the buffer zone in 2006. Although there were delays in providing housing because of the buffer zone rule, most households saw the prospect of better housing because of this policy.

IPS-TS 2005 results found that most houses that were destroyed were smaller than the minimum floor area of 500 square feet specified for new houses under the donor-driven program; in other words, a majority of households would get superior replacement houses, at least in terms of floor area.[10] Moreover, while all new houses were to be built with permanent housing materials, a large share of destroyed houses had been made of temporary housing material.[11] Also, households that did not have legal ownership of land were given houses under the donor-driven program.[12] These factors may have outweighed the costs incurred by many households due to delays in housing progress caused by the 2005 buffer zone rule.

But there was widespread popular opposition on many levels to the buffer zone policy. By end-2005, the government had largely abandoned the idea of enforcing the buffer zone restrictions. In particular, the scarcity of land with which to relocate affected households highlighted the impracticality of enforcing such a zone in the face of the need to ensure permanent housing within a reasonable period of time. A more relaxed buffer zone policy was announced in May 2006 along with a 'Revised Tsunami Housing Policy'.[13] It was essentially aimed at ensuring that all tsunami-affected people return to their houses or get new houses by the end of 2006. The policy document promised 'a house for a house, regardless of land ownership'. It defined two zones (not buffer zones)[14] and four housing options, with the cost being shared by the government and donors (Box 5.2).

The revised housing policy pushed the total housing needs to around

---

BOX 5.2   REVISED TSUNAMI HOUSING POLICY

1. Government land + donor-built house under the donor-driven housing program primarily for all those who previously lived within the buffer zone.
2. Government land + government cash grant (SLRs250000) to construct a new house + regulated donor assistance provided to complete the houses (not less than SLRs250000 depending on costs to meet the minimum standard house) through co-financing agreement.
3. Government cash grant (SLRs150000 for three divisions in Ampara and SLRs250000 for Colombo) to purchase land + government cash grant (SLRs250000) to construct a house + regulated donor assistance provided to complete (not less than SLRs250000, depending on costs, to meet the minimum standard house) through co-financing agreement.
4. Housing reconstruction grant (SLRs250000 for fully damaged homes and SLRs100000 for partially damaged homes) + regulated donor assistance provided to complete only fully damaged houses as required for meeting the minimum standard house through co-financing agreement.

Source: RADA (2006).

110000 units. The key change was a decision to extend house eligibility to those without legal ownership of land outside the former buffer zone and to offer housing to extended family members living in the affected households.

Secondly, in contrast to the earlier policy, the government and donors were to jointly provide for a minimum of SLRs500000 (US$5000) cash support to a tsunami-affected family to build a house. The significant cost escalation of construction material and labour, already clearly visible by end-2005, undoubtedly forced a revision of the earlier estimates. Under the revised policy, the GOSL was to provide the cash grant, initially reimbursed by different development banks and bilateral donors.[15] The grant of SLRs250000 (US$2500) each from the government and donors was to be given in instalments; a first instalment of SLRs50000 (US$500) by the government matched equally by the donor and thereafter followed accordingly. The beneficiary was to receive full title to the property in the resettlement area (while retaining legal ownership of property within the re-designated buffer zone).

Table 5.7   Housing requirements

	Original (2005)	Revised (2006)	Completed (end-2006)
Homeowner-driven program	55 525	79 184	46 531
Partially damaged	32 497	39 823	34 988
Fully damaged	23 028	39 361	11 543
Relocation Housing Program	43 000	29 830	14 488

Source: GOSL (2006).

Finally, under the donor-built reconstruction program, standard building requirements were set down by the GOSL of a floor area of 500 square feet; the donor was to make available common infrastructure for housing clusters, and the government was to provide services up to the relocation site. The technical specifications were revised to ensure a more equitable basis. This was primarily a response to the initial experience where donors built houses of widely varying quality, with some houses costing only SLRs400 000 and others being valued at over SLRs1 million (US$4000 to over US$10 000), causing friction amongst recipients.[16]

The new housing policy requirements were identified under a homeowner-driven program and a relocation housing program. Overall, revisions to the housing policy (involving a higher cash grant component and a significant increase in the number of housing units deemed necessary) meant that questions would be raised about the ability to meet the costs of reconstruction within the commitments made by donors. It also created much confusion amongst the beneficiary households. Only about a quarter of the households surveyed in the IPS-TS 2006 were clear about their housing entitlements. Close to 60 per cent indicated that they would like legal advice regarding their rights as a homeowner.

As of November 2006, 46 531 partially or fully damaged houses had been rehabilitated, recording an 85 per cent completion rate (Table 5.7). Nevertheless, a funding gap of US$107 million had been identified to complete most of the fully damaged houses (GOSL 2006). In contrast to the progress in the homeowner-driven rehabilitation, progress in relocating tsunami-affected families was much slower at only 50 per cent of required units having been completed by November 2006. As the target in this scheme was reduced substantially, the government estimated that sufficient funds were available to successfully complete this program (GOSL 2006).

The lack of clarity regarding housing entitlements and distribution was

Table 5.8   Housing situation as at July 2006 (by eligibility under the 2005 housing program)

Eligibility	Rebuilt	Relocated	Donor built on old site	Temporary housing	NI[a]	Total
Donor-driven	52	25	11	175	5	268
%	19	10	4	65	2	100
Owner-driven	76	25	22	26	8	157
%	48	16	14	17	5	100
Not eligible[b]	34	17	24	59	0	134
%	25	13	18	44	0	100
Total	162	67	57	260	13	559

Notes: [a] No information; [b] households not owning a house before the tsunami (70% of 134) and households owning a house on encroached land (30% of 134) outside the buffer zone were not eligible for a new house under the 2005 housing policy.

Source: Authors' calculations based on IPS-TS 2005 and IPS-TS 2006 data.

apparent from the survey results. The IPS-TS 2005 and 2006 data give information on the location of households with respect to the 2005 buffer zone, and house and land tenure for 559 households. Of these, 268 were eligible for the donor-driven new housing and 157 were eligible for owner-driven housing reconstruction. A total of 134 households were not eligible for a new house either because they were not homeowners before the tsunami (70 per cent of 134) or because they were outside the 2005 buffer zone, and were homeowners without land tenure (30 per cent of 134).

The survey found considerable inequities in the distribution of new houses. Housing progress was worst for people who were actually eligible for donor-driven new housing. About 65 per cent of such households were still to be found in temporary housing as of mid-2006. At the same time, about 56 per cent of households who were not eligible for a new house had received a house. There appeared to be inconsistencies between official government policy on housing and actual practice. Some households eligible to relocate under the donor-driven housing program had rebuilt (19 per cent), while others eligible to rebuild under the owner-driven housing program had relocated (16 per cent). Some households had received houses outside both these programs, and others who were not eligible to receive a house under either program had also received houses (see Table 5.8). This is consistent with the observation by the World Bank (2008) that in some areas, the actual number of houses built exceeded the number destroyed.

Table 5.9   Status of housing progress by region (end-November 2006)

District/Province	Homeowner-driven		Relocation	
	Requirement	Completed	Requirement	Completed
Galle	11405	9590	3720	2793
Matara	6048	5409	2120	1372
Hambantota	1469	1344	4643	4162
Southern Province	18922	16343	10483	8327
Colombo	60	53	1387	107
Gampaha	253	234	436	218
Kalutara	5290	4537	2862	1687
Western Province	5603	4824	4685	2012
Ampara	21347	10298	3721	871
Batticaloa	19499	9581	2961	850
Trincomalee	3635	3378	2872	884
Eastern Province	44481	23257	9554	2605
Jaffna	4424	1720	4257	1348
Mullaitivu	5193	387	458	53
Killinochchi	611	0	393	143
Northern Province	10228	2107	5108	1544
Total	79184	46531	29830	14488

Source: GOSL (2006).

There were coordination problems across various donors, especially those who provided houses without adhering to government plans. According to local-level government officials, the reluctance of local non-government agencies to share information on aid distribution and their beneficiaries exacerbated the problem of coordination and monitoring.

Table 5.9 confirms the significant regional variation in housing progress across the country. The uneven progress was, in part, due to the resurgence of conflict in the north and east of the country from end-2005 (Figure 5.1). The Eastern Province with the highest requirement of housing lagged well behind. The survey results were consistent with national data and showed that housing progress was best in the Southern Province for those outside the 2005 buffer zone. Less than 6 per cent of surveyed households in this region were in temporary housing. Housing progress was worst for those in the Eastern Province – for households both within and outside the 2005 buffer zone. Progress was especially poor for households affected by the conflict. Progress was fastest in the South. The Western Province lagged

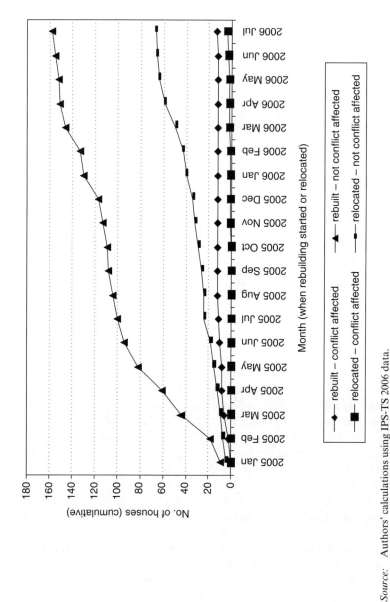

Source: Authors' calculations using IPS-TS 2006 data.

Figure 5.1 Survey results on housing progress by effect of conflict

Table 5.10   Quality of housing before and after tsunami for relocated households

	No	Better now (%)	Worse now (%)	No difference (%)
House design	69	42	41	14
Construction materials used for housing	69	27	49	21
Access to services (water, electricity, road)	69	14	63	20
Primary school within 1 km	73	10	62	29
Clinic within 1 km	73	1	59	40

Source: Authors' calculations using IPS-TS 2005 and 2006 data.

behind the Southern Province, most likely due to greater difficulties in obtaining suitable land but also because of more favourable political factors operating in the South.

Key reasons cited for the overall slow progress in housing relocation included a lack of commitment by NGOs, impact of the conflict, lack of infrastructure in new locations, and poor communications strategies. In the case of donor housing, it was pointed out that many donors that had large amounts of funds at their disposal and had pledged to build large numbers of housing units failed to meet even 50 per cent of their original targets (GOSL 2006).

These findings are consistent with the survey results: lack of land and delays in obtaining donor assistance were cited as the main reasons for the slow progress in the donor-driven housing program. The survey results also suggested that some people found that they were worse-off in terms of quality of housing and access to services (Table 5.10). There were claims that people's lifestyles were not taken into consideration when designing the new houses. For instance, the percentage of households using expensive sources of fuel for cooking such as gas and electricity increased from 10 per cent to 18 per cent, primarily because many of the new houses did not include a kitchen with a chimney to allow use of firewood for cooking.

The relatively smooth progress of the homeowner-driven housing program vis-à-vis the relocation program encouraged the Reconstruction and Development Agency (RADA) to consider converting donor-driven housing projects to owner-driven programs. Owner-driven housing programs were reportedly more effective because families got the funds directly into their own hands.[17] Owner-driven housing projects not only progressed faster but also proved to be cheaper than donor-driven projects. The cost of a single donor-assisted housing unit was estimated to range between SLRs0.4 and SLRs1.6 million (US4000–16000) even without the additional costs of site preparation, land-filling, drainage, and infrastructure provision (GOSL 2006).

Considering these factors, RADA urged the international NGOs (INGOs) to transfer their tsunami reconstruction funds to the Treasury so that the government could direct funds to the victims. Additional funding of around US$50 million was needed to shift house construction previously under donor-driven programs into owner-driven programs (MFP 2006). RADA argued that this would be the most practical way of resolving the logistical problems that INGOs faced in constructing houses themselves. Many donors had concerns about allowing the government to choose beneficiaries. To address those concerns and to ensure transparency, it was proposed that donors who opted to convert to the owner-driven program could be given a list of beneficiaries, so that they could verify their needs and make payments directly to those families. However, with the sole exception of the Red Cross (which had complied with the request to cooperate with the government and converted two-thirds of their pledges (US$25 million)), INGOs showed no enthusiasm to transfer funds to the government.[18]

Escalating costs of building materials and skilled construction labour may also have contributed to slow progress in housing. All interviewed key informants reported that the cost of building materials and the wages of carpenters and masons had increased since the tsunami, with more than three-quarters stating that construction costs had increased by 'a lot'.

Livelihoods

An estimated 150000 people lost their main source of income because of the tsunami.[19] About 50 per cent of these were in the fisheries sector, with others distributed among agriculture (4–5 per cent), tourism, and small and micro enterprise-related sectors (GOSL 2005a). In all surveyed districts, people received some livelihood support. Types of livelihood assistance included grants in kind (income-generating assets such as fishing boats and equipment), cash grants, loans, training (vocational, business support, and the like), cash-for-work, and temporary employment.

According to official sources, around 75 per cent of the affected families had regained their main source of income by end-2005 (GOSL 2005a). This was supported by the survey results where 71 per cent of interviewed households claimed they had regained their previous source of livelihood. Only 8 per cent of heads of households had changed their livelihood,[20] while 21 per cent were still unemployed.[21] Thus, within a year of the tsunami, most people were back in their previous occupations. However, this did not mean that people regained their previous level of income. According to household-level survey data, on average close to 60 per cent of households considered their real family income – in terms of their ability to cover basic needs such as food and health – to be lower than their pre-tsunami income.

There were regional variations in income recovery patterns. Compared to the Southern Province, a higher proportion of Eastern Province households felt that they were worse off.[22] According to the survey data – in both the Southern and Eastern Provinces – poor distribution of livelihood-related assets, the buffer zone rule, and damages to work places have affected livelihood recovery. In addition to these, inability to participate in employment training (due to security reasons) has slowed down livelihood recovery in the Eastern Province.

The damage to tourism infrastructure was quite significant and affected tourism-related livelihoods. A total of 53 (out of 242) large hotels and a further 248 small hotels were damaged or destroyed. In terms of hotel rooms, about 3500 out of a total of 13 000 rooms available in medium to large-scale hotels were out of service in February 2005. Approximately 210 small enterprises that relied on the tourism industry were also destroyed along the coastline. They were mostly enterprises engaged in informal sector activities, and 190 of them were not formally registered with the tourist board. Of the 53 large-scale hotels damaged, 41 were back in operation by end-2005.

Despite the gradual restoration of infrastructure damage to tourist facilities, recovery in livelihoods in the sector was slow. Sri Lanka saw the largest ever number of tourist arrivals in 2004 and although recorded 'tourist' arrival numbers did not fall steeply in 2005, many of those counted as tourists were aid workers visiting the country rather than genuine tourists. Tourism earnings, in fact, dropped sharply in 2005. This suggests that many potential tourists were discounting Sri Lanka as a desirable travel destination in the aftermath of the tsunami. Recovery in tourism was further constrained by an escalation in ethnic conflict-related incidents from the end of 2005 that deterred the return of tourists in numbers comparable to pre-tsunami levels. Thus, while damage to infrastructure was relevant, it was the negative psychological impact of the tsunami and the subsequent political conflicts that seem to have played a more significant role in hampering recovery in the tourist sector.

By contrast, the recovery of fisheries-related livelihoods was relatively swift despite the fact that this was the most badly affected sector. Those engaged in fishing or related activities made up over one-third of the

Table 5.11   Fishing boats destroyed and damaged

Boat type	2004 Fleet	Damaged (No.)	Repaired[a] (No.)	Destroyed (No.)	Replaced (No.)
Multi-day	1 581	676	780	187	0
One-day boats	1 493	783	904	276	29
FRP boats[b]	11 559	3 211	4 258	4 480	4 321
Traditional craft	15 934	2 435	3 479	11 158	8 636
Beach seine craft	1 052	161	134	818	204
Total	31 619	7 266	9 555	16 919	13 190

Note: [a] See note 23 for a discussion of why the number of boats repaired is higher than the number damaged. [b] FRP = fiberglass reinforced plastic.

Source: MFAR (2006).

affected households. In total, over 100 000 people in the fisheries sector were displaced, 16 434 houses were damaged and 13 329 destroyed, and nearly 4870 fishers lost their lives with a further 136 reported missing (MFAR 2006). In terms of equipment (Table 5.11), an estimated 75 per cent of the fishing fleet (32 000 boats) had been totally destroyed or severely damaged (around 23 per cent were made unseaworthy and 54 per cent were destroyed), and one million fishing nets were lost. Apart from these, the basic infrastructure of the fishing industry, such as boatyards, cold rooms, ice plants, and fish markets, was damaged. Damage to fishery harbours and other infrastructure facilities, government services facilities, coast conservation structures, and so on, was placed at US$275 million, while repair and replacement costs for the damaged fleet were estimated at US$60 million.

By end-2006, the fisheries harvest had been restored to 70 per cent of the pre-tsunami level with most of the affected fishers returning to their occupation (GOSL 2006) and in the conflict-free areas recovery was complete by 2008. The relatively rapid recovery of the fisheries sector can be attributed primarily to the relatively rapid progress in replacement of the fishing boats and equipment. The fisheries sector received more immediate assistance than other affected sectors and was able to replace most of its productive assets fairly quickly. A large proportion of destroyed boats had been replaced, and all damaged boats were repaired by end-2005.[23]

However, there were complaints about the poor quality of repairs. According to results of a survey carried out in December 2005, 8 per cent of the repaired boats were not being used due to dissatisfaction with the repairs.[24] Inadequate technical inputs and/or supervision, lack of boat-building knowledge and expertise on the part of NGOs (as well as the fishers), and the absence of proper contracts for after-sales services were blamed for poor-quality repairs, with boat-builders using low-quality material, reducing the thickness, and the like, to meet deadlines and profit from the opportunity.

By end-2005, 78 per cent of the destroyed fishing fleet had been replaced (this figure had risen to 95 per cent by mid-2006)[25] with pledges for more than 6000 boats still outstanding. But 19 per cent of the new boats provided were found to be not seaworthy. Lack of coordination in distribution efforts also led to conflicts and problems over the increasing numbers of boats, the quality of boats, and so on. For many NGOs, the provision of small fishing boats was seen as an 'attractive' tsunami aid program that had high visibility but was easy to implement and not too expensive.

The result of this focus on providing small fishing boats, however, was an oversupply of boats in some places. Such oversupply had unhealthy longer term implications for the fisheries sector raising the prospect of over-fishing. The oversupply was due to several factors. There was no reliable data on the fishing fleet prior to the tsunami, and the damage assessments done by a large number of agencies had their weaknesses. Sometimes, people who were not familiar with the community of fishers were responsible for gathering data on previous boat ownership; this permitted many non-fishers to acquire boats. Misidentifications and overlaps occurred as a result of delays in issuing Entitlement Cards by MFAR. Also, the same beneficiary list was sometimes provided to more than one NGO to speed up the recovery process. There was a lack of coordination between the fisheries authorities and the NGOs, poor coordination between NGOs themselves, and competition amongst these agencies which led to errors and miscalculations (MFAR 2006). Anecdotal evidence from district-level authorities indicated that reluctance to share information on the part of some NGOs made the task of coordinating even more difficult.

Many genuine beneficiaries did not receive new boats because allocations were not properly targeted. Based on extrapolations from the findings of a survey done by the authorities in December 2005, only 6067 of the 13 190 (46 per cent) boats distributed went to 'genuine' beneficiaries. Some small, local agencies had provided boats to 'friends and relatives' and had bypassed the fishing authorities.[26]

Access to credit is a vital element for livelihood recovery after a disaster. Most of the tsunami-affected businesses were informal, small-scale industries – an estimated 25 000 micro-enterprises were damaged in the disaster. In addition, 15 000 tsunami survivors were previously involved in self-employed and informal sector activities such as food processing, coir manufacture, carpentry, and tailoring. While over forty organizations were involved in a host of microfinance programs established to assist small- and medium-sized enterprises (SMEs), the primary sources of credit were two major government finance schemes.

Prior to the tsunami, the Central Bank of Sri Lanka had been implementing a microfinance scheme (*Susahana*) through the two state-owned commercial banks. The *Susahana* loan had been provided with no repayment required for the first year and interest at a fixed rate of 6 per cent thereafter. The National Development Trust Fund (NDTF) also offered similar terms through its partner organizations. Following the tsunami, lending escalated, and by June 2006 25 735 loans and grants of SLRs4769 million (US$47 million) had been provided to micro-, small-, and medium-sized enterprises (RADA 2006). The majority of these loans were disbursed in the south and west of the country. The *Susahana* scheme had reportedly disbursed US$36 million to 8000 borrowers in the tsunami-affected areas by September 2005. Of these loans, 75 per cent were in the south and west of the country. Sixty per cent of the NDTF scheme was also disbursed in the south, with only 40 per cent going to the north and east of the country (GOSL 2005a).

Unfortunately, the procedures and processes associated with loan approval and disbursement seemed weighted against those worst affected by the tsunami, with the emphasis placed on ensuring high probability of repayment or loan recovery rather than on meeting the credit needs of those most in need. Despite claims to the contrary, and its stated intention to reach the micro-entrepreneurs, the *Susahana* lending scheme had been set up in a way that made it very difficult for small tsunami-affected micro-entrepreneurs to obtain access to the loans. The conditions for access were quite onerous. Guarantors with a permanent income above a certain threshold level were required before a loan was approved. Collateral was required, for which land within the buffer zone was not acceptable. Loans were only to be given to businesses registered before the tsunami, which ruled out many smaller, unregistered businesses. These conditions ruled out, in most cases, people hoping to take up new livelihoods in response to their changed post-tsunami circumstances, from causes such as, for example, the death of the main earner, disability, or new responsibilities for the care of family members.

In fact, it was acknowledged that the many affected businesses in the buffer zone were especially hard hit because they were unable to access bank credit, and that banks were reluctant to relax their collateral requirements (GOSL 2005a). It was also found that very few new clients were reached by the subsidized schemes and a considerable number of small entrepreneurs were left with no access to credit. The survey results confirmed these findings: only a few households (16 per cent of the sample) even applied for credit. Many households did not apply for loans because they were not aware that they were eligible to receive them, or because they felt that their applications would be rejected. Most of those who applied did receive a loan, but they had to provide collateral and sometimes a guarantor in order to obtain it. The average size of the loan was fairly small at less than SLRs100 000 (US$1000).

On a positive note, there is evidence to suggest that microcredit providers improved cooperation and coordination in an attempt to try to maintain the microcredit culture that the post-tsunami supply of microcredit funds at low interest rates was in danger of undermining.

In the immediate aftermath of the tsunami, a cash grant livelihood assistance program was announced in January 2005, offering a monthly cash grant of SLRs5000 (US$50) to each tsunami-affected household for a period of four months. Over 250 000 households received the first two instalments on time immediately following the introduction of the program.[27] However, concerns were soon expressed in some quarters about the need for proper targeting. The Ministry of Finance Directives then directed local government officials to revise the lists of eligible beneficiaries according to a set of eligibility criteria.

There were complaints from both affected families and even some government officials that the criteria were not very clear, or were not in the public domain. This created much confusion and payments halted at a time of acute need. The government circulars announcing the revised criteria were quite broad. This meant that local government officers had considerable room to exercise discretion, resulting in wide variations in interpretation, allegations of corruption, and delays and long backlogs of appeals. Interviews with relevant stakeholders, including both affected families and government officials, suggested that households having access to 'regular income' were no longer eligible. It took several months to draw up new lists of those eligible to receive the grant, with the number of recipients eligible for the third payment declining by 25 per cent to 165 000 while the fourth monthly payment was still 'on-going' a year after the tsunami (GOSL 2005a).

In assessing the value and benefits of changes to this program, it should be noted that even households with a 'regular' post-tsunami income had suffered a major loss of wealth in terms of property and possessions, and were cash poor. There was a high probability that they would have to borrow from high interest, informal sector lenders to meet many pressing needs. The decision to take recipients with a regular income off the list after only two monthly payments generated perverse incentives, effectively penalizing not only those who had held on to previous jobs, but perhaps, even more importantly, those who had managed to obtain regular employment after the tsunami. If donor assistance was available for this program – and it is hard to see why funds were not available if the May 2005 pledges were honoured – these cutbacks seem hard to justify. Moreover, since bank accounts had to be opened for the cash grant transfer, the system was extremely cost effective – many other tsunami livelihood projects had far higher transactions costs with as much as 30 per cent spent on administrative overheads.

This experience with trying to shift the livelihoods grants program to a targeting scheme soon after the disaster (only a couple of months after) holds lessons of much wider applicability for post-disaster situations. By all accounts, the initial grants scheme was very effective in reaching most of the affected population. It provided cash at a time of great need, and even helped to link people with little prior engagement to the formal financial sector because they had to set up bank deposit accounts to receive the funds. Unfortunately, the scheme only provided two timely grants before the emphasis shifted to targeting. In theory, it seems obvious that grants should be distributed to those who are 'truly needy', and therefore that grants should be properly targeted. But, in practice, the costs of such narrow targeting must also be taken into account. In the immediate aftermath of a major disaster, particularly in a poor country, the vast majority of affected people are 'truly needy'. Markets are dislocated, assets have been destroyed, and records are destroyed or missing. In such circumstances, the cost of trying to exclude a relatively small proportion of people from the small temporary grants scheme through targeting can far exceed any benefits.

In Sri Lanka's case, grants were delayed for all recipients, including those in dire need; administrative resources were diverted away from the urgent tasks of recovery and reconstruction, which created room for petty officials to engage in corruption and aggravated community divisions and tensions. Expectations of benefits from the rush to implement targeting, only two months after the tsunami, should have been tempered by the experience with targeting achieved in Sri Lanka's long-established national poverty alleviation program (*Samurdhi*): the leakage in the *Samurdhi* program has been estimated to be 40 per cent!

Trauma and Stress

The IPS-TS surveys found some limited evidence of mental and physical health problems related to the tsunami. About 11 per cent of the households knew someone who had committed suicide because of the tsunami.

There were reports of more sleeping difficulties, and children experiencing nightmares that were linked to trauma associated with the tsunami. A large number of households – 33 per cent of households in the sample – had been offered or given counselling for distress. The percentage of people who received counselling was higher in the Eastern Province, possibly because counselling was already taking place in those areas for sufferers of conflict-related mental health problems.

Twelve per cent of households had family members who had been injured in the tsunami or whose health had deteriorated afterwards: a large proportion of such households (77 per cent) claimed that this affected their income-earning capacity and/or day-to-day activities.

In many cases, the decline in school attendance after the tsunami was not fully reversed and attendance was reported to be poor even at the end of 2006, with over 25 per cent of children still not attending school (GOSL 2006). The IPS-TS surveys also found that nearly 30 per cent of households had children who had not restarted schooling nearly two years after the tsunami. The schooling problem existed in areas other than just those affected by conflict, indicating that the problem cannot solely be attributed to the conflict. Thirty-one per cent of the households reported that the performance of children who were attending school had fallen.

Assistance

There was a strong international public response to the appeal for recovery assistance. Multilateral and bilateral donors and NGOs pledged US$3.4 billion for post-tsunami recovery activities at the first Sri Lanka Development Forum held in May 2005 (MFP 2005; GOSL 2006).[28] This comprised (concessional) loans amounting to US$798 million and the balance in grants. NGOs pledged a total of US$853 million on a grant basis. The International Monetary Fund pledged US$268 million by way of both emergency relief and a debt moratorium. Bilateral donors extended the debt moratorium providing further relief of US$263 million.

The government reported that around US$2.2 billion (of the total pledges of US$2.8 billion, which excluded debt relief) could be considered as firm commitments from the international community (GOSL 2005a). In addition, an estimated US$150 million was reportedly received as contributions from domestic sources, without taking into account relief disbursements (for which figures are not available).

However, actual committed funds made available to the government appear to have fallen over time to US$2 billion from the previous 'firmly committed' of US$2.2 billion (Table 5.12). At the end of the second year of reconstruction, total foreign grant expenditure relative to commitments

Table 5.12 Sources of foreign assistance and expenditures (US$ million)

	Pledges	Commitments	Expenditure
International NGOs	378	272	171
International organizations	444	319	76
United Nations	240	109	65
National NGOs	31	22	9
Private sector	16	16	7
Bilaterals	492	912	261
Multilaterals/IFIs[a]	339	396	125
Total foreign grants	1940	2046	714
Total foreign loans	1458	940	377
Government funding[b]	1462	944	381
Total foreign grants and government funding	3402	2990	1095

Notes: [a] IFI=international financial institution. [b] Funding by the Sri Lankan government to finance reconstruction.

Source: GOSL (2006).

was only 35 per cent and foreign loan expenditure was 40 per cent. While individual agencies varied in performance, the bilateral and multilateral agencies had spent, on average, 29 per cent and 32 per cent, respectively, of committed funds by end-2006. In addition, although the initial needs assessment was placed at US$2.2 billion and a total of US$2.9 billion was secured as committed funds, the funding gap for the reconstruction process as at end-2006 was estimated at US$247 million (Table 5.13).

This low rate of expenditure (absorption of available assistance) is not surprising and highlights the constraints that hinder rapid reconstruction. Sri Lanka's past performance in aid absorption has been poor: the rate of aid utilization in recent years has been only around 20–22 per cent, having improved from around 13–15 per cent towards the end of the 1990s. Many reasons have been cited for such low levels of aid utilization, including political interference with regard to planning, implementation and allocation of funds; staffing and related problems in project management; implementation delays (including infrastructure bottlenecks, complex and costly procurement procedures), and excessive conditionality imposed by donors. Another important factor was the non-availability of adequate counterpart funds (local funds with appropriation).

Despite the initial euphoria in the aftermath of the tsunami about the volume and adequacy of foreign assistance, it became clear over time that

Table 5.13   Sector allocation overview (US$ million)

	Funding gap	Commitments	Expenditure
Housing	107	486	162
Livelihood	20	416	186
Social service	85	393	137
Infrastructure	35	861	134
Other		833	476
Total	247	2990	1095

Source: GOSL (2006).

a substantial proportion of reconstruction would have to be domestically financed. In 2006, the government had committed US$1.5 billion in domestic funds (over one-third of total reconstruction costs as initially estimated) for tsunami reconstruction. Here it should be noted that this gap emerged even though the reconstruction program in parts of the East and the North – areas where damage was severe – were effectively stalled. Thus, at the end of two years, two problems with the funding of the reconstruction effort could be identified: the inability of the country to utilize available foreign assistance in a timely manner, and a widening gap between the actual amount of foreign assistance received and reconstruction requirements. While some donor agencies, such as the World Bank, expressed relative satisfaction with their expenditure levels over the next two years, these issues remained important, though pushed into the background by political developments related to the escalating conflict in 2008.

Delivery and Coordination of Assistance

Coordination of the relief and reconstruction effort emerged as a key issue from the beginning of the relief effort, and it continued to be a major issue as the reconstruction and recovery phase started. In Sri Lanka, coordination was required across three groups: (a) among the various government agencies, (b) between the numerous donor agencies, and (c) with the LTTE which was in *de facto* control of a part of the country that was heavily affected by the tsunami. Sri Lanka's governance structure is such that provincial government agencies have considerable powers, and this meant that coordination was required not only between the various central government agencies, but also between the central government and local government agencies. The involvement of major bilateral and multilateral donor agencies naturally required that their activities be coordinated, both among themselves and with the government. Sri Lanka has long experience working with major donor agencies and several INGOs maintain long established operations in the country. There had been some welcome moves towards donor coordination even prior to the tsunami in the context of conflict-related donor reconstruction programs. Thus, the World Bank, ADB, and JBIC had already established a partnership that enabled a needs assessment to be done immediately after the tsunami. However, coordination with donor agencies and NGOs became a vastly more complicated issue due to the numbers and practices of the numerous international NGOs (not counting large numbers of individuals and small groups) who came in after the tsunami. Before long, some 180 NGOs were operating in the tsunami-affected regions of Sri Lanka, making coordination a difficult and complex task. In addition, establishing effective coordination with the LTTE raised difficult and sensitive political and constitutional issues.

As mentioned previously, the government initially set up a Centre for National Operations (CNO) and three task forces to address the coordination challenge. Subsequently, the Task Force for Rebuilding the Nation (TAFREN) became the lead agency charged with the task of overseeing the recovery and reconstruction phase.[29] While an overarching authority such as TAFREN was clearly necessary to coordinate post-disaster reconstruction, the structure and composition of TAFREN was such that it was not able to be fully effective in that role. TAFREN was dominated by private sector representatives, and lacked links to line ministries and clear lines of authority. This greatly hampered its ability to efficiently coordinate activities among government agencies. Reconstruction activities had been divided into sectors, such as housing and water and sanitation. This meant that coordination across several agencies, often falling under different ministries, was needed to implement even relatively minor reconstruction activities. For example, three different agencies had to be brought together to ensure that new housing units could get access to water, sanitation, and electricity supplies. Though TAFREN attempted to monitor the line agencies and to play a coordinating role as a 'one-stop-shop', its effectiveness was limited because its role and authority remained unclear.

In November 2005, a decision was taken to amalgamate TAFREN, The Task Force for Relief (TAFOR) and the Task Force for Logistics and Law and Order (TAFLOL) into the Reconstruction and Development Agency (RADA). RADA was given wide powers by an Act of Parliament. It was given authority over organizations working on post-tsunami reconstruction and development, and could monitor and control their activities as well as issue 'licenses' that would provide legal authority for them to carry out specific activities. In theory, this enabled RADA to exercise efficient coordination. However, there were potential drawbacks to the vesting of such wide powers in a single, centralized body. Arguably it could overly limit the powers of all other agencies and actors, ignore inputs and feedback from line ministries and local-level agents, reduce flexibility and scope for local initiatives and actions, and make the reconstruction effort too centrally driven. Field observations confirmed that lack of adequate coordination resulted in considerable mal-distribution of aid. This was clearly visible, for example, in the way that the distribution of new boats had been conducted, and – as described in a report by the Auditor General – in payment of housing assistance.[30] Large payments were made for houses with minor or no damage, NGOs provided houses to families who were not at all affected by the tsunami, and government grants were given to people who had already received houses constructed by NGOs. In practice, RADA's performance in addressing these issues appears to have been reasonably satisfactory – though there were occasional reports of coordination and implementation problems.

The lack of adequate coordination was not only due to weaknesses on the part of the government-established coordinating bodies. A major problem was that some NGOs were simply not willing to be 'coordinated', preferring to act alone pursuing their own agendas. INGOs, as well as some domestic NGOs (particularly those with good foreign links), had access to relatively large amounts of money. With their own funds secure, they saw few incentives to improve coordination. In fact, some were openly hostile to any government action that seemed to place 'controls' on their independence.

Further, the presence of large numbers of donors/NGOs at times led to competitive behaviour. In several places deep mistrust developed between local NGOs (who had often been working in the local area for many years) and some INGOs and other foreign agencies that came to distribute tsunami assistance. Local NGOs claimed to have been 'crowded out' by some of the better financially endowed larger INGOs, who 'poached' staff and resources. INGOs varied widely in experience, skills, and operating styles. Many 'new' INGOs lacked experience and local knowledge, and in their haste to spend funds and disburse goods and equipment often disregarded local circumstances and community needs. Certainly some INGOs and agencies had valuable expertise in large-scale disaster relief (such as provision of transitional shelters and other relief measures), but domestic NGOs (and INGOs that have operated in Sri Lanka for a long period) usually had a much greater appreciation of local conditions and sensitivities. Greater interaction, engagement and coordination between them would have clearly benefited the overall relief and reconstruction effort. New mechanisms were put in place to improve coordination of donor activities at regional and local levels through regular meetings and consultations held by regional administrative officers. However, at the end of 2006 it was still too early to judge their effectiveness.

The problems caused by some INGOS should not, however, be seen as typical of all INGOs. In fact, in many cases INGOs played a very positive role. About 44 per cent of the households surveyed felt that INGOs were more effective in delivering aid, while only 11 per cent felt that the local NGOs were more effective.

Coordination with the LTTE proved to be the most difficult and contentious issue. While discussions to establish a mechanism for aid-sharing began soon after the tsunami, a mutually acceptable arrangement for aid-sharing to enable assistance to flow into the LTTE-controlled areas proved elusive. Sections within the government and within the majority community were opposed to any deal that even appeared to provide *de facto* recognition of the LTTE as the administrative power in regions controlled by it. The LTTE, for its part, was unwilling to accept an arrangement that diluted its administrative and political power in areas under its control. After long, drawn-out negotiations, a Memorandum of Understanding (MoU) setting out an aid-sharing deal between the GOSL and the LTTE, the Post-Tsunami Operation Management Structure (P-TOMS), was signed in June 2005. The P-TOMS agreement envisaged the setting up of a Regional Fund to allow donors to channel tsunami funds directly to the Northern and Eastern Provinces. A multilateral agency (anticipated to be the World Bank) was to be appointed as the custodian.

However, this agreement promptly ran into political opposition. It was challenged in the courts through a fundamental rights petition and the Supreme Court ruled in July 2005 that certain elements were to be put on hold pending clarification,[31] though the overall mechanism was not unconstitutional. The situation was aggravated further by the fact that several major donors who had supported the idea of a joint mechanism for aid distribution between the GOSL and the LTTE declined to channel aid directly to the Regional Fund once the MoU was signed, claiming that the LTTE remains a 'proscribed terrorist organization' in their countries. After the November 2005 election of a new President who publicly opposed the agreement, P-TOMS became totally inoperative. The conflict between the GOSL and the LTTE intensified soon after. The renewed violence disrupted not only the lives of the tsunami-affected people in the area, but also led to a sharp increase in internally displaced persons, placing further pressure on aid agencies. There can be little doubt that these problems led to inequitable distribution of aid, with the most severely affected North and East missing out on their fair share.

While these political factors affected the distribution of aid across regions, there was no strong evidence of widespread corruption in the distribution of aid within the provinces (though some petty corruption appears to have affected the distribution of cash grants once targeting was introduced).[32]

Cost Escalation

As mentioned, at the time of the May 2005 meeting of the Sri Lanka Development Forum, the aid promises of the international community seemed to more than cover all reconstruction financing needs. Unfortunately, there was a fundamental flaw in the estimates: they were based on costs and prices that prevailed immediately after the tsunami disaster, adjusted for some expected national-level inflation. These estimates proved to be gross underestimates; clear evidence soon emerged that construction costs were rising rapidly over time. This was, of course, not surprising. The scale of construction that was envisaged was several times larger than that undertaken in a normal period, and naturally implied sharp increases in demand for construction labour and materials.[33]

Total construction costs for the planned houses for tsunami-affected families had already risen by 30–50 per cent by August 2005, according to data obtained from companies and organizations involved in house building and from field interviews (Table 5.14). By September 2006, costs had exceeded initial estimates by 60–80 per cent or more.

Information from field interviews indicated that these increases are driven primarily by higher wages for skilled labourers (such as carpenters, painters, and masons), whose wages have doubled in some locations. This is confirmed by data from the construction industry body, the Institute for Construction Training and Development (ICTA) (Figure 5.2).[34]

Prices of particular building materials, such as cement, sand and bricks, saw a sharp increase (Figure 5.3). However, it should also be noted that price increases for importable materials were significantly lower than overall construction cost increases (Figure 5.4). These data are consistent with survey information: more than three-quarters of the surveyed key informants said that wages of carpenters and masons and prices of building materials increased 'a lot' after the tsunami. This has some important implications: increased local demand can be met without major price increases when construction materials are importable, but price increases are unavoidable for domestically sourced ('non-tradeable') materials and labour. The faster the reconstruction program, the higher the price and cost escalation will be, with less 'construction' actually occurring for a given amount of expenditure.

Table 5.14 Cost escalation in housing construction

Donor	Unit area (sq ft)	Initial estimate (SLRs)	August 2005		September 2006	
			Estimate (SLRs)	Comments	Estimate (SLRs)	Comments
Red Cross[a]	600	625000 (March)	1000000	Houses with all basic infrastructure facilities (electricity, water supply, sanitation for each house, roads, etc.)	1250000–1300000	Cost per housing unit with a tiled roof, basic infrastructure. Price escalation since last year is about 22% due to increase in prices of factors like fuel and labour.
CARE International	550	450000 (March)	850000 600000 550000–650000	Jaffna Hambantota All other areas (houses with little basic infrastructure)	700000–800000	This is the average. However, the value differs from district to district.
Aitken Spence Co. Ltd	550	450000 (March)	> 500000	With basic infrastructure (with electricity but no water supply)	550000[b] (Sept. 2005)	A basic housing unit

	Sq. ft.					
World Vision Lanka[c]	500	550 000 (March)	700 000	With basic infrastructure	750 000–800 000	With basic infrastructure
CARITAS Sri Lanka	500	500 000 (May)	650 000	A basic house (no mention of infrastructure)	800 000	A basic housing unit only
Sarvodaya Movement[d]	500	500 000 (May)	650 000	With only a few basic infrastructure facilities	600 000	South
					700 000	North and East
						The cost of a basic housing unit only
Forut Institute	550	500 000 (April)	550 000	Only for the house (not with basic infrastructure)	700 000–900 000	North – with basic infrastructure
					800 000	South – with basic infrastructure

Notes: [a] Estimates said to be costlier because of higher specifications (e.g., use only imported timber); [b] September 2005 estimates; [c] Initial estimates based on 500 sq. ft. New estimates based on 515–550 sq. ft; [d] Initial estimates based on 500 sq. ft. New estimates based on 540 sq. ft.

Source: IPS surveys.

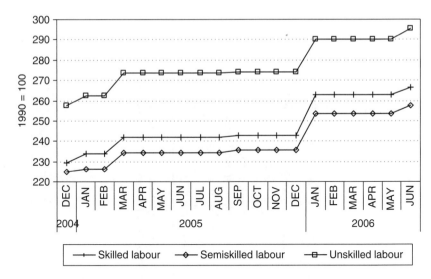

Source: Data from the Institute of Construction, Training and Development, June 2006.

Figure 5.2   *Price indices for labour wages*

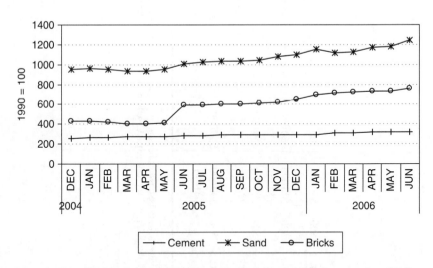

Source: Data from the Institute of Construction, Training and Development, June 2006.

Figure 5.3   *Prices of raw materials for building*

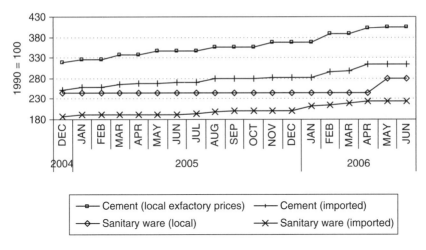

Source: Data from the Institute of Construction, Training and Development, June 2006.

Figure 5.4   *Imported and local prices of building materials*

Broader Economic Impacts

The typical pattern for economies struck by unanticipated natural disasters has been to experience a brief deceleration in growth, followed by a rebound as a result of the stimulus from reconstruction programs. GDP growth dipped in the first quarter of 2005 but subsequently showed a strong resurgence. Predictably, the fisheries and hotels and restaurants sub-sectors experienced a sharp contraction in output while the construction sub-sector experienced strong growth (Table 5.15). The recovery was better than initially anticipated, and was broad-based. There was continued expansion in industry and services, as well as a recovery in agriculture following improved weather conditions, and this good growth performance continued into 2006.

The tsunami reconstruction undoubtedly brightened prospects for Sri Lanka's short-term economic outlook. The total investment/GDP ratio increased by 1.5 percentage points in 2005, much of it driven by government investment. In fact, the investment/GDP ratio improved to 28.7 per cent in 2006. This was reflected in higher imports of investment goods and construction activities.

While the additional tsunami-related expenditure was budgeted to be met by foreign grants, financing needs increased owing to cost escalation and the increase in the numbers of housing units required. Despite added

Table 5.15   GDP growth rates (in per cent)

	2004	2005	2006
Agriculture	−0.3	1.9	4.7
Fishing	1.6	−42.2	51.7
Industry	5.2	8.3	7.2
Construction	6.6	8.9	8.0
Services	7.6	6.2	8.3
Hotels & restaurants	13.1	−27.5	6.3
GDP	5.4	6.0	7.4

Source: Central Bank of Sri Lanka, *Annual Report 2006.*

Table 5.16   Post-tsunami fiscal outlook

(As % of GDP)	2004	2005	2006
Revenue	15	16	17
Expenditure	23	25	25
Current	19	19	19
Capital	4	6	6
Fiscal deficit	−8	−9	−8
Financing			
Foreign loans	2	2	2
Foreign grants	...	1	1
Domestic	6	5	6

Source: Central Bank of Sri Lanka, *Annual Report 2006.*

fiscal pressures, there was little effort to curtail spending in other areas, fuelling inflationary pressures from policies unrelated to tsunami reconstruction (Table 5.16).[35] Fiscal profligacy in the face of higher spending on tsunami-related rehabilitation aggravated inflationary pressures in the economy. The initial response to rising inflationary pressure was slow, and interest rates remained unchanged allowing credit growth to expand at a rate of over 20 per cent. Broad money growth in 2006 was 17.8 per cent, and inflation rose from 11.6 per cent in 2005 to 13.7 per cent in 2006.

The Sri Lankan electorate has traditionally been very sensitive to inflation. Elections were scheduled for late 2005 and the government was keen to keep inflation in check. This generated political pressures to resist any exchange rate depreciation which could have intensified domestic inflation. There is some evidence to suggest that the tsunami-related capital inflows were used to prop up the nominal exchange rate in 2005, and this

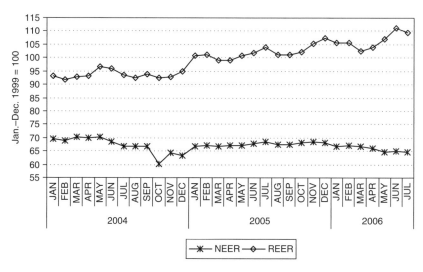

Notes: The nominal effective exchange rate (NEER) and real effective exchange rate (REER) are based on trade composition with 24 trading partners.

Source: Central Bank of Sri Lanka (www.centralbanklanka.org).

Figure 5.5   Nominal and real effective exchange rate

may have been a factor in the slow absorption of aid flows. There was also a significant increase in inward remittances from 6.7 per cent of GDP in 2004 to 7.7 per cent by 2006. While some of the increase may reflect assistance provided to affected family and friends, the increase could also reflect better earnings performance of the majority of migrants employed in the oil rich Middle Eastern countries. Sri Lanka managed to record an overall surplus of US$500 million on the BOP in 2005 (compared with a deficit of US$205 million in 2004) and official reserves showed a sharp improvement.

The influx of increased foreign capital reversed the sharp depreciation of the rupee vis-à-vis the US dollar at end-2004, leading to a nominal appreciation of over 5.5 per cent in the week following the disaster (Figure 5.5).[36] The nominal effective exchange rate (NEER) appreciated by 7.7 per cent in 2005 (compared to a depreciation of 11 per cent in 2004). The higher nominal appreciation in the context of relatively high domestic inflation led to a real effective exchange rate (REER) appreciation of 12.7 per cent (as against a depreciation of 1.1 per cent in 2004). To the extent that this real appreciation was a result of tsunami-related aid flows, it would have had the standard Dutch Disease effects on Sri Lanka's exports.

Aid flows following a disaster are, by their nature, temporary. As the tsunami-related capital inflows eased over time, the government was compelled to seek other forms of external funds to finance the expanding fiscal deficit. In December 2005 Sri Lanka sought a sovereign credit rating as the first step to raising an estimated US$0.5–1 billion in the international bond market. Sri Lanka was assigned a BB− (below investment grade) and a B+ by two rating agencies. But, with the escalation in domestic hostilities the credit outlook was downgraded from stable to negative in April 2006. In 2006, for example, the government raised US$580 million by issuing 2–3-year maturity dollar bonds (Sri Lanka Development Bonds) at rates of 120–140 basis points above the London Inter-Bank Offer Rate (LIBOR) despite the inherent risks involved in recourse to foreign commercial borrowings.

Thus, the overall macroeconomic trends raised serious concerns about the sustainability of the country's post-tsunami burst of GDP growth once the temporary aid flows ceased. However, other developments – such as the massive increase in military expenditure and other forms of government expenditure – soon dwarfed the negative impact of reduced tsunami aid flows on economic activity.

Social Cohesion

The spontaneous solidarity that united communities immediately after the tsunami rekindled hopes that the ethnic divisions that had cost the country so dearly in recent years might finally be on the wane. But the post-tsunami relief and reconstruction activities contributed to increased social tensions among various groups in affected communities. Many poor households who were unaffected by the tsunami were unhappy because they were ineligible for tsunami aid. This was particularly important in the conflict-affected Eastern Province where large numbers of people have suffered from the two-decade-long conflict and have been internally displaced for long periods of time. The subsequent escalation in hostilities between the GOSL and the LTTE plunged the country back into large-scale conflict, which finally ended in a military victory for the government but may not have produced greater ethnic harmony. This was in sharp contrast to what happened in Aceh, Indonesia, where the tsunami created conditions for the cessation of a long-running secessionist war and a sharp lowering of community tensions.

There were several reasons why the relief and reconstruction activities aggravated social tensions in Sri Lanka. In some instances the manner in which tsunami-damaged physical assets were replaced exacerbated pre-existing tensions and rivalries. In other places, tensions developed between fishers and other groups because the latter felt that the fishing industry received greater attention. Similar tensions emerged in the housing sector. The substantial quality differences between different types of houses built by different organizations, and the different levels of grants given to different groups created perceptions of inequity.[37]

OVERALL ASSESSMENT AND CONCLUSIONS

For Sri Lanka, facing a totally unanticipated major natural disaster and coping with the subsequent reconstruction and recovery needs was a unique experience. In the circumstances, the initial relief effort can be assessed as quite satisfactory. An unusually large amount of aid, from a very large number of organizations, arrived in a very short time. Also, a large proportion of aid flowed through individual, private, and non-government organization hands instead of through the traditional donor agencies or the United Nations. This facilitated rapid relief and early initiation of reconstruction activities, but also raised issues of coordination and aid absorption, and posed some unique challenges. The problems and issues that emerged included:

- Problems related to the absorptive capacity of government and households;
- Very high transaction costs and major coordination problems caused by a large number of donor organizations;
- Rapid increases in demand for labour and raw materials leading to construction cost escalation;
- Excessive focus on the quantity of aid disbursement that undermined the effectiveness of aid (for example, mal-distribution, poor quality fishing boats, and the like);
- Lack of adequate local capacity to provide the information necessary for effective coordination and monitoring of aid distribution;
- Lack of clear and transparent information-sharing mechanisms between various governmental and non-governmental agents; and
- Differences in levels of assistance provided to tsunami-affected households and conflict-affected households in the North and the East.

It must also be pointed out that many initial fears about a range of likely problems either proved to be not well founded or were resolved effectively. In particular, large-scale corruption did not become a major problem, perhaps because the reconstruction did not involve large-scale infrastructure projects. Cases of petty corruption were recorded, such as officials abusing discretionary powers (for example, determining eligibility for different types of housing aid and cash grants). In several such cases the government took disciplinary action. There were also fears that large-scale imports of food as aid would depress domestic producer prices and hurt farmers. But the government ensured that new food purchases by the World Food Programme were domestically sourced to help farmers recover and maintain rural incomes.

The Sri Lankan experience suggests strongly that the mode of assistance must take into account the stage of the relief effort. In the initial relief stage, what is most important is to ensure delivery of basic food, clothing, medicines, and shelter. At this stage, the provision of aid in kind is probably essential. But even just a short period later, aid in kind may not be the most effective mode of assistance. Except in very remote locations, markets and links with the rest of the economy get re-established very quickly and allow supplies to be brought in from surrounding areas and from existing stocks. Cash grants enable people to access markets and obtain needed supplies more efficiently and effectively. In fact, substantial amounts of aid in kind were often wasted because they did not meet the requirements or the preferences of the affected households. In contrast, cash grants allowed households the flexibility to spend on goods and services they actually desired.

Another issue often raised in disaster relief is whether assistance should be narrowly targeted to the 'most needy' groups only, or provided to all affected people. In Sri Lanka, experience suggests that the costs of narrow targeting may outweigh benefits in the early phase of relief. The beneficiary lists drawn up by government agencies not only delayed distribution of grants, but also became, at times, an inefficient, corruption-prone process. In principle, systems can be created where the most needy 'self select', and these can work fairly effectively in some circumstances. But it is not clear that the savings made justify the costs in delays, the incentives for corruption, and the likelihood that some truly needy groups miss out altogether.

A major challenge in Sri Lanka was to devise appropriate administrative mechanisms to ensure effective coordination between central government and local agencies, and to ensure that central coordination did not end up stifling local initiatives. Decision-making in disaster situations requires a complex balance of roles between the central government and the locally affected areas, and the central government must be responsive to the concerns and feedback from local agents. Sri Lanka initially tended to have an overly centralized system. There were concerns that local governments were not given enough freedom to make decisions and implement them. Also, the central government seemed to have rushed to establish new institutions specifically to deal with tsunami-related aid distribution, ignoring or bypassing existing institutions, resulting in the reduced effectiveness of reconstruction efforts.

The aftermath of the tsunami disaster also raised issues of macroeconomic management of relevance for countries affected by a major disaster. Sri Lanka was faced with the challenge of absorbing a large but necessarily temporary inflow of foreign funds. In itself this is a complex task. But the task was made even more difficult by the need to direct those funds efficiently to emergency relief, and then to rehabilitation and reconstruction of damaged assets and infrastructure.

Sri Lanka's experience highlights the need for factoring in major construction cost increases when assessing needs following major disasters, and the need for the formulation of reconstruction programs which take into account supply side constraints. The initial assumption that foreign financing was adequate for reconstruction was quickly dispelled. The large reconstruction program quickly raised demand for construction inputs that produced sharp increases in construction costs. In turn, this produced funding gaps that had to be filled either by the government – widening the already larger fiscal deficit – or by additional foreign assistance. Arguably, the institutional weaknesses and political factors that slowed absorption of foreign assistance may have helped to restrain such cost increases, thereby allowing a larger share of tsunami expenditures to be effective in asset rehabilitation rather than be captured by construction input owners.

The Sri Lankan reconstruction program took place in a context of sharpening political conflict. This posed problems with aid distribution that aggravated perceptions of regional/ethnic bias in policy and regional disparities. When it comes to an assessment of the overall success of the reconstruction effort in Sri Lanka, these problems resulted in what the World Bank (2008: 16) rather coyly described as 'lingering concerns about the overall tsunami reconstruction effort'. It is to be hoped that with the end of the violent conflict there can be a revival of attention to the reconstruction needs of these areas so that affected groups will be finally able to leave the trauma and suffering inflicted by the tsunami behind them.

NOTES

1. Dushni Weerakoon, Sisira Jayasuriya, Nisha Arunatilake and Paul Steele were primarily responsible for this chapter, which draws on Weerakoon et al. (2007).
2. Sri Lanka had no effective domestic hazard warning system, and had not felt the need to be part of international early warning systems, such as the Tsunami Warning System (TWS) in the Pacific (which has 26 member countries).
3. The significant differences between total recovery needs and damages in some sectors

were due to the fact that the recovery strategy for those sectors focused on long-term development targets rather than merely on restoration.

4. The GOSL identified its needs for a three- to five-year rehabilitation phase.
5. For example, while food rations were generally available, there were problems with the provision of adequate variety and quality in some locations; complaints emerged about the application of different rules in different areas for the distribution of rations and cash grants.
6. An assessment of the initial response to the tsunami at the Sri Lanka Development Forum 2005 can be found at www.erd.gov.lk/DevForum/
7. As of end-2006, 42 096 of the 57 057 shelters originally constructed had been decommissioned with only 14 961 shelters remaining occupied (GOSL 2006).
8. For details on methodology and coverage of the surveys, see Weerakoon et al. (2007).
9. A village level administrative unit.
10. About 53 per cent of the surveyed houses made unusable by the tsunami were less than 450 square feet, while only 10 per cent were bigger than 600 square feet.
11. About 32 per cent of roofs of the surveyed houses were made of cadjan or metal sheets, while close to half of the surveyed houses had walls made of temporary material.
12. About 13 per cent of surveyed households inside the buffer zone owned houses on government land, while a further 9 per cent owned houses built on other people's private land.
13. The new boundaries were set according to the Coast Conservation Department (CCD) Coastal Management Plan of 1997.
14. Zone 1 referred to any state reservation within tsunami-affected areas while Zone 2 is any area outside Zone 1.
15. Extended since then to co-financing arrangements through local and foreign NGOs as well.
16. *Sunday Times*, 14 May 2006. About 3 per cent of the households surveyed in the IPS-TS 2006 had shifted from one NGO-allocated list to another. The most common reasons for switching were: expectation of better assistance, to move closer to the sea, or because the first NGO had failed to deliver a house.
17. *Daily Mirror*, 28 January 2006.
18. *Sunday Observer*, 27 August 2006.
19. RADA estimates those who lost livelihoods at 200 000 with a further 125 000 jobs being lost indirectly (see www.rada.gov.lk).
20. About a half of the household heads that had changed their livelihoods came from one GND, in the Eastern Province.
21. Further, the current housing situation does not appear to have any effect on livelihood recovery.
22. Key informants in almost all surveyed districts in the Southern Province, and in around half of the surveyed districts in the Eastern Province, thought people were better off because of aid, training, and more employment opportunities. There were also considerable differences between clusters of villages.
23. There is some debate about the exact numbers of boats damaged and repaired. For most boat types, the number of crafts repaired exceeded the numbers reported as damaged. It has been suggested that boat owners in non-tsunami-affected areas may have transferred their boats to these areas to take advantage of the opportunity to get minor repairs done, that there may have been miscategorization of beach seine crafts as traditional crafts, and that boats classified as destroyed may have been repaired and put back to sea.
24. Cited in MFAR (2006).
25. RADA (2006).
26. The efficiency implications of the misallocation of these fishery assets may be corrected over time because those who were mistakenly given boats or the like may have been able to subsequently sell them to genuine fishers who could make use of them. But this

would not be much consolation for people who had lost assets and lacked the necessary finances to buy them, even at discount prices.

27. This had some other cash grant components too, including a grant for a family death. According to the IPS-TS 2005 data (collected in April/May 2005), all surveyed districts had received funds of SLRs15 000 for deaths, SLRs2500 for kitchen equipment, and a SLRs5000 livelihood grant and food/cash coupon.

28. The US$3.4 billion included debt relief/moratorium and IMF support.

29. After one month, with the conclusion of immediate relief operations TAFRER and TAFLOL were amalgamated to a single entity – the Task Force for Relief (TAFOR) – to implement all relief measures, and the operations of the CNO were scaled down. In February, the CNO was dissolved and officials returned to line ministries. TAFOR and TAFREN took over the responsibilities of the CNO. With the completion of transitional housing, TAFOR was expected to wind down operations and pass its responsibilities to the line ministries.

30. This report on the tsunami rehabilitation covers the period 26 December 2004 to 30 June 2005. See GOSL (2005b).

31. Specifically, these elements were the Regional Fund and the location of the regional committee in the rebel-held Kilinochchi city.

32. According to the household survey respondents, very few households had paid bribes to government or NGO officials to receive aid, and very few were aware of instances where politicians had interfered directly.

33. There were varying estimates of the extra demand for house construction, but they all pointed to a massive increase in demand for scarce construction labour and materials. According to the Chamber of Construction Industry, as reported in the *Daily Mirror*, 21 February 2005, it was estimated that at least 100 000 additional workers would be required, including about 13 000 masons, 2000 carpenters, 2500 painters, and nearly 54 000 unskilled labourers.

34. Organizations involved in tsunami housing construction were required to use ICTA registered contractors.

35. For example, adding workers to the government pay-roll saw payments on salaries and wages rising from 5.2 per cent of GDP in 2004 to 5.9 per cent of GDP in 2005; transfers and subsidies over time increased from 4 per cent of GDP in 2003 to 5.4 per cent of GDP in 2005.

36. The currency depreciated to SLRs105.47 per US dollar on 17 December 2004 – the highest rate in the interbank market. It had appreciated to SLRs98.11 by 12 January 2005. The appreciation of the rupee for the rest of the year was also partly influenced by the movement of major currencies as the US dollar appreciated against them.

37. The government was forced to lay down specific standards for new houses because of large differences in size, quality, and so on, among donor-built houses.

REFERENCES

Asian Development Bank (ADB), Japan Bank for International Cooperation (JBIC) and World Bank (WB) (2005), *Sri Lanka 2005 Post-Tsunami Recovery Program: Preliminary Damage and Needs Assessment*, Colombo, Sri Lanka, 10–28 January 2005.

GOSL (Government of Sri Lanka) (2005a), *Sri Lanka: Post Tsunami Recovery and Reconstruction*, Joint Report of the Government of Sri Lanka and Development Partners, December 2005.

GOSL (2005b), *Interim Report of the Auditor General on the Rehabilitation of the Losses and Damages Caused to Sri Lanka by the Tsunami*, September 2005.

GOSL (2005c), *Post Tsunami Recovery and Reconstruction Strategy*, May 2005.

GOSL (2005d), *Rebuilding Sri Lanka: Action Plan*, February 2005.

GOSL (2006), *Post Tsunami Recovery and Reconstruction*, Joint Report of the Government of Sri Lanka and Development Partners, December 2006.

IPS (Institute of Policy Studies) (2005), 'Survey and analysis of rebuilding and relocation of tsunami affected households in Sri Lanka', mimeo, June 2005.

Jayasuriya, Sisira, P. Steele and D. Weerakoon (2006), *Post-Tsunami Recovery: Issues and Challenges in Sri Lanka*, Research Paper no. 71, ADB Institute, Japan.

MFAR (Ministry of Fisheries and Aquatic Resources) (2006), *Recovery Assessment in the Fisheries Sector*, Draft Report, June 2006.

MFP (Ministry of Finance and Planning) (2005), *Annual Report 2005*, December 2005.

MFP (2006), *Mid Year Fiscal Position Report*, June 2006.

RADA (Reconstruction and Development Agency) (2006), *Post Tsunami Recovery and Reconstruction: Mid Year Review*, June 2006.

Weerakoon, Dushni, S. Jayasuriya, N. Arunatilake and P. Steele (2007), *Economic Challenges of Post-Tsunami Reconstruction in Sri Lanka*, Tokyo: Asian Development Bank Institute, http://www.adbi.org/discussion-paper/2007/08/31/2354.sri.lanka.post.tsunami.reconstruction/, accessed 31 October 2009.

World Bank (2008), *Country Assistance Strategy for the Democratic Socialist Republic of Sri Lanka for the Period FY 2009–2012*, Report no: 43471-LK, Washington, DC: World Bank.

APPENDIX 5A.1 SUMMARY OF METHODOLOGY FOR IPS TSUNAMI SURVEY 2005 AND 2006

Eight districts that were most severely affected by the tsunami in the Northern, Eastern, and Southern provinces were selected for the survey. These consisted of the Trincomalee, Batticaloa and Ampara districts from the Eastern Province, the Jaffna and Mullaitivu districts from the Northern Province, and the Hambantota, Matara and Galle districts from the Southern Province.

In these eight districts, Grama Niladhari Divisions (GNDs) were first identified using Department of Census and Statistics (DCS) data as those where more than 50 per cent of houses were made unusable due to being completely or severely damaged.

The 16 GNDs for the study were distributed across the eight districts based on the level of housing damage in each district (Table 5A.1). Within the districts, GNDs were chosen based on socio-economic data so as to select a representative set of GNDs considering ethnicity, religion, livelihoods, and the location with respect to the 2005 buffer zone (the 'no-build' zone). Socio-economic data for this purpose were obtained from the 2001 Census by the DCS for the Southern districts. Since census data did not extend to the districts in the Eastern and the Northern provinces, socio-economic information for these provinces was obtained through key informants from those areas. Key informant information was also used to select GNDs with households both within and outside the 2005 buffer zone. (Information given by key informants in this regard was not entirely

Table 5A.1   Distribution of GNDs[a] across selected districts

District	Number of unusable houses	No of GNDs selected for survey
Jaffna	3 686	1
Mullaitivu	5 137	1
Trincomalee	4 643	2
Batticaloa	9 905	4
Ampara	10 566	4
Hambantota	1 290	1
Matara	2 401	1
Galle	6 169	2

Note: Information from Mullaitivu was not available for the selection process. [a] Grama Niladhari Divisions.

accurate, and, as a result, some GNDs that were mostly within the no-build zone remained in the sample.)

A sample of 45 households from the list of unusable houses for each GND was randomly selected for the household survey, with 30 households outside the no-build zone and 15 within. However, in some GNDs there were less than 30 houses outside the buffer zone. In these instances, more households from within the buffer zone were interviewed to make up the sample. The households were selected using DCS tsunami census data where available. For the two GNDs where DCS data were not available, household lists obtained from Grama Niladharis (GNs) were used as a frame.

Due to delays in obtaining access, the survey could not cover the Jaffna and Mullaitivu districts of the Northern Province. Therefore, information is only available for 14 GNDs in the Southern and Eastern provinces. Information from the selected GNDs was collected at several levels in April 2005. To obtain community-level perspectives on rebuilding, relocation, and land issues, focus groups were conducted in all GNDs. In addition, community-level information to ascertain community characteristics and information on rebuilding, relocation, and land issues was obtained through key informant interviews based on a structured questionnaire. In addition to these interviews, information on land supply in the GNDs was obtained from the relevant Divisional Secretary's Office, also based on a structured questionnaire. The household-level interviews were conducted using a structured household questionnaire. The questionnaires were drafted in English and translated to Sinhala and Tamil for use in different GNDs.

In July 2006, an attempt was made to resurvey all the 622 households that were interviewed for the April 2005 survey with the view of gaining updated information on the progress of the reconstruction effort. The survey was designed to address issues of permanent housing paucity, recovery in livelihoods, and so on, to get a clearer picture of where Sri Lanka stood in the reconstruction process one and a half years after the tsunami disaster. In addition to the housing survey, three key informant interviews in each GND were conducted. When a household could not be located, randomly selected replacement houses were surveyed from the GND. The resulting database consisted of 595 households, of which 564 were from the original 622 households.

6.   Thailand[1]

INTRODUCTION

The tsunami that hit six southern provinces of Thailand on 26 December 2004 is the worst natural disaster Thailand has ever experienced in terms of human tragedy, bringing incalculable misery to affected communities and massive damages to their livelihoods. It killed over 8000 people and injured thousands more; it damaged or destroyed thousands of houses, other buildings, roads, bridges, and other physical infrastructure. Because the tsunami hit some of Thailand's most popular beach tourist resorts, a large number of foreign tourists were among the dead and injured.

Total damages were assessed at around US$508 million, while losses were estimated at US$1.69 billion, totalling US$2.2 billion (1.4 per cent of GDP).[2] The impact on the affected provinces was quite severe: it was assessed to be equivalent to one half of the combined gross provincial product (GPP). In some cases, such as that of Phuket, damage and losses equalled 90 per cent of GPP, and in Krabi and Phang Nga, they were around 70 per cent.[3]

Though the impact of the tsunami was quite severe, after accepting technical assistance at the early stages, Thailand relied mostly on its own resources in coping with the reconstruction tasks, unlike Indonesia and Sri Lanka. Thailand's experience with the wider economic effects of large-scale reconstruction activities also seems to have differed from that of other affected countries in some respects. Overall Thailand appears to have been more successful than Indonesia and Sri Lanka in overcoming the economic effects of the tsunami. This provides an interesting contrast to the experience of Indonesia and Sri Lanka, which relied heavily on international assistance in their reconstruction efforts.

This chapter provides a descriptive and analytical narrative of the post-tsunami relief efforts and reconstruction activities in Thailand in the first two years after the disaster to the end of 2006. This approach facilitates comparative analysis of the experiences of the three countries. The chapter is organized as follows: the first section after this introduction describes briefly the damage and costs of the tsunami, and is followed by an examination of the immediate response after the disaster. The third section discusses short-term economic effects of the tsunami, and the fourth discusses the experience of rehabilitation, reconstruction and recovery. In the fifth section the issues related to adequacy, efficiency, and effectiveness of aid and assistance are considered. The above discussions are based largely on secondary data. As part of this study, fieldwork was carried out in the tsunami-affected areas and primary data was collected from a sample survey of displaced and non-displaced individuals, visitors, and seven NGOs in the three most severely affected provinces. This information is presented in the sixth section. In the final section the main findings of the study and some policy implications are summarized.

DAMAGE AND COSTS

In the cases of Indonesia and Sri Lanka, the largest economic losses from the tsunami were caused by damage to physical infrastructure and property. In contrast, Thailand's biggest source of losses occurred in the productive sectors, particularly tourism, because the most severely affected areas were key tourism destinations. As a result, initial estimates of analysts led to forecasts of significant reductions in the GDP growth rate. JP Morgan, for example, revised the first quarter growth rate of 2005 to zero from the previous projection of 3 per cent. The 2005 annual GDP growth rate was also revised downward by 0.3 per cent to 5.7 per cent. Similarly, Morgan Stanley reduced its annual growth projection from 6 per cent to 5.7 per cent, citing, in particular, the dampening multiplier effects on the economy of the damage caused by the tsunami on the tourism industry.

Of the six Thai provinces hit by the tsunami (Table 6.1), Phang Nga, Phuket, and Krabi were the most severely affected. Phang Nga – in particular the Kao Lak and Ban Nam Kem areas – suffered the most in terms of human and economic losses (79 per cent of the total 5395 casualties) (Table 6.1). Krabi sustained the second heaviest loss of life (13 per cent) but damage to infrastructure and the business sector were higher in Phuket, which suffered the most serious damage to infrastructure of around US$100 million. Ranong, Trang, and Satul, which are not tourist destinations like the other three provinces, suffered mainly from damages to aqua culture and destruction of fishing boats and equipment.

The initial relief efforts in Thailand were complicated by the need to deal with a large number of dead, injured, and missing foreigners. In most locations, casualties amongst Thai nationals were higher than those among foreigners. However in Phang Nga, a major centre of tourism and with the tourist season at its peak, foreign casualties exceeded Thai casualties (Figure 6.1). In addition, foreign casualties in Phang Nga also included

Table 6.1 Numbers of dead, injured, and missing due to the December 2004 tsunami

Province	Dead				Injured			Missing		
	Thai	Foreigners	Unidentified	Total	Thai	Foreigners	Total	Thai	Foreigners	Total
Phuket	151	111	17	279	591	520	1111	245	363	608
Phang Nga	1389	2114	722	4225	4344	1253	5597	1352	303	1655
Krabi	357	203	161	721	808	568	1376	314	230	544
Ranong	153	6	–	159	215	31	246	9	–	9
Trang	3	2	–	5	92	20	112	1	–	1
Satul	6	–	–	6	15	–	15	–	–	–
Total	2059	2436	900	5395	6065	2392	8457	1921	896	2817

Source: Department of Disaster Prevention and Mitigation (DDPM), Ministry of the Interior.

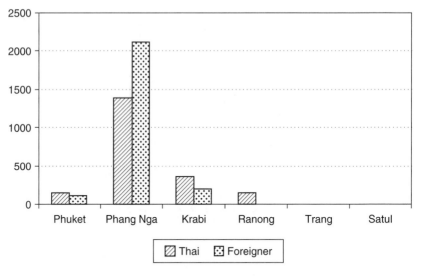

Source: Department of Disaster Prevention and Mitigation (DDPM).

Figure 6.1   Thai and foreign death toll

a large number of migrant workers from Myanmar. The 2817 missing persons, most likely dead, suggests that large numbers were dragged into the sea by the giant waves.

The impact of the tsunami was spread over a large number of villages in these provinces. This made the provision of immediate relief difficult. Krabi had the highest number of affected villages but not the largest number of casualties (Table 6.2).

In total, the tsunami directly affected 12 815 households comprising more than 58 550 people. A total of 3302 houses were destroyed and 1504 were damaged (Table 6.2). Phang Nga accounted for 52 per cent of total house destruction, followed by Phuket with 21 per cent, and Krabi with 14 per cent.

Damages to business properties accounted for most of the damage in Phang Nga, Phuket, and Krabi while damages to the fisheries sector were the most important in the other three provinces (Table 6.3). These differences in the nature of damages between the two groups of provinces meant that they required quite different rehabilitation and reconstruction activities: Phang Nga, Phuket, and Krabi needed urgent measures to restore tourism and business properties, while Trang, Ranong, and Satul required assistance to restore the fisheries industry.

Most of the losses inflicted on people's livelihoods (88 per cent) came

Table 6.2   Impact on housing

Province	Number of people affected		Residences affected (number of houses)			Affected villages (number)
	persons	households	destroyed	damaged	total	
Phang Nga	19 509	4 394	1 904	604	2 508	69
Krabi	15 812	2 759	396	262	658	112
Phuket	13 065	2 616	742	291	1 033	58
Ranong	5 942	1 509	224	111	335	47
Trang	1 302	1 123	34	156	190	51
Satul	2 920	414	2	80	82	70
Total	58 550	12 815	3 302	1 504	4 806	407

Source: DDPM.

Table 6.3   Damage to livelihoods (US$ mn)

	Fishery	Livestock	Agriculture	Business property	Total damage
Phang Nga	22.8	0.3	. . .	161.4	184.6
Krabi	4.8	. . .	. . .	67.1	71.9
Phuket	8.6	. . .	. . .	87.8	96.4
Ranong	4.3	. . .	. . .	. . .	4.4
Trang	1.7	. . .	. . .	0.2	1.9
Satul	3.0	. . .	. . .	–	3.0
Total	45.2	0.4	0.2	316.4	362.2
Per cent	12	. . .	. . .	87	100

Source: DDPM.

from the damage to business properties in Phang Nga, Phuket, and Krabi. Most of these properties were hotels, critical to the tourism industry. Fisheries was the second most affected sector (12 per cent) while damage to livestock and agriculture was negligible. In Phang Nga, though most of the damage was to business properties, the fisheries sector was also significantly affected (Table 6.4). Many fishing boats were lost or damaged, and there were extensive damages to fish cages and shrimp hatcheries (which in turn affected the wider southern shrimp industry, which relied on supplies of post-larvae from these hatcheries).

The total damage to roads and bridges was relatively minor (estimated

Table 6.4   Tsunami damage to fisheries

Province	Fish cage culture	Shrimp hatchery	Damage
	Area affected ('000 m²)	Area affected ('000 m²)	(US$ mn)
Phang Nga	141	16	22.9
Krabi	66	0	4.8
Phuket	53	76	8.6
Ranong	856	0	4.3
Trang	24	0	0.4
Satul	85	0	3.0
Total	1 224	92	43.9

Source: DDPM and Department of Fisheries.

at less than US$2 million). This also meant that emergency relief and assistance could be delivered relatively quickly immediately after the tsunami. The more costly damage to infrastructure came from the numerous damaged piers, which delayed fishermen from returning to their normal livelihoods (Table 6.5). Twelve schools were either destroyed or severely damaged, while another twelve suffered mild damage.

IMMEDIATE RESPONSE: DESCRIPTION AND ASSESSMENT

The emergency response following the disaster naturally focused on the provision of basic shelter, food, and medical assistance, and search and rescue missions for survivors. It was the neighbouring communities who first rushed to the assistance of the tsunami victims.[4] These community actions were followed by government initiatives and international assistance. The Tsunami Victim Relief Center was established on 26 December 2004 to coordinate mobilizing relief efforts from all sectors of society. The Center provided an international and domestic call centre to provide information to relatives of both Thai and foreign disaster victims. It also acted as a 24-hour donation centre for both cash and essential supplies, which were transported by container trucks to the six provinces. Other donation centres were also established by government and non-government agencies.

The relief efforts focused on areas along Patong and Kamala beaches in Phuket, Khao Lak, Phi Phi Island, and Ban Nam Kem – the areas

Table 6.5 Infrastructure and public utility damage

	Piers		Concrete bridges		Wooden bridges		Box culvert and dykes		Roads	
	Units	US$ '000	Units	US$ '000	Units	US$ '000	Units	US$ '000	Units	US$ '000
Phang Nga	5	206	11	454	3	31	2	5	44	3562
Krabi	2	762	2	180	–	–	–	–	3	179
Phuket	3	200	7	160	1	12	–	–	13	592
Ranong	27	231	8	192	2	10	11	69	27	231
Trang	1	...	1	2	–	–	–	–	8	23
Satul	–	–	–	–	–	–	–	–	3	177
Total	38	1400	29	988	6	53	13	74	98	4764

Source: DDPM.

177

that were hardest hit. Over 30 000 people, comprising military personnel, policemen, volunteers, and 36 helicopters and six vessels from the Royal Navy, participated in the emergency relief activities. Rescue teams with search equipment came from a variety of places, including France; Germany; Hong Kong, China; Japan; Singapore; the Republic of Korea; Taipei,China; Italy; and the US. Local roads were repaired almost immediately to allow delivery of aid to the disaster areas. Telephone communications and electricity distributing systems in Phuket, Phang Nga, and Krabi were quickly restored and were back to normal within a few days. This immediate restoration of logistic infrastructure helped to improve the speed and coordination of aid delivery.

The search for bodies and human remains was also undertaken immediately. Searches were carried out to locate bodies buried under damaged buildings, in the sea, and in the mangrove forest areas. An extensive process of identifying human remains using DNA techniques was undertaken to deal with the large number of unidentified bodies. The identification process was supported by volunteers and NGOs, who worked tirelessly in a corpse-clearing centre established at the temple of Wat Yanyao in Phang Nga. By October 2005, the forensic teams had been able to identify 4148 bodies, while 1247 bodies still remained unidentified.[5] The next priority was to set up a centre to take care of over 34 000 tourists, including both Thai and forty foreign nationalities, and to help them return home. (Some tourists were provided with airfares to return home.)

The United Nations warned that the secondary impacts of the disaster could be deadlier than the first: people faced health risks due to contamination of drinking water and devastation of health care infrastructure. Close monitoring by the Ministry of Health helped to contain infectious diseases, while a mental health care program was successful in preventing suicides of traumatized survivors.

The scale of the disaster in Thailand was relatively small compared to other tsunami-affected countries such as Indonesia and Sri Lanka. Nevertheless Thailand faced complex logistical tasks and coped relatively successfully with the challenges. Thailand's success in the immediate relief effort was attributed to a number of factors such as (1) the synergy generated by the Thai community in the provision of many forms of assistance, (2) the close collaboration among civil, military, and police authorities, NGOs, charitable foundations, and civil volunteers, and (3) the influx of support and humanitarian assistance from international communities and NGOs (World Conference on Disaster Reduction (WCDR) Thailand Country Report (2006)).

The challenge following the successful delivery of immediate relief was to implement rehabilitation and reconstruction activities to help the tsunami survivors to cope with immediate economic problems and move on to rebuild shattered livelihoods.

SHORT-TERM ECONOMIC IMPACT

The immediate economic impact of the tsunami was felt most acutely in the tourist industry, and to a lesser extent in the fisheries sector. The extensive damage to buildings – particularly tourist hotels – and the negative impact on potential tourists of the traumatic events associated with the death and destruction following the tsunami was expected to have a substantial negative effect on the overall economy. The consequences of an absence of tourists for even one year would have been devastating for both the tourist industry and the wider regional economy because each occupied hotel room translates into many related economic activities, generating employment for both local and migrant workers.

The initial assessments of the impact of the tsunami on the Thai economy can be gauged by the movements in the Thai stock market. Stock prices reflect investor expectations about the present value of the expected future stream of dividend payouts derived from corporate profits. The tsunami had an immediate impact on the Thai stock market. The overall security exchange index (SET) fell during the first few trading days after the disaster, reflecting concerns about the longer term impact on the Thai economy. But market participants, after this initial (over)reaction to the tsunami, revised their assessments and concluded that the economy would not suffer much from the tsunami in the long term. The SET index rebounded within a week, though the stock price index relating to the tourism industry was depressed longer, faced with a continuous bombardment of bad news. Nevertheless, as the market reassessed the damage even the tourism industry index recovered within a month. By the end of January 2005 it had even exceeded its pre-tsunami level, rising in line with the SET index.

The investor assessment of the long-term economic impact of the tsunami was, however, more optimistic than the early assessments of most official and private sector analysts. As already mentioned, JP Morgan predicted a zero growth rate for the first quarter of 2005, while both JP Morgan and Morgan Stanley revised downward their annual growth forecasts by 0.3 per cent. The Bank of Thailand also projected a reduction of annual GDP growth by 0.3 per cent due to the tsunami, even after taking into account the growth momentum of the last quarter in 2004, and expected compensating effects of soft loans and other assistance. In the

worst-case scenario, if no tourists were visiting the affected areas, GDP
was projected to decline by 1.3 per cent.

The tourism industry in the affected provinces experienced a significant
negative impact in the immediate post-tsunami period. This was caused
mainly by a fall in tourist arrivals rather than because of damage done to
hotels and other tourist infrastructure (Table 6.6). The key issue therefore
was not so much the rebuilding of tourism infrastructure – important as it
was – but how to encourage tourists to return.[6]

The first quarter growth rate of 2005 turned out to be a robust 3.3 per
cent, but the annual growth rate fell to 4.5 per cent, significantly lower
compared to the 6.2 per cent growth achieved in 2004, and much lower
than predicted by analysts.[7] The current account recorded a deficit of
US$6.4 billion in the first seven months of 2005 compared with a surplus
of US$3.4 billion a year earlier.[8] Inflation rose from 2.7 per cent in 2004 to
4.5 per cent in 2005 and the trade deficit widened to 8.5 per cent of GDP.
The current account surplus of 1.7 per cent of GDP in 2004 turned into a
4.4 per cent deficit in 2005.

However the downturn in tourism alone could not have caused the
very large fall in the GDP growth rate. The tourism industry contrib-
utes only 6 per cent to Thai GDP and the six tsunami-affected provinces
accounted for only 30 per cent of Thailand's total tourism income. The
tsunami did not destroy all hotels (or the fishing industry) in the six provinces. Moreover, other tourist attractions on the east coast of the Gulf
of Thailand remained intact and the industry as a whole proved to be
resilient. But in 2005 the Thai economy was badly affected not only by the
tsunami but also by drought, ongoing insurgency in the south, rising oil
prices, and a slowdown of global trade. The main cause of higher inflation
was high oil prices. The combined effect of these problems was reflected

Table 6.6   Hotel industry six months after the tsunami (Jan.–June)

	Phuket			Phang Nga			Krabi		
	2004	2006	%	2004	2006	%	2004	2006	%
No. hotels	616	457	−26	149	55	−63	290	288	−1
No. rooms '000	31	29	−6	5	1	−69	10	9	−11
Occupancy rate %	63	27	−57	56	31	−45	51	21	−59
Duration (day)	3.57	3.16	...	1.66	1.41	...	2.86	1.94	−1

Source: Tourism Authority of Thailand.

in a sharp deterioration in the trade and current account. According to several estimates, the tsunami was probably responsible for only a 0.3 per cent reduction in Thailand's GDP growth in 2005.

Thus the early predictions tended to exaggerate the expected adverse economic impact of the tsunami. Indeed, arguably the overly pessimistic forecasts made in the immediate aftermath of the tsunami may have had the unintended consequence of eroding consumer and business confidence and depressing business activity, contributing to the aggravation of the economic slowdown.

REHABILITATION, RECONSTRUCTION AND RECOVERY

In the immediate aftermath of the tsunami, relief and reconstruction became the focus of a massive national effort. The overall government budget allocation for tsunami relief and reconstruction was nearly US$1.7 billion (Table 6.7). The government set aside US$112 million for immediate tsunami relief, 76 per cent of which was allocated to emergency relief and mitigation measures in the six provinces. Around 14 per cent of the relief budget went to projects for reviving the tourism industry in the Andaman areas, 10 per cent for rehabilitation of natural resources, and a relatively small proportion (less than 1 per cent) for installing an early warning system. Subsequent rehabilitation measures were allocated an additional US$73 million.

The Thai government initially allocated only US$8.3 million to public infrastructure reconstruction. This relatively small budget reflected the low level of assessed damage to infrastructure. The largest budget allocation was to provide assistance to large entrepreneurs by way of soft loans.[9]

Table 6.7   Budget allocation for tsunami relief classified by measures[a]

Measures	US$ mn
Emergency measures	112
Relief measures for large entrepreneurs	1487
Rehabilitation measures	73
Reconstruction of infrastructure	8
Total	1681

Note: [a] As of 16 November 2006.

Source: Tsunami Help and Recovery Information System (THRIS).

Relief measures for large entrepreneurs included the Bank of Thailand's soft loans, which were extended to commercial banks for lending to large companies in the three provinces. These loans amounted to around 90 per cent of the total budget.

A US$75 million ten-year tsunami recovery fund was set up in February 2005. The fund was managed by Mutual Fund Corporation Asset Management and funded by the Government Savings Bank, the Stock Exchange of Thailand, and the Thai Bankers' Association. Tsunami-affected firms could get assistance either in the form of loans or by sharing equity with the fund. The loans were made available at a 1 per cent interest rate for the first five years before reverting to market interest rates. The expectation was that reconstruction of hotels would be completed before the tourist high season at the end of 2006. In total, this fund amounted to around 6 per cent of total relief measures for large entrepreneurs.

Public Infrastructure

Figure 6.2 shows the actual expenditures on various categories of public infrastructure reconstruction compared with estimated values of damages in November 2006. In every category, the allocated funds exceeded actual expenditures, suggesting that the availability of finances was not a critical constraint on reconstruction. The expectation was that infrastructure reconstruction would be completed without any major funding problems.

Various government and private agencies were allocated responsibility for repairing or rebuilding houses in each province. Households could also

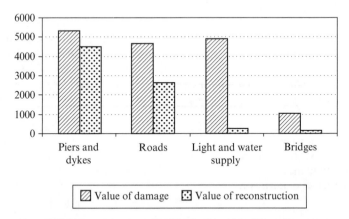

Source: Tsunami Help and Recovery System (THRIS), November 2006.

Figure 6.2   Infrastructure damage and reconstruction (US$ '000)

opt to get US$750 in aid to rebuild their own houses. As shown in Table 6.8, residential house construction was largely complete by mid-2006.

In Satul, where housing damage was small, the local government took on the house-building responsibility, while in Trang, where there were only 39 requests for new houses, the National Housing Authority undertook the task. Private companies were allocated the rebuilding of 127 new houses in Phuket. In Ranong, the Air Force took care of building 167 houses while the Defence Ministry took charge of building 375 houses in Krabi. The Army and the Navy were responsible for completing the construction of 2850 houses in the worst-damaged area, Phang Nga.

However, as we shall discuss later, although the physical demand for new houses was met, villagers who moved into these new houses were not always entirely happy with their new living quarters.

Cost Escalation

An interesting feature of Thailand's reconstruction experience is the fact that the physical reconstruction effort had little discernible effect on increasing construction costs. In fact, construction costs actually declined during 2005. This contrasts sharply with the experiences of Indonesia and Sri Lanka.[10]

The reconstruction activities certainly increased demand in the affected regions for construction materials and labour. This was reflected in the opening of a large number of construction material shops in the affected areas. However, higher demand did not lead to price increases. It is

Table 6.8 Housing reconstruction

Province	Destroyed (units)	Damaged (units)	New houses	
			Demand	Completion
Krabi	396	262	375	375
Phuket	742	291	127	127
Phang Nga	1 904	604	2850	2850
Trang	34	156	39	39
Ranong	224	111	167	167
Satul	2	80	–	–
Total	3 302	1 504	3 558	3 558

Note: 552 households opted for US$750 in aid to rebuild their own houses.

Source: DDPM (damage data reported on 15 February 2005, rates of completed construction data reported in June 2006).

important to note that the tsunami-affected areas were not very far from the metropolitan Bangkok region and that the overall reconstruction activity was small relative to the size of the Thai economy. Moreover, the higher demand for inputs into the construction sector came at a time when the construction sector at the national level was somewhat depressed because an overall slowdown in economic activity was tending to push prices down. There was considerable excess capacity in the main input markets for construction. Substantial excess capacity in the steel industry led to declining prices of steel products while prices of wood and wood products rose less than 5 per cent during 2005. Even though higher oil prices exerted some upward pressure on most materials, prices of essential raw materials such as cement and steel remained subdued during the reconstruction period. Overall, the magnitude of the demand effect was not sufficient to increase prices because of the elastic supply of construction inputs.

Livelihoods

The second-round effect of the tsunami hit when victims lost their livelihoods. This occurred either because the capital equipment they used in their jobs was destroyed (as in the fisheries sector) or because they lost jobs in the tourist sector due to hotels being damaged or cuts in employment following falls in tourist numbers (even though some workers were willing to accept pay cuts to keep their jobs).

The government addressed the plight of unemployed workers through various employment programs (Table 6.9). The employment project, averaging an expenditure of US$130 per person, was the most active program set up to generate short-term livelihood support; as of November 2006, it had cost around US$3 million and benefited almost 24000 workers. In terms of total expenditure, the second most important project for the unemployed was the job training project, which cost US$43 per head. However, unemployment was expected to be essentially short-term and it is not clear whether workers temporarily displaced from their normal occupations (tourism industry and fisheries, for example) were likely to gain much benefit from training for alternative occupations. The job creation project had the highest cost per head (US$254) but could accommodate fewer than 1000 workers, while the project supervised by the Department of Labour and Welfare Protection spent only US$30 per head.

Impact on the Tourism Industry

Tourism was the key industry in terms of employment. It had been on a steady growth path prior to the tsunami. Revenue from tourism in Phuket,

Table 6.9   Thai government support to unemployed workers

	Totals	
	(Dec 2005)	(Nov 2006)
Employment project		
Budget (US$ '000)	2809	3110
Number of beneficiaries	22000	23958
Job provision		
Budget (US$ '000)	10	10
Number of beneficiaries	23000	23000
Labour transferring service		
Budget (US$ '000)	9	9
Number of beneficiaries	1200	1200
Job creation project		
Budget (US$ '000)	222	238
Number of beneficiaries	760	936
Job training project		
Budget (US$ '000)	1096	1097
Number of beneficiaries	10000	25751
Dept of Labour Protection and Welfare		
Budget (US$ '000)	980	1024
Number of beneficiaries	28340	34340
Total		
Budget (US$ '000)	5126	5487
Number of beneficiaries	85300	109185

Source: THRIS, 23 November 2006.

Krabi, and Phang Nga had been increasing steadily. But the December 2004 tsunami sharply interrupted this growth. Following the tsunami, revenues fell dramatically in 2005 (Figure 6.3).

The primary reason for the drop in tourism was not actual physical damage to tourism infrastructure but the reluctance of tourists to visit the tsunami-affected areas. Phuket suffered the steepest fall despite the fact that its hotels were less damaged than those in the other two provinces. The number of tourists in Phuket dropped sharply in January – when there were almost no tourists – and continued to be low throughout 2005 (Figure 6.3). The drop in tourism led to considerable unemployment in these areas.

Fortunately the falls in tourism in the affected regions were to some

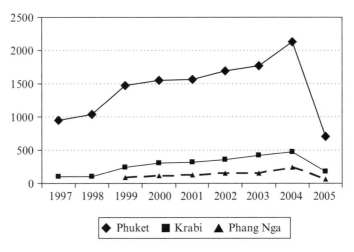

Source: Tourism Authority of Thailand.

Figure 6.3   Tourism revenue in three provinces (million US$)

extent compensated for by increases in tourist arrivals in other parts of the
country because only a small portion of Thailand's hotel industry was seriously affected by the tsunami. There are other beaches in different parts of
Thailand, particularly along the Gulf of Thailand, which are reasonable
substitutes for those of the Andaman areas. Tourists also had the option
of switching their visits to northern Thailand.

The consequence was that while there was a significant decline in the
hotel occupancy rate in the south, there were increases in occupancy rates
in other parts of Thailand – particularly Bangkok (Figure 6.4). The result
of the substitution of the Gulf of Thailand for the Andaman coast as a
tourist destination can be seen by the tourism boom in Koh Samui and
some other resort areas on the east coast of Thailand. In 2005 the hotel
occupancy rate in Pataya grew by 28 per cent. The result was a boom in
demand for land in these alternative tourist destinations. By March 2006,
the land price in Koh Samui had gone up nearly sevenfold from 37 500 to
250 000 baht per rai (0.625 hectare). Hotel chain operators and investors
drove up property values as the demand for hotel accommodation in these
areas exceeded available supply.

Tourist arrivals numbers in the tsunami-affected areas began to increase
in 2006. Two years after the tsunami the tourism industry was close to
regaining its earlier level of activity. Airlines that cancelled flights to
Phuket after the tsunami had returned, including those from Australia,
the Republic of Korea, Singapore, and Europe. In addition, new airlines

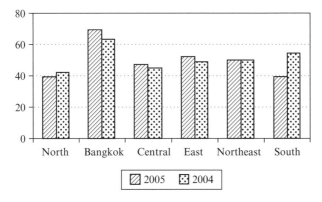

Source: Tourism Authority of Thailand.

Figure 6.4 Hotel occupancy rate in 2004 and 2005 (per cent)

started direct flights to Andaman areas. In the second half of 2006, Hong Kong Express started to operate two flights a week from Hong Kong, China to Phuket. Thai Airways resumed twice-weekly flights from the Republic of Korea to Phuket in an attempt to encourage high-end Korean tourists to return to Phuket. Targeted tourists included golfers, spa visitors, honeymooners, and families. Phuket's private sector went on a road show to attract tourists from new markets in India, the Middle East, and Russia. All of these private sector initiatives helped the industry recover within a year of the disaster.

The return of many airlines and the arrival of new airlines reflected a recovery in the tourism sector. Another indicator of the rapid recovery in tourism was the low level of non-performing SME loans. The SME Bank reported in March 2006 that 523 business operators had borrowed special loans totalling 19 million baht from the SME banks. These were loans with a concessionary interest rate of 2 per cent per year. Thirty-one operators had repaid all their debt within one year. All borrowing enterprises paid interest on schedule.[11]

Damage to Coral Reefs

Initially, there were fears about the impact of the tsunami on the coral reefs. The reefs are a precious natural resource important for both the tourism and fisheries industries as well as for the wider ecosystem. Fortunately, according to the Phuket Marine Biological Center, only coral reefs in shallow waters were damaged by the tsunami, meaning that only 5 per cent of the coral reefs in Phuket were destroyed. Moreover, some corals, such as 'branchy' corals, were expected to recover within three years, while 'bunchy' corals were expected to recover within ten years. Hence the indications were that there was no serious long-term damage to the quality of coral reefs. However, the Food and Agriculture Organization (FAO) warned that there could be other long-term impacts on the coastal ecosystem. The dense mangrove forests hit by the tsunami were damaged, and the freshwater swamp forests were also destroyed by saline water intrusion. These needed rehabilitation to ensure long-term sustainability of the ecosystem and protection from future disasters (FAO 2005).

Tsunami Warning System

On 26 December 2004 the Pacific Tsunami Warning Center detected the massive earthquake that triggered the tsunami and warned of the approaching giant waves. However there was no official alert system in the region. There is now widespread recognition that an early warning system is an essential part of preparations for coping with disasters. The National Disaster Warning Center (NDWC) has an agreement with the Asian Disaster Preparedness Center (ADPC) to exchange real-time data from sea-level observations and seismic monitoring systems. Cooperation among countries in the Andaman region to share information can provide a valuable public good that can save lives and mitigate unwarranted fears of future tsunamis. In early December 2006, a 'Deep Ocean Assessment and Report of Tsunami' (DART™) buoy costing US$5 million was installed in the centre of the Andaman Sea, 1100 kilometres west of Phuket and 925 kilometres east of India.[12] The deep-sea buoy was designed to detect tsunami waves and send signals to warning centres in countries in the region. The NDWC is responsible for alerting the public in Thailand after receiving a signal from the buoy.

But a high-tech network of sensors and buoys will not be effective if there is no effective communications link to coastal communities at risk of being hit by a tsunami. In an effort to build up an 'alert system' in local communities, the Thai Public Works Department completed the construction of 55 tsunami warning towers by June 2006 in the six provinces. The construction of ten warning towers along the Andaman coast was also planned. The total budget for the construction of the towers was less than 1 per cent of the total budget for the warning system, reflecting the capital intensive approach of the installed system.

The extent to which this warning system will build confidence among village communities and tourists over the longer term is unclear. Observation towers and signs pointing to escape routes may generate a confidence among villagers and tourists. It remains to be seen whether tourists, encouraged by this warning system, will feel safer and will return to these locations.

AID AND ASSISTANCE

Thailand was not as severely affected as Indonesia or Sri Lanka by the tsunami but it attracted much international media attention because of the large number of foreign tourists caught up in the tragedy. Furthermore, the areas hit by the tsunami included famous tourist destinations. Thus Thailand was inundated with offers of assistance from governments, multilateral donor agencies, corporate and community groups, and individuals. Philanthropy was shown to exist among both large and small corporations, and among both the rich and the poor.

The immediate response to the disaster can be considered a success. However poor coordination among aid donors hampered effective delivery and distribution. There were many instances of wasteful aid. Some donations of food and clothing were wasted because they were not appropriate for Muslims. Some houses constructed by the military were not appropriate for the lifestyle of fisherfolk. Many of the inefficiencies in aid programs reflected the problems of supply-driven assistance which sometimes passed over the particular needs of people whom the donors said that they wished to assist.

The Thai government turned down offers of financial assistance from foreign governments, including offers of debt relief from Europe, though it accepted technical assistance. The rationale given was that Thailand wanted funds to be given to other countries in more difficult circumstances, such as Indonesia. It is also likely that the government wanted to send a message to the global investor community concerning its financial stability, fearing that acceptance of debt relief might hurt Thailand's credit rating and thus raise Thai borrowing costs and discourage capital inflows.

Foreign Assistance

However, as seen in Table 6.10, following the tsunami Thailand received significant assistance from a range of foreign donors. This included technical assistance from foreign governments. The total amount of aid committed was US$131 million, ranging from contributions of US$5000 to US$27 million. This foreign commitment was around 10 per cent of Thailand's tsunami-related budget. The government also received

The Asian tsunami

Table 6.10   Contributions from international donors at end-2006 (US$)

International partner	Committed (US$ mn)	Disbursed (US$ mn)	Disbursed (%)
Main donors			
FFEM (Fond Francais pour l'Environnement Mondial)	27.4	–	–
United States Agency for International Development	21.1	3.0	14
World Vision	20.0	7.0	35
Australia, Department of Foreign Affairs and Trade	12.2	12.2	100
United Nations Children's Fund	9.8	9.8	100
Norway	7.9	7.9	100
Other donors			
Adventist Relief and Development Agency (ADRA)	0.5	0.5	100
The Asia Foundation	0.5	0.5	96
AusAID	0.8	0.8	100
Danida	3.2	1.4	45
Embassy of Italy	1.2	1.2	100
Entraide et Solidarite	0.1	0.1	98
GTZ	1.1	0.4	38
IOM (International Organization for Migration)	0.2	0.1	57
International Labour Organization	0.8	0.7	85
Office for Coordination of Humanitarian Affairs (OCHA)	0.5	0.1	22
Swiss Agency for Development and Cooperation (SDC)	2.3	1.3	55
Terre des Hommes – Italy	0.7	–	0
Sustainable Tourism Development Consortium (STDC)	1.2	1.2	100
The Australian Federal Police (AFP)	3.1	3.1	100
The Austrian NGO Hilfswerk, Austria	0.8	–	0
UN OPS	0.2	0.2	100
United Nations Development Programme	5.2	5.2	100
United Nations Population Fund	0.9	0.8	89
World Bank	4.9	4.9	100
World Food Programme	0.5	0.5	100

Table 6.10 (continued)

International partner	Committed (US$ mn)	Disbursed (US$ mn)	Disbursed (%)
World Health Organization	3.0	3.0	100
World Vision Canada	1.5	1.5	100
All others (13 agencies)	0.6	0.4	63
Total	132.0	67.6	51

Source: Thailand International Development Cooperation Agency (TICA).

substantial donations from the corporate sector, estimated at US$50–60 million in 2005 (Bernhard et al. 2005).[13] This amount is quite substantial when compared with the amount contributed by international donors. Nearly all large foreign companies operating in Thailand provided some type of contribution within a short period following the disaster. Overall, around 80 per cent of the total amount donated came from donations larger than US$250 000. These larger donations came primarily from large organizations and corporations. Contributions of less than US$25 000 accounted for about 8 per cent of total contributions.

Delivery of Assistance: Speed and Efficiency

Emergency assistance to tsunami survivors was delivered quickly. Government officials and volunteers were able to reach affected areas immediately after the tsunami because basic infrastructure was not totally damaged and access to affected areas remained open. Moreover, relief agencies and individuals were able to reach disaster areas without having to obtain prior permission from provincial governments.

In the early relief phase, aid disbursement was rapid. Disbursement was 20 per cent of the total fiscal budget within two months of the disaster. The rate went up to 70 per cent by the end of the first year, an acceptable rate in the circumstances. However, disbursement in the second year slowed down. It seems that by the end of 2006 it may not have been higher than 80 per cent.

Of course some types of financial assistance can and should be spent faster than others. The disbursement rates of government funds for various categories varied (Table 6.11). Funds to provide aid to foreign tourists (medical care, helping those who lost their belongings, helping them to return home, and so on) were completely utilized. On the other

Table 6.11   Financial assistance provided by the Thai government

Sub-Committee on Assisting	PM Office Assistance Fund and Central Budget (US$ mn)	Amount disbursed (US$ mn)	Disbursement (%)
1 Foreign tourists	2.2	2.2	100
2 Affected victims	20.5	19.5	95
3 Affected fishers	20.7	14.5	70
4 The unemployed	5.3	5.4	97
5 Small vendors	5.3	5.2	99
6 Accommodation	2.5	2.3	89
7 Affected students	21.3	11.3	53
Total	78.1	60.4	77

Source: Office of Prime Minister Website, November 2006.

hand, assistance to students – less urgent – had the lowest disbursement. Disbursement was also slower for assistance to fishers.

The disbursement rate of foreign pledges varied a great deal. As of November 2006, the disbursement was only 50 per cent. Some pledges (Table 6.10) had not been disbursed at all. Larger donations with commitments of US$20 million or more (for example, FFEM, USAID, World Vision) seem to have had a slower disbursement rate. It is not surprising that large donations tended to be disbursed more slowly because the objective of the pledges was to achieve longer term rehabilitation. Further, speeding up the disbursement of the large amounts of money with no effective monitoring and careful evaluation would have created problems of accountability. Zero disbursement rates were related to small amounts of donations.

Aid Delivery: Equity Issues

Issues arose over the way in which assistance was to be distributed. As noted earlier, damage to fisheries accounted for about 12 per cent of total damage while various organizations contributed compensation of about 32 per cent of total fishery damage. However the distribution of compensation did not correspond to the actual damages. Fishers in Phang Nga who suffered 50 per cent of the total damage received only 30 per cent of the total value of aid. In contrast, Satul's share of damage was only 6.6 per cent but the area received 39 per cent of total compensation. Krabi fisheries, with 65 per cent of total compensation, also received much more than their fair share. It may be noted here that Phang Nga is the home of minority ethnic groups who may not be given the highest priority. In addition, some

Table 6.12   Financial assistance to enterprises

	Units	US$ mn
Large enterprises		
Soft loan	7 014	997
Financial institution credit	2 068	31
Mutual fund	36	60
Social security fund	6	2
Total	9 124	1 089
Small and medium enterprises		
Financial aid	10 718	5

Source: THRIS, 23 November 2006.

of them had not obtained Thai citizenship or other necessary documents. Uneven disbursement might also have been due to the allocation of budgets by central and local governments among affected provinces.

Arguably, there may be a similar issue with regard to the provision of loans supplied to firms to help revive businesses. Large hotels that suffered heavy losses received government subsidies in the form of loans at concessionary rates; in total, large enterprises received financial injections of over US$1 billion (Table 6.12). In contrast, around 10 000 SMEs received a total of around US$5 million. It is not clear what criteria were employed in deciding the allocation of funds between large enterprises and SMEs, whether this was the best means of helping to revive the tourism industry of the Andaman coast, or whether the marginal product of capital injected into large enterprises is higher than that of SMEs. The employment effect of assisting SMEs versus large enterprises, too, was a factor that might have been considered.

Public Assistance, Insurance, and Credit Markets

This raises a longer term issue about the impact of public sector provision of assistance to business enterprises. The question is whether private sector enterprises will bother looking for private insurance if they are provided with (or can assume that they will get) public assistance for disasters. Kunreuther and Pauly (2006) show that public disaster assistance is a form of insurance that is suboptimal when compared to insurance purchased before the disaster. Firms maximize expected profits by taking into account insurance premiums and the expected extent of public assistance. Mandatory comprehensive private disaster insurance with risk-based rates can help minimize costly and poorly targeted disaster assistance. An *ex ante* public coverage program to cover catastrophic losses and to subsidize insurance coverage for small and medium firms can be more efficient than costly *ex post* relief programs. From a public policy perspective, preparations for disasters should involve assessments of how disaster insurance markets can be developed and how private firms can be induced to invest in disaster insurance.

In this context, policies to cope with natural disasters need to address issues raised by the underdeveloped nature of financial and capital markets in developing countries and the restricted access of the poor to such markets. Natural disasters typically hit the poor hardest. Those engaged in small and micro-enterprises, including craftspeople, small shopkeepers, and fisherfolk, require credit to replace their equipment and inventories to re-start businesses. In this context, microfinance appears to have a major role to play. However, the Grameen Foundation USA, which looked into the availability of microfinance in the tsunami-affected areas, did not find NGOs or other organizations offering micro-lending services. The Foundation believes that poverty hindered the development of effective micro-lending initiatives, particularly in the south (Counts et al. 2005).[14] We revisit this issue below.

Assistance to Children

Thousands of children lost both parents following the tsunami. The Thai government provided financial aid to almost 1500 orphans and almost 27 000 other children (Table 6.13). Most of those orphaned were from the six affected provinces; some were from other locations whose parents had been working in the tsunami-hit areas. The government provided orphans with clothes and educational materials, including scholarships through to university level. The response of the government in terms of providing access to education was swift. Most schools were able to re-open almost immediately (on 4 January 2005). Attendance was initially low but soon returned to pre-tsunami levels. However for these affected children, particularly orphans, the impact of the tsunami was obviously not confined to the short term. Recognizing this, psychological support was provided through a broad community-based psychosocial recovery program to mitigate the negative impact on children's learning.

Assistance for Trauma and Stress

The impact of the tsunami was not confined to physical and economic losses. The trauma associated with loss of family members, relatives, and

Table 6.13   Financial assistance from Thai Ministry of Education

Province	Orphans		Affected children	
	Number	Aid (US$)	Number	Aid (US$)
Krabi	119	73 800	5 577	2 091 050
Phang Nga	630	393 175	6 127	2 297 625
Phuket	177	110 625	2 608	977 675
Ranong	87	54 375	2 278	852 950
Satul	13	8 125	5 116	1 918 500
Trang	29	18 125	4 432	1 662 000
Other provinces	441	275 625	854	320 250
Total	1 496	933 850	26 992	10 120 050
($ per child)		624		375

Source: THRIS.

Table 6.14   Mental health services for tsunami victims (26 December 2004–
4 May 2006)

Province	No. of services	Types of services		
		Psychiatric drugs	Counselling	Medical treatment
Krabi	3 664	839	3 799	1 114
Phang Nga	9 984	3 349	9 898	3 335
Phuket	2 600	634	2 669	833
Ranong	1 484	178	1 364	316
Satul	704	273	226	458
Trang	614	6	594	156
Total	19 050	5 279	18 550	6 212

Source: Mental Health Center for the Thai Tsunami Disaster.

friends, as well as loss of physical assets and livelihoods, imposed heavy economic and psychological pressures on survivors. It was reported that some fishers, for example, suffered from hallucinations and paranoia and were unable to go back to sea. Attempted suicides and symptoms of acute stress and other mental problems were also widely reported (Table 6.14).

Social Tensions

Many disputes threatened social cohesion in the affected communities. Many villagers, already depressed by misfortune, faced disputes over land ownership. More than 20 per cent of affected villages experienced some land disputes. Many traditional owners – villagers and ethnic communities – did not have secure legal title to their land. In the aftermath of the tsunami many found themselves locked into disputes, both with local governments (who wanted to maintain land for public use and to protect the environment) and with developers (who wanted to obtain prime land along pristine beaches for commercial purposes).

Conflicts also arose because of perceptions that assistance had not been delivered in a fair way. In the early phase of relief assistance, there was a strong emphasis on speedy delivery of aid which sometimes meant that some needy people missed out on assistance. In some cases when the aid distributors arrived in a village, some people did not receive assistance because they were elsewhere searching for their family members. Irrespective of the reason, for people already traumatized by the disaster, perceptions of unfair treatment tended to exacerbate community tensions.

COMMUNITY PERCEPTIONS AND BEHAVIOUR: RESULTS FROM A FIELD SURVEY

A key part of this study was a field survey of affected communities in the three most severely affected provinces. The aim was to try to understand behavioural adjustments of families affected by the tsunami so as to draw lessons of wider relevance for policy formulation for natural disaster management.

Primary data was obtained from a sample survey of 262 displaced and non-displaced individuals, 37 visitors (tourists), and seven NGOs. The survey was designed to gain insights into aspects of the disaster management process from the point of view of affected communities, tourists, and non-government agents such as NGOs. In particular, we were interested in obtaining community perceptions regarding the effectiveness of aid in terms of availability, distribution, speed, and targeting among various groups of occupations, and whether assistance may have adversely affected incentives for self reliance by creating an 'aid-dependency' syndrome.

Survey Methodology

The survey was conducted in June 2006. It covered the three provinces severely affected by the tsunami and included 296 respondents. There were

Table 6.15   Survey sample: composition and distribution

	Phuket	Phang Nga	Krabi	Total	%
Diversified households (H)	6	53	13	72	24
Fishers (F)	8	23	5	36	12
Entrepreneurs (E)	11	17	8	36	12
Labourers (L)	11	17	8	36	12
Beach vendors (B)	11	17	8	36	12
Tourists (T)	11	18	8	37	12
NGOs	0	7	0	7	2
Moken (M)	0	36	0	36	12
Total (numbers)	58	188	50	296	
Per cent (%)	20	64	17		100

Source: Thailand tsunami survey, three Thai provinces, conducted by chapter author, June 2006.

eight individual sample categories: Diversified Households (H), Fishers (F), Entrepreneurs (dependent mainly on tourism) (E), Labourers (L), Beach Vendors (B), Tourists (T), and Moken (an ethnic minority tribe of 'sea gypsies' who comprise a small fishing community in Phang Nga) (M), as well as seven NGOs from Phang Nga province. The sample distribution is shown in Table 6.15. The sample size in each province was roughly proportional to the loss of life in each province, taken as an indicator of the severity of the impact of the tsunami. The group sample sizes do not strictly correspond to their proportions in the population.

The families included in the Diversified Households group had family members engaged in a variety of occupations, including general service providers, fishers, housewives, and traders. Thus, while some of these household members followed occupations similar to those of the main income earners in the various occupational categories, the households as a whole had more diversified income sources. Twenty-three fishing households (Fishers) were randomly selected from Phang Nga, eight from Phuket, and five from Krabi. Those in the Entrepreneur category were mainly small business operators involved in tourism-related businesses such as restaurants, shop houses, and guest houses. The Labourer category included those who were employed in hotels, restaurants, shop houses, department stores, and local administration. Beach Vendors provided various services to tourists on the beach such as renting out beach umbrellas and chairs and selling food. The activities of NGOs were concentrated primarily in Phang Nga province where the need for assistance was deemed to be strongest. The sample was drawn entirely from that province. The aim was to ensure that NGOs could provide their own perspective to balance that provided by community groups. The Moken are fisherfolk who also provide construction labour and engage in petty trade. They were included as a separate category to assess their perceptions as an ethnic minority group regarding any bias or discrimination in the provision of assistance.

Overall, the sample was reasonably gender balanced (52 per cent males, 48 per cent females) but there was considerable variation among different groups. There were significantly more male respondents than females in the Fisher and Labourer categories (81 per cent and 58 per cent, respectively) while there were more females within the Entrepreneur (64 per cent) and the Moken categories (56 per cent). In other categories (Diversified Households and Beach Vendors) the gender numbers were approximately equal.[15]

Half of the surveyed Entrepreneurs and around a third of Diversified Households and Beach Vendors were new migrants to these areas, in contrast to nearly 80 per cent of the Fishers and almost all of the Moken being natives of the areas.

Tsunami and Asset Losses

The survey provided a household-level perspective on how the tsunami affected households (Figure 6.5). Some families in each group lost family members while most lost some assets. The way in which affected families adjusted to post-tsunami life and coped with the many economic and non-economic challenges they had to face was conditioned by these two, key, traumatic driving forces: loss of family members and asset destruction. Respondents were asked to approximate the damage on their property as a percentage of their total assets. In relative terms, Moken were the worst affected by asset losses, losing almost 80 per cent of their total assets. Labourers lost 40 per cent of their assets. In the sample, less than 20 per cent of Fisher families lost family members – the lowest rate among the six groups – but Fishers were hit hard by asset losses.

Adjustment and Coping with Post-tsunami Reality

Table 6.16 presents information about how families adjusted to the loss of incomes and livelihoods after the tsunami. Eighteen months after the tsunami, the incomes of the large majority of families (68 per cent) were below their pre-tsunami level, while a small minority (15 per cent) experienced an increase in income level.

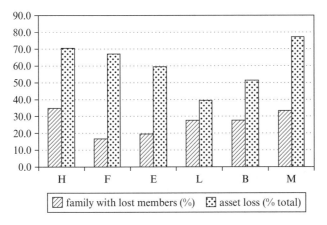

Note: H: households; F: fishers; E: entrepreneurs; L: labourers; B: beach vendors; M: Moken minority.

Figure 6.5   Death and destruction

Table 6.16   Income changes and patterns of adjustment by category (%)

	Diversified households (H)	Fishers (F)	Entre-preneurs (E)	Labourers (L)	Beach Vendors (B)	Moken (M)	Total
Incomes							
Lower	69	72	86	64	92	53	68
Unchanged	15	17	6	6	6	36	17
Higher	15	11	8	31	3	11	15
Total	100	100	100	100	100	100	100
Of whom:							
Borrowed money	54	58	53	44	53	19	48
Changed occupation	42	36	31	47	33	31	39

Source: Thailand tsunami survey, three Thai provinces, conducted by chapter author, June 2006.

But there were significant differences within the sample categories. Those who depended heavily on incomes from tourism were the hardest hit: 92 per cent of Beach Vendors and 86 per cent of Entrepreneurs experienced a decrease in income, followed by Fishers (72 per cent) and Diversified

Households (69 per cent). Surprisingly, the Moken minority suffered the least from the reduction in income. Only a little over half of them experienced a decline in income level, 36 per cent of them were able to maintain the same level of income, and 11 per cent actually earned higher incomes. While 64 per cent of families belonging to the Labourer group had lower incomes, some 30 per cent reported that their incomes were higher.

More insights into the reasons for these differences can be gleaned from the ways in which families adjusted their income-earning activities after the tsunami. Overall, 40 per cent of the sample reported that they had changed their main occupation. The largest change was in the Labourer group of whom nearly half took up a new occupation. In contrast, only 30 per cent of Entrepreneurs and the Moken changed occupations.

A variety of factors to do with occupational skill-specificity, adjustment costs, and alternative job opportunities appear to have been important. Many Entrepreneurs probably felt that they were able to cope with a temporary fall in income based on the expectation that tourist arrivals would soon recover. Regarding the Moken, not only were many of them less dependent on markets for their incomes, but with limited skills they may also have had fewer opportunities to move into other jobs.

Consumption Smoothing and Access to Credit

An event like the tsunami can be thought of as a temporary shock that reduces income for a period of time. Of course, if significant asset damage also occurs, then there is a longer-term impact that reduces household wealth. However, the large-scale assistance programs generated a perception that asset damages would be more or less fully compensated through government and other donor aid. One likely response to income reductions, particularly when the decline is expected to be temporary, is an increase in borrowing as families attempt to smooth their consumption.

In the post-tsunami period, despite the availability of some aid and assistance, nearly half of all households across the different categories went into debt. However, though over half of the Moken families experienced an income fall, less than 20 per cent of them went into debt. In contrast, the number of families who borrowed was highest among the Fishers. It is possible that some families who wanted to borrow may have been unable to access credit markets and thus became liquidity-constrained. This is particularly likely to be the case for those who were asset poor and hence unable to borrow because of lack of collateral. Arguably, most Fishers expected that their assets and equipment would be replaced and hence expected that their income levels would recover after some time. This expectation may have been shared by many lenders. On the other hand, many Moken families were more likely to be liquidity-constrained because they were probably not seen as good credit risks and hence were more likely to have been denied access to credit. Further research is required, however, before any firm conclusions can be reached.

Determinants of Loan Demand

The demand for credit within households was explored using a model where the demand for credit (amount of borrowing) was considered to depend on the following factors: the pre-tsunami monthly income (YB) multiplied by the number of months of unemployment (to proxy the income gap needed to maintain the pre-tsunami expenditure level), the cost of borrowing or the interest rate, the loan purpose (business or non-business), the availability of collateral, and the total amount of financial aid (TOTAL-AID) obtained from direct aid, relatives and friends. The detailed results are given in Equation (6A.1) in Appendix 6A.1.

The results indicate that credit demand was positively related to direct aid amount, availability of collateral, and whether the loan was for business purposes, and (as expected) negatively related to the interest rate. Interestingly, the total cash aid that was received complemented rather than substituted for total credit demand. The significance of the availability of collateral as a determinant of credit demand indicates that tsunami victims who suffered loss of assets, and thus loss of adequate collateral, were likely to be liquidity-constrained. Poorer households with no collateral were also likely to be forced into the informal credit market where interest rates are higher. Such high-interest credit raises the cost of credit and thereby further reduced the capacity of the asset poor households to use the credit market for consumption smoothing. In this context, effective microfinance programs can play an important role by providing credit to restart microenterprises to those who cannot afford the high interest loans.

Financial assistance from friends and relatives – from social networks – can be very important for cash-strapped tsunami victims experiencing income shortfalls. In the survey, assistance from friends and relatives accounted for about a third of total financial assistance to households. However, this was not evenly spread across household categories.

Beach Vendors received the bulk of their financial assistance from relatives and friends while Diversified Households and Labourer households received about a third of their total assistance from relatives and friends. On the other hand, outside assistance was by far the most important source for Moken and Entrepreneur households. In the case of Entrepreneurs, it is possible that the low proportion of financial assistance from relatives

Table 6.17   Changes in income and occupations (%)

Income	Diversified households (H)	Fishers (F)	Entre-preneurs (E)	Labourers (L)	Beach vendors (B)	Moken (M)
New occupation:						
Decrease	72	85	83	94	77	42
Constant	15	8	8	0	15	25
Increase	12	8	8	6	7	33
Totals	100	100	100	100	100	100
Maintain previous occupation:						
Decrease	60	61	83	42	91	42
Constant	23	26	8	5	4	50
Increase	17	13	8	53	4	8
Totals	100	100	100	100	100	100

Source: Thailand tsunami survey, three Thai provinces, conducted by chapter author, June 2006.

and friends was related to several factors: their need for handouts from friends and relatives to meet living expenses may have been lower; they had better access to savings; and credit markets and outside agencies, including the government, may have provided large scale assistance to restore business assets destroyed by the tsunami.

The Moken community was in a very different situation. If families and friends were also affected by the disaster, or if their friends and relatives were quite poor anyway, their capacity to help each other would have been constrained. In this context, being a migrant may have been an advantage. Migrants had some chance of assistance from relatives and friends living at a distance and unaffected by the tsunami. In fact, after the disaster, the Moken community seems to have recognized the value of being more integrated with the broader Thai society. Moken people have obtained Thai citizenship and thereby have better access to formal education for their families.

Households whose livelihoods have been badly hit by a disaster can seek alternative employment, provided such employment opportunities exist. As Table 6.16 shows, a significant number of households changed occupations. Table 6.17 presents data which shows changes in occupations enabled the maintenance of income levels within different household groups. Most households were forced to accept lower incomes whether or not they remained in the same occupation. This does not mean that changing jobs was of no benefit; those who changed jobs did so because the alternative would have been an even lower level of income or unemployment, and the cost of changing jobs was more than compensated for by the expected earnings in the new occupation.

For many people employed in the tourism industry, or who depended on it, there was considerable pressure to change jobs. As described earlier, the tourism industry was badly hit by the tsunami. As the number of tourists declined, tourist-related businesses were adversely affected and many hotels and restaurants closed down or scaled back their operations. Job losses followed. In some cases, workers accepted lower wages in order to keep their jobs. Those who lost their jobs needed to find new ways to earn a living. But if their skills were industry-specific it was difficult to find new jobs that allowed them to maintain their previous incomes. Hence, many workers who remained in their previous occupations were obliged to accept lower incomes. Only a small percentage could maintain their previous income levels.

As tourism began to recover, wages improved for those employed in the hotel business. There were shortages in specific skilled labour categories because some of the skilled workers had been killed by the tsunami. Many Labourer households who were employed in the tourism industry and remained in their occupation experienced an increase in income by the time of the survey in mid-2006. But the recovery in tourism was not yet sufficient at that stage to restore business for Beach Vendors to previous levels. Over 90 per cent of those who remained in that occupation continued to have lower incomes even in mid-2006. There was a similar story in the case of Fishers whose income declined for several reasons. The tsunami destroyed their boats and fishing nets, limiting their capability to fish. In the first few months after the tsunami, fish consumption in Thailand fell because of public fear that the fish were feeding off corpses in the sea. Further, the oil price shock in 2005 raised the price of diesel, a major cost component in the fishing industry. Thus, even when Fishers were given fishing gear, these various factors constrained their capacity to fully recover their earlier income levels quickly.

Figure 6.6 shows the share of households in each group that engaged in borrowing and the share that did not change their pre-tsunami occupation. Among those who remained in the same occupation, the percentage of families with debts was high. The share ranged from less than 25 per cent among the Moken people to more than 50 per cent among Beach Vendors, Entrepreneurs, Fishers, and Diversified Households. The Moken families, despite their income reduction, incurred lower debts (possibly, however, because they could not access credit) and experienced serious distress. The other surveyed households, in general, had better access to

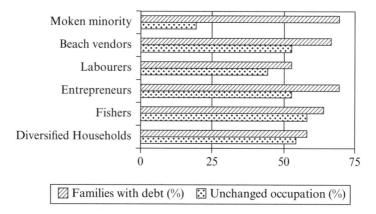

Figure 6.6   Debt and unchanged occupation (%)

credit, thus easing the hardship despite their inability to change occupations. Furthermore, many of those who did not change occupations were
prepared to remain in their occupations in expectation of the recovery of
the tourism and fishery industries. In this case, access to credit was useful
because it helped them to tide over the expected temporary shortfall in
income.

    To sum up, it is clear that whether or not they changed occupations,
households affected by the tsunami experienced significant income losses.
But most people saw the tsunami as a temporary shock and expected the
situation would return to more normal levels after time. Because of this,
many felt that it might be best to stay in the same job while waiting for a
recovery. A new occupation was perhaps seen as useful to make ends meet
in the short term but it was unlikely to be seen as the best option in the
long run.[16]

    These patterns of job movements raise the issue of the effectiveness of
the occupational training for the tsunami victims provided by many agencies. These job training programs may not actually have been of much
help. In the first place, people are less likely to look for new occupations
if the current bad situation is seen as only temporary. In any case, for
people to be attracted to new training programs they need to be able to
see a market for the new skills that will provide compensation for the costs
of long-term occupational change. The survey responses reported here
indicated that many people were not convinced that the benefits from such
training were enough to compensate for the costs. There may be a lesson
of general relevance for job training programs in disaster situations: if the
disaster is seen as only a temporary shock, there may be little incentive for

people to undertake substantial training to prepare for alternative long-term occupations.

Mental Health Issues: Post-traumatic Stress Disorder, Anxiety and Depression

A group of Thai and international medical researchers associated with the Thailand Post-Tsunami Mental Health Study Group documented the significant mental health problems that affected many tsunami victims. Their work was based on surveys conducted in February 2005, only a few weeks after the tsunami, and a follow-up survey in September 2005 (van Griensven et al. 2006). They found a significant incidence of anxiety, depression, and post-traumatic stress disorder (PTSD) eight weeks after the disaster. Nine months after the disaster, these problems had diminished but had not entirely disappeared.

The issue of mental health is not examined in detail in this chapter. Nevertheless, because information on the mental health problems of survey respondents was likely to be useful, several questions were included in the survey for this study that made it possible to construct an index of mental health.[17] Hallucination and paranoia, for example, are symptoms of post-traumatic disorder. Admittedly, the index constructed in the survey was not as comprehensive as the Harvard Trauma Questionnaire and the Hopkins Checklist-25 to detect symptoms of anxiety and depression. Further, respondents may not have revealed the true state of mental stress, depression and PTSD eighteen months after the tsunami. For a group, a mental stress index computed as an average equal to 100 indicated that the group had resolved its depression and could cope with the stress in a stable manner. An index closer to 200 suggests that the group members were still quite saddened by the traumatic experience. A high group index indicated that hallucinations and paranoia were common, suggesting acute PTSD.

Table 6.18 shows the group averages of the mental stress index along with some other indicators associated with mental stresses or concerns. The group averages suggest that, on average, people in the survey group coped with the effects of the tsunami. They were still affected – 'sad' – but were able to accept the tragedy and cope with it. Even the Moken families, who had a higher stress index (144), were not in an acute state of stress or paranoia. However, certainly some individuals within each group suffered from acute mental problems.

People who lost their assets and properties experienced higher mental stress. Moreover, in all groups, anxiety and fear of another tsunami continued to be present among around half of the respondents. In each group some people reported knowing someone who had attempted suicide, but

Table 6.18   Mental health and related factors

	Diversified households (H)	Fishers (F)	Entre-preneurs (E)	Labourers (L)	Beach vendors (B)	Moken (M)
Mental stress index	101	94	100	100	125	144
Received consultation visit	0.69	0.81	0.53	0.61	0.58	0.78
Participated in tsunami drill	0.39	0.58	0.42	0.39	0.53	0.50
Believed that community became more united	0.33	0.36	0.26	0.47	0.33	0.26
Knew someone who attempted suicide	0.21	0.08	0.17	0.11	0.19	0.06
Expected another tsunami	0.56	0.61	0.54	0.43	0.53	0.60
Asset loss (% total)	70.35	67.08	59.58	39.58	51.53	76.94

Source: Thailand tsunami survey, three Thai provinces, conducted by chapter author, June 2006.

the proportion was somewhat lower among Fishers and the Moken people. Only around half the respondents reported participating in a tsunami drill; it is not clear if this helped alleviate anxiety and stress.

As mentioned earlier, mental stress was aggravated if social tensions increased within communities due to perceptions of inequitable distribution of assistance. Respondents were asked about community unity after the tsunami (with a score of 1 if it had strengthened, 0.5 if it was unchanged, and 0 if it had deteriorated). An average group score below 0.5 would suggest, therefore, community cohesion had deteriorated after the tsunami. In fact, the group average was less than 0.5 in all cases indicating a widespread view – though the extent differed between groups – that community cohesion had deteriorated after the tsunami.

An Ordered Probit regression was used to explore the relationship between mental health and a number of likely explanatory variables.

The index (MENTAL) was constructed as described earlier. This index was regressed on the percentage of total assets destroyed by the tsunami (LOSSASSET), expectations of a future tsunami (EXPTSUNAMI), interactions with other victims who attempted to commit suicide (SUICIDE), age (AGE), the number of family members lost in the disaster (LOSSFAMILY), consultation or visits provided by health officials (CONSULT), and perception of community unity (UNITY).

The results (Equation (6A.2) in Appendix 6A.1) suggested that economic loss was a key factor significantly affecting mental health. This finding was consistent with results reported by van Griensven et al. (2006), who found that the loss of livelihood was independently and significantly associated with symptoms of all three mental health outcomes (PTSD, anxiety, and depression). Loss of family members and expectations of future tsunamis, too, adversely affected mental health. On the other hand, a perception that community unity had been strengthened helped reduce mental distress, as did visits or consultations by health officials. Age and knowing someone who had attempted suicide were not significant. These results have obvious policy implications. They highlight the importance of adequate and equitable financial assistance, and the value of visits by health officers to provide counselling and advice.

The Tsunami and Tourist Attitudes

Given the importance of tourism to the regional economy, responses obtained in the survey from a small sample (37) of tourists visiting the three provinces were analysed. The aim was to explore their views and gain insights into ways in which the tourism industry could recover rapidly (Table 6.19). The sample was evenly distributed between new visitors and previous visitors who had returned to the tsunami-affected beaches.

Views expressed by tourists provided grounds for optimism about the recovery of the Thai tourist industry. Some two-thirds of the respondents did not expect another tsunami to hit the area within the next few years. And importantly, they all agreed that the early warning system installed by the government could improve levels of safety. Despite the fact that 22 per cent of the tourists surveyed had known someone who had died in the tsunami, these visitors had nevertheless opted to return to the Andaman area. During the first quarter of 2005, unlike western visitors, Asian visitors reportedly tended to stay away from the affected areas because they felt uneasy about tsunami ghosts. In our sample, more than 80 per cent of the visitors said that they were not afraid of tsunami ghosts. A slight majority (57 per cent) agreed that the media had discouraged tourists, and two-thirds of visitors still saw some traces of the tsunami's destruction.

Table 6.19   Interviews with tourists

	Yes (%)	No (%)
Have you been to Andaman before?	49	51
Do you think that the media has scared visitors away?	57	43
Are you scared of tsunami ghosts?	19	81
Do you think that the next tsunami will hit again within the next few years?	32	68
Do you think that our early warning system can improve safety?	100	0
Do you still recognize any traces of tsunami destruction in this area?	65	35
Did you know anyone who lost their lives here?	22	78

Source: Thailand tsunami survey, three Thai provinces, conducted by chapter author, June 2006.

Respondents were asked to rate the rehabilitation performance of the Thai government in three areas: infrastructure reconstruction, environment restoration, and assistance given to tsunami victims. The overall rating on a scale of 1 to 5 across all three areas was relatively similar and satisfactory: 3.32 (66 per cent) for infrastructure rehabilitation, 3.38 (68 per cent) for environment restoration, and 3.68 (74 per cent) for victim assistance.

In addition, a hypothetical question was included in the survey to gauge the impact of a tsunami in terms of visitor perceptions of safety ('fear'): how many months would it take the respondents to return to the areas if another tsunami were to strike in the future? If visitors had no fear, it can be presumed they would return without hesitation if they had the opportunity. But some visitors may have been deterred from a return visit by several factors – such as the fear of another tsunami; the grim picture painted by the media; a poor reconstruction effort by the government; or perhaps fear of tsunami spirits and ghosts. While recognizing that the sample included only visitors who had already returned and was therefore biased, a multiple regression model was used to get some indication of the extent to which these factors may influence tourists to delay returning to the region, taking the measure of 'fear' as a proxy.

The results suggested that grim pictures presented by the media were likely to have a significant deterrent effect, interacting with the perception of tourists about the rebuilding effort of the government (see the detailed results in Equation (6A.3) in Appendix 6A.1). The fear of tsunami ghosts, interacting with the number of previous visits, was the most significant variable in the equation. This variable was more important than other variables representing expectations of a future tsunami and the positive effects of successful government efforts in rebuilding.

Even if tourists did return, a critical issue for the Thai tourist industry was the duration of stay. Another regression was used (using the number of days visitors would stay in the area as the dependent variable), hypothesized to test the fear factor, the media scare variable, and an Asian dummy variable, given that Asian visitors tend to have different behavioural characteristics to other visitors. The results (Equation (6A.4) in Appendix 6A.1) suggest that, as expected, fear reduced the expected duration of stay. Further, media scare was particularly important as a negative factor for Asian tourists. This finding – if confirmed by other studies of a more representative sample – would indicate that efforts to promote tourism through discount holiday packages and marketing promotions may not work well for Asian markets. On the other hand, favourable media coverage, highlighting the successful rehabilitation of the areas and the tourism industry overall, may have been expected to have a more positive impact on Asian tourism.

ASSISTANCE ASSESSMENT

Quality, Level, and Effectiveness of Assistance

A major aim of the field survey was to obtain the views of the tsunami victims on the impact of the aid program for relief, reconstruction and recovery. Respondents were asked to evaluate the assistance from various organizations on a scale of 1 to 4.[18]

The survey results indicated that respondents in all categories received assistance from government, foundations, and private corporations. In many cases, the role of government assistance was complementary to corporations and charity foundations. The government and other organizations sometimes pooled their resources to provide, for example, housing for families whose houses had been destroyed. Similarly, private corporations contributed to financing housing construction done by army units. None of the survey respondents reported any systematic bias in the provision of government assistance.

However, the overall level of satisfaction was not very high (Figure 6.7). Still, this response must be treated with some caution. It is possible that respondents may have rated the overall assistance not very highly in hope of getting more aid in future. Moreover, there was substantial variation among the groups in their assessments of the various donor

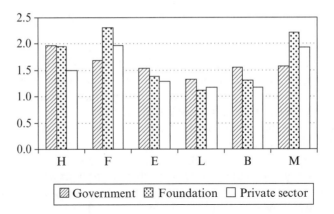

Note: H: households; F: fishers; E: entrepreneurs; L: labourers; B: beach vendors; M: Moken minority.

Figure 6.7   Comparative evaluation of donors

agencies. While Diversified Households, Entrepreneurs, Labourers, and Beach Vendors ranked assistance from the government equal to, or higher than the assistance from the private sector and foundations, Fishers and Moken people rated assistance from foundations and private corporations as superior.

A series of questions was asked about cash needs, the amount received, the speed of disbursement, and adequacy (Figure 6.8). Again, the responses have to be treated with caution because respondents are likely to have felt that their answers might affect the amount that they would get in the future so they may have tended to overestimate their need for cash aid while underestimating the amount they had received.

Respondents rated the amount of cash grants they had received on the following scale: 0 for no grant, 1 for little, 2 for moderate, 3 for large (high), and 4 for very high. In addition, they were asked to rate their need for future cash grants on the same scale. While there were differences between the categories, the overall responses indicated that what they had received was low to moderate, and that low to moderate levels of cash assistance were still needed.

As for the speed of cash disbursement, respondents who did not get any cash were assigned a score of 0, 1 if arrangements took more than a month, 2 if two weeks, 3 if within one week, and 4 if cash was provided immediately. Most people got cash aid within a month. The average rating for speed of cash delivery was 1.5, implying that cash aid, on average, was received within about three weeks of the tsunami, but in the case of some

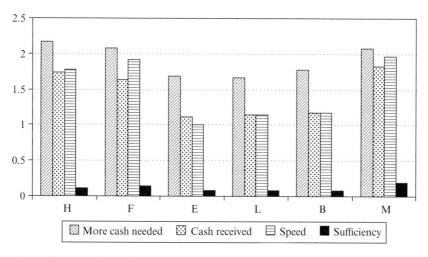

Note: H: households; F: fishers; E: entrepreneurs; L: labourers; B: beach vendors; M: Moken minority.

Figure 6.8 Cash grants: sufficiency and speed

groups it was faster (one to two weeks) – including Fishers and Moken people – but for others, including Beach Vendors and Labourer households, it was closer to a month.

As to the question whether they received a sufficient amount of cash aid, if the respondent answered no, the score given was 0, and if yes, the score given was 1. (Note the difference in the scale for this question when interpreting the height of the column in Figure 6.8.) The score for this sufficiency question was very low, ranging from 0.08 (Labourers) to 0.19 (Moken). Again, these scores may have been highly influenced by the perception that responses might influence future assistance levels.

As mentioned earlier, the provision of job training was another aspect of assistance. According to the survey responses, assistance with job training was provided at a relatively late stage – about seven to twelve months after the tsunami.

In Figure 6.9 the survey responses across groups to questions on areas of need for future assistance are shown. Respondents ranked each category of demand on a scale of 0 to 4. Leaving aside the question on business assistance, which was only directed to respondents in the Entrepreneur group, the type of assistance that respondents ranked as being most important was cash grants, followed by job training, housing, and health care.[19]

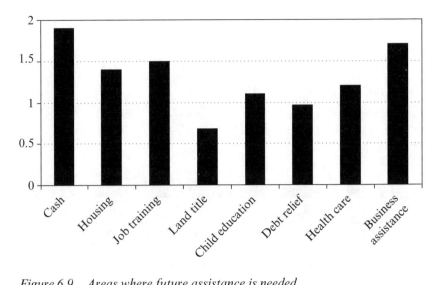

Figure 6.9   Areas where future assistance is needed

Build Back Better

In all the main tsunami-affected countries reconstruction activities have
been conducted under the slogan 'build back better'. The basic idea was
that new construction would not simply replace what existed previously
but would be superior in quality. Community perceptions of the effectiveness of this approach were investigated by focusing on a key component
of the reconstruction effort: the reconstruction of damaged or destroyed
houses. Respondents who had received housing assistance were asked to
indicate whether the quality of their newly constructed house was better
than their old house.

There were reports both in Thailand and in other tsunami-affected
countries of many instances where communities were not happy with their
new houses. It is admittedly not easy to interpret these reports. People
traumatized by the experience of a disaster might react to new homes in
different ways. In a depressed state, they might view a new house as being
an inferior replacement to their old dwelling even if the new house was in
fact a superior structure. Alternatively, they might rate it as better because
they had lowered their expectations due to reduced circumstances of
unemployment, debt, and so on.

This matter was investigated using a model with a dummy dependent
variable, Build Back Better (BBB), which was assigned the value of 1 if

the new house was perceived as a better house than the old one and 0 if otherwise (see Equation (6A.5) in Appendix 6A.1). The probit regression results suggest that the economic circumstances of households may indeed have been related to how they viewed their new houses. Households which suffered serious economic losses, or had experienced a long period of unemployment, or were in pressing need of more cash assistance (a proxy for being liquidity-constrained) were more likely to rate their new house as better.

Psychological factors (mental distress and loss of family members) ranked lower in the model than economic factors.[20] While the results are not conclusive, it does appear that those who lost almost everything tended to appreciate the value of their new houses while those who did not lose much had higher expectations of the quality of the houses offered to them. Those who suffered relatively smaller losses tended to deny the notion of build back better.

Role of NGOs

Information from the perspectives of the NGOs was obtained in interviews with NGO representatives.

NGOs were involved in a range of assistance activities in Thailand. Some of them provided livelihood equipment and job training, initiated health consciousness campaigns, and set up organic farms and child care centres. They also provided education-related assistance such as providing English teaching, giving student scholarships to tsunami-affected children, and building community libraries.

But there were problems. Many of the NGOs interviewed reported that gaining cooperation from villagers was sometimes a problem. There was sometimes a perception in the communities that the NGOs would only be active for a short period and thus could not be relied on for longer-term assistance.[21] This made people reluctant to contribute to or participate in NGO programs. Some NGOs admitted that lack of coordination between them has produced overlap, leading to inequitable and inefficient delivery of assistance. The result has been to produce a sense of unfair treatment among recipients and to contribute to a deterioration of social cohesion among villagers.

However the story was complicated because there was another side to it. Many NGOs encountered avaricious aid recipients who resorted to deception with fake claims of damages and injury – sometimes even using corpses that belonged to other families – to claim compensation and assistance. With assistance focused on material and cash handouts, some children were reportedly disappointed that they were not orphaned because they received less assistance from the NGOs.

Aid Dependency?

In the literature on aid, a frequently expressed concern is that aid recipients can develop an 'aid dependency' attitude that constrains them from taking private initiatives to move beyond aid recipient status. While eighteen months after the tsunami may be a relatively short period to assess attitudes on this matter, a preliminary analysis of survey responses was conducted to see if any sign of such a syndrome was apparent. Some indications of the existence of an 'aid dependency' syndrome may be considered to be present if people who had received substantial assistance continued to rate their assistance needs as high (even though they should have had lower assistance needs). When respondents were asked if they still needed additional cash aid in 2007, those who suffered greatly from asset destruction and income reduction were more likely to reply 'yes'. But those who had received a new house and a secured land title were surely unlikely to have really required more cash and should have needed to depend less on financial aid. We explored whether these types of propositions were supported by the survey responses.

An index (in log values) was constructed to measure the degree of cash dependency. The ratio of desired cash in 2007 was compared to the cash aid that respondents had received in 2006. If value of the ratio of need for cash (NMCASH) to the cash received (RECASH) was negative, households' expressed need for cash aid was considered lower. If the value was positive, the expressed need was considered higher, suggesting a tendency towards growing aid dependency. As seen in Figure 6.10, the kernel density distribution was tilted to the positive region indicating that there was indeed evidence supporting the aid dependency view. However, this matter needs further analysis to examine why respondents continued to ask for cash aid.

This was tested further undertaking a multivariate analysis. A dependent variable MORECASH was defined as the difference between cash 'needed' in 2007 and the sufficiency of cash previously received.[22]

The results (Equation (6A.6) in Appendix 6A.1) show that those who believed they had received adequate cash (SUFCASH) tended not to express a need for more financial assistance. Also, it is interesting to note that those who had borrowed tend not to seek more money. A possible explanation is that the fact that they had borrowed indicates that they had access to credit markets and hence were not highly credit-constrained and did not seek more handouts from donors. Looking at variables that are statistically significant and positive, only people who lost their livelihoods through mental depression and suffered a large income loss after the tsunami appear likely to have continued to demand more cash aid.

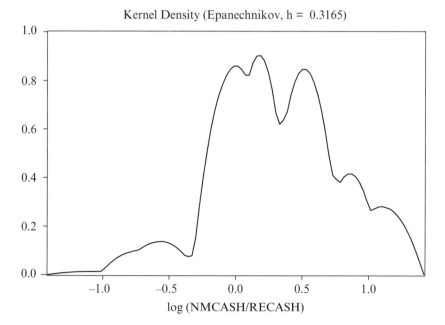

Figure 6.10   Distribution of demand for aid with respect to aid received

In sum, weighing these factors up, there is no strong evidence to support the aid-dependency view. The finding that those who were able to adjust through borrowing tended not to ask for continuing handouts is significant. The indications are that once difficulties in the immediate aftermath of the disaster were overcome, tsunami victims were not likely to become aid dependent provided they had access to credit markets. In addition, employment-generating programs – which would enhance their capacity to both borrow and repay – were likely to give tsunami victims a better chance to lead normal lives without having to depend on long-term aid.

Other Impacts of Assistance

Several other aspects related to aid and assistance have not been explored. There were concerns, for example, that the cultural heritage of the minority Moken people might be lost due to the provision of large amounts of assistance which some feared might erode their traditional way of life. Moken children, some argued, no longer cared about their language and culture, and money and material belongings had become the dominant objectives in their lives. They blamed this on the fact that their rebuilt community was located near the road linked to city areas. Donors certainly need to be sensitive to such unintended impacts of large-scale assistance and reconstruction activities.

CONCLUSION

This chapter has discussed the responses to the December 2004 tsunami disaster in Thailand. In 2006, two years after the tragedy, the human dimensions of the disaster were still acute but it was clear that Thailand had made major steps towards recovering from the worst economic effects.

There is a consensus that the initial relief effort was satisfactory given the unpredicted nature of the disaster and the further complications created by having a very large number of foreign tourists among the victims. The huge international media coverage of the tsunami led to an outpouring of offers of assistance from governments and communities around the world. Thailand, however, refused to solicit official financial assistance for the recovery and reconstruction phase, preferring to rely on domestic sources and organizations. The domestic community and corporate sector response was very positive leading some analysts to argue that the decision to rely on domestic finances probably ensured a stronger overall response than would otherwise have been the case.

The largest economic impact was on the tourism industry followed by the impact on the fisheries sector in southern Thailand. In contrast to the situation in Indonesia and Sri Lanka, economic losses were not primarily caused by damage to physical assets and infrastructure but by losses from forgone earnings in the tourism sector. In the tourism industry, the tsunami did not completely destroy all hotels and other facilities even in affected regions. However large losses were caused by the sharp fall in tourist arrivals. The immediate impact on the regional economy was severe. But the overall effects of the tsunami on the wider national economy – even in the short term – were muted by the fact that there were alternative destinations available for tourists within Thailand. Overall, initial estimates of the negative impact on the economy were quickly revised. Indeed, in the two years following the tsunami there was a general recovery in tourist arrivals in Thailand even though many Asian tourists were somewhat reluctant to return.

The relief and subsequent reconstruction efforts were facilitated by the relative proximity of the affected areas to the Bangkok metropolitan region. Relatively easy access to the region meant that emergency assistance could be provided quickly. The availability of a large pool of construction labour and materials allowed reconstruction activities to be undertaken without major supply-side constraints. In particular, with a construction sector that had yet to recover fully from depressed demand in the wider economy, the demand generated by reconstruction efforts in the tsunami-affected region did not produce the kinds of cost increases seen elsewhere. In other words, reconstruction efforts in Thailand were not affected by cost increases associated with Dutch Disease effects of a construction boom seen, for example, in Indonesia.

Though the immediate response to the disaster within the first few weeks of the tsunami can be considered a success, poor coordination among aid donors, NGOs, and aid recipients hampered effective delivery, and sometimes led to inequities and waste in aid distribution. Some job training programs did not lead to employment because they did not provide skills that were in demand in regional labour markets. In any case, the fact that the disaster was seen as a temporary (one-off) shock meant that most people were not interested in undertaking costly training for a new occupation. The assistance they sought in the short term was primarily for financial assistance (cash) or for access to credit markets so that they could cope with the immediate problems caused by loss of incomes and livelihoods. In the longer term, they primarily sought aid to restore their damaged or destroyed assets.

The overall reconstruction effort, despite some of these limitations, was seen by most people in Thailand as reasonably successful. However, the experience of the post-tsunami reconstruction effort suggests that greater direct cash aid, improved access to credit markets (including microfinance), and better coordination among aid agencies is needed. The provision of these kinds of assistance can also address concerns about aid dependency. The survey reported on in this chapter did not find any evidence that aid dependency was a problem in Thailand following the Asian tsunami. Most people who continued to ask for aid did so because they genuinely needed financial assistance. Most of these people had lost their livelihoods, were unemployed, or had little or no access to credit markets.

Many of the inefficiencies in aid programs reflected the problems of supply-driven assistance. Beyond the immediate emergency relief stage where food, medicine, clothing and basic shelter were priorities, direct cash assistance would have allowed most households to obtain what they required from nearby markets. While supply-oriented assistance cannot be avoided during the immediate response phase because donating agencies and corporations are most efficient in utilizing their core competencies, the reconstruction experience highlighted the need to adopt a more demand-oriented, participatory approach during the period of rehabilitation and reconstruction. More participatory approaches are needed so that aid can be effectively channelled into areas of greatest need in cooperation with local communities.[23]

Broader issues have been raised about the need for greater preparedness to face natural disasters. These include establishment of early warning systems, development of greater community awareness about natural disasters and how to prepare for them, and use of market instruments on the part of the private sector and households to insure against damages from such disasters. Subsidized insurance policies covering catastrophic losses, through providing tax incentives to market participants, can encourage the development of disaster insurance markets and induce private firms to get involved. This public subsidy would be less costly than supporting post-disaster relief programs. Some progress has already been made with early warning systems. However, the relative infrequency of megadisasters may mean that in the absence of any similar huge disaster in the near future, community recognition of the need to prepare for future disasters may not be sustained.

There are also broader lessons for the international community. The Thai government did not seek financial assistance from the international community; indeed it encouraged international donors to direct their assistance to countries such as Indonesia and Sri Lanka which suffered more than Thailand and which were less able to generate the financial resources needed for reconstruction. However Thailand did ask for a different form of assistance from developed countries: it requested the lifting of barriers that prevented access to donor markets for Thailand's exports. Thailand argued that the removal of tariff and non-tariff barriers is the best kind of assistance developed countries can give to developing countries hit by disasters. Such market access would give developing countries a chance to achieve sustainable recovery. Regrettably, this request was largely ignored, despite the oft-repeated rhetoric of many foreign governments that trade is better than aid as a form of development assistance.

NOTES

1. Bhanupong Nidhiprabha was primarily responsible for this chapter which draws on Nidhiprabha (2007).
2. See Telford et al. (2006).
3. United Nations and World Bank (2005): p. 19.
4. Telford et al. (2006).
5. By December 2006, the last 440 unidentified bodies, believed to be migrant workers from Myanmar, had been buried in the cemetery for unidentified tsunami victims in Kao Lak. Their DNA samples had been collected for possible future identification.
6. Phang Nga suffered most in terms of destroyed hotels. Although the number of hotels in Krabi did not fall much, the number of rooms in operation was reduced by almost 12 per cent because some large hotels were badly affected.

7. JP Morgan thus underestimated the first quarter growth, while both JP Morgan and Morgan Stanley overestimated the annual growth rate.
8. This led the World Bank in November 2005 to reduce its growth forecast from 5.2 to 4.2 per cent, and the Asian Development Bank, also highlighting the role of tourism, warned that the current account deficit in 2005 would worsen further if tourist arrival numbers did not recover during the peak season in the last quarter of 2005 (ADB 2005).
9. Note that some of these expenses may be subsequently recoverable in the form of paid-back principal and investment returns. In addition, these measures may yield subsequent tax revenues as they indirectly generate employment.
10. See Nazara and Resosudarmo (2007) and Jayasuriya et al. (2006).
11. Ironically, the SME Bank had the highest rate of non-performing other loans among financial institutions in Thailand – at 35 per cent of total outstanding loans amounting to 16 billion baht in 2006.
12. The NDWC paid six million baht to the Navy to install the buoy and patrol the area to prevent approaching vessels from getting too close to the beacon.
13. Bernhard et al. (2005) have argued that the Thai government's rejection of official aid from other countries may have encouraged corporate donors to make a larger contribution.
14. There are a number of microfinance organizations operating in Thailand, including the Small Enterprise Development Corporation, which serves 15 000 clients in the northeast region of Thailand. Coleman (2006) found that microcredit may not reach the core poor of northeast Thailand because wealthier villagers participate more than the poor and become committee members who borrow significantly more than rank and file members.
15. There were significantly more male respondents than females in the Fisher and Labourer categories (81 per cent and 58 per cent, respectively) while there were more females within the Entrepreneur (64 per cent) and the Moken categories (56 per cent). In other categories (Diversified Households and Beach Vendors) the gender numbers were approximately equal.
16. People were apparently likely to move into areas where they did not have comparative advantage if they changed occupations.
17. The index was constructed on the following basis. If a person able to carry on with their normal way of life as if nothing had happened, a score of 0 was given. If a person accepted their misfortune, but acted with resolve and coped well with the crisis, a score of 100 was given. The score was raised to 200 if they were still in a state of acute sadness; to 300 if they suffered from hallucinations; and to 400 if they were paranoid. All scores were assigned by enumerators after interviews with respondents.
18. Scores used were 0 when there was no help at all, 1 for a low level of assistance, 2 for medium assistance, 3 for high assistance and 4 for the highest level of help.
19. The F-tests of means and variances indicate statistical differences at a 0.01 level of significance.
20. It must be recognized that there is a co-linearity problem between the number of family members lost and mental health deterioration, which may lead to the coefficient of psychological factors becoming statistically non-significant.
21. More than 70 per cent of the NGOs interviewed were not planning to stay in the areas longer than three years.
22. A Tobit model was used because respondents are likely to overstate their amount of cash aid needed, hoping to receive more cash, and are likely to understate the amount of aid they received. Hence we used a censored model with extreme values, -3 and 3, resulting in three observations left censored and ten observations right censored.
23. The pattern of financial assistance provided to tsunami victims has set the standard for mitigating the impact of other natural disasters. Thailand is prone to frequent floods and droughts. In early 2006, the victims of flash floods and mudslides were given US$600 000 from a contingent budget earmarked for natural disaster relief.

REFERENCES

ADB (Asian Development Bank) (2005), 'An initial assessment of the impact of the earthquake and tsunami of December 26, 2004 on South and Southeast Asia', online Note, January.

Bernhard, Richard, Y. Yritsilpe and O. Petchkul (2005), 'Corporate philanthropy in Thailand', in *Philanthropy in Disasters: Tsunami and After*, Conference Proceedings of the Asian Pacific Philanthropy Consortium, Kenan Institute, Phuket, 28–30 November.

Coleman, Brett E. (2006), 'Microfinance in Northeast Thailand: who benefits and how much?', *World Development*, **34** (9),1612–38.

Counts, Alex, L. Collins, G. Octavio and V. Rai (2005), *Recovery from the Tsunami Disaster: Poverty Reduction and Sustainable Development through Microfinance*, Special Report, 26 May, USA: Grameen Foundation.

FAO (2005), *Tsunami Impact on Fisheries and Aquaculture in Thailand*, Joint Report of the NACA, FAO, SEAFDEC and BOBP-IGO, 14 January.

Jayasuriya, Sisira, P. Steele and D. Weerakoon (2006), *Post-Tsunami Recovery: Issues and Challenges in Sri Lanka*, ADB Institute Research Paper 71, January.

Kunreuther, Howard and M. Pauly (2006), *Rules Rather than Discretion: Lessons from Hurricane Katrina*, NBER Working Paper 12503, August.

Nazara, Suahasil and B.P. Resosudarmo (2007), *Aceh-Nias Reconstruction and Rehabilitation: Progress and Challenges at the End of 2006*, ADBI Discussion Paper 70, http://www.adbi.org/files/dp70.acehnias.reconstruction.rehabilitation.pdf, accessed 31 October 2009.

Nidhiprabha, Bhanupong (2007), *Adjustment and Recovery in Thailand Two Years after the Tsunami*, ADBI Discussion Paper 72, http://www.adbi.org/files/dp72.thailand.tsunami.adjustment.recovery.pdf, accessed 31 October 2009.

Telford, John, J. Cosgrave and R. Houghton (2006), *Joint Evaluation of the International Response to the Indian Ocean Tsunami: Synthesis Report,* London: Tsunami Evaluation Coalition.

United Nations and World Bank (2005), *Tsunami Thailand, One Year Later–National Response and the Contribution of International Partners*, http://www.reliefweb.int/rwarchive/rwb.nsf/db900sid/RMOI-6KF8KS?OpenDocument&Click=, accessed 31 October 2009.

van Griensven, Frits, M.L. Somchai Chakkraband, W. Thienkrua, W. Pengjuntr, B. Lopes Cardozo, P. Tantipiwatanaskul, P.A. Mock, S. Ekassawin, A. Varangrat, C. Gotway, M. Sabin and J.W. Tappero (2006), 'Mental health problems among adults in tsunami-affected areas in Southern Thailand', *Journal of American Medical Association*, **296** (5), 537–48.

World Conference on Disaster Reduction (WCDR) (2006), *Thailand Country Report 2006*, WCDR.

APPENDIX 6A.1

(1) Demand for Credit (CREDIT)

Method: Least Squares, 85 observations
White Heteroskedasticity-Consistent Standard Errors & Covariance

$$\text{CREDIT} = 1.845 - 0.002 \text{ INTEREST} + 0.507 \text{ LOG (TOTAL-AID)}$$
$$\quad\quad (1.070) (-1.967)^{**} \quad\quad\quad (3.332)^{***} \quad\quad\quad\quad (6A.1)$$

$$+ 0.507 \text{ BUSINESS-LOAN} + 0.771 \text{ COLLATERAL}$$
$$(1.750)^* \quad\quad\quad\quad\quad (2.996)^{**}$$

$$+ 0.245 \text{ LOG(YB*UNEMPLOY)}$$
$$(2.082)^{***}$$

Adjusted R-squared: 0.255
F-statistic: 6.755
Prob (F-statistic) 0.000

(2) Mental Health Problems (MENTAL)

Method: ML – Ordered Probit (Quadratic hill climbing), 252 observations
Number of ordered indicator values: 5

$$\text{MENTAL} = 0.366 \text{ EXPTSUNAMI} + 0.286 \text{ SUICIDE}$$
$$(2.122)^{***} \quad\quad\quad\quad (1.550) \quad\quad\quad\quad\quad (6A.2)$$

$$+ 0.016 \text{ LOSSASSET} - 0.005 \text{ CONSULT*LOSSASSET}$$
$$(4.171)^{***} \quad\quad\quad\quad (-2.260)^{***}$$

$$- 0.334 \text{ UNITY} + 0.281 \text{ LOSSFAMILY} + 0.006 \text{ AGE}$$
$$(-2.083)^{***} \quad (1.857)^* \quad\quad\quad\quad\quad (1.217)$$

LR statistic (7 df) 40.0442
LR index (Pseudo-R2) 0.063
Probability (LR stat) 1.23E-06

(3) Tourist Attitude (FEAR)

Method: Least Squares, 37 observations

$$FEAR = 5.853 - 4.953\ MEDIASCARE*REBUILDING$$
$$(3.340)\ (-2.596)*** \hspace{3cm} (6A.3)$$
$$+\ 2.460\ EXPTSUNAMI + 16.14\ GHOST*VISIT$$
$$(1.040) \hspace{3cm} (7.005)***$$

Adjusted R-squared   0.321
F-statistic   6.697
Prob(F-statistic)   0.0011

(4) Stay Length (STAY-LENGTH)

Method: Least Squares, 37 observations
White Heteroskedasticity-Consistent Standard Errors & Covariance

$$STAY\text{-}LENGTH = 18.68 - 0.472\,FEAR - 10.86\,MEDIASCARE*ASIAN$$
$$(5.030)\ (-2.209)*** \quad (-3.227)*** \hspace{2cm} (6A.4)$$

Adjusted R-squared   0.201
S.E. of regression   10.559
F-statistic   5.551
Prob (F-statistic)   0.008

(5) Build Back Better (BBB)

Method: ML – Binary Probit (Quadratic hill climbing)
Sample: 146, 58 observations with B=0, 88 observations with B=1
QML (Huber/White) standard errors & covariance

$$BBB = 5.998 - 1.253LOG(LOSSASSET) + 0.205\ NMCASH$$
$$(2.638)\ (-2.359)*** \hspace{2.5cm} (1.749)* \hspace{1.5cm} (6A.5)$$
$$-\ 0.159\ LOSSFAMILY - 3.18E\text{-}06\ DEBT - 0.102\ MENTAL$$
$$(-0.668) \hspace{2.5cm} (-1.731)* \hspace{1.5cm} (-1.281)$$
$$-\ 0.047\ UNEMPLOY$$
$$(-2.357)***$$

Z-statistics in parentheses
LR statistic (6 df)   22.159
McFadden R-squared   0.112
Probability(LR stat)   0.0011

(6) Aid Dependency (MORECASH)

Method: ML – Censored Normal (TOBIT) (Quadratic hill climbing), 252 observations

$$\text{MORECASH} = 0.346 - 8.05\text{E-07 DEB} + 8.52\text{E-07 UNEMPLOY*YB}$$
$$\quad (3.312)\ (-2.542)^{***} \qquad (3.172)^{***} \qquad\qquad (6A.6)$$

$$+ 0.132\ \text{MENTAL} - 0.763\ \text{SUFCASH}$$
$$\quad (2.508)^{***} \qquad\qquad (-3.380)^{***}$$

Adjusted R-squared   0.120
S.E. of regression   1.098

***, **, and * significant at the 1, 5, and 10 per cent level, respectively.

Definition of Variables

AGE	Age of respondents
ASIAN	Dummy variable = 1 if Asian visitor, 0 otherwise
BBB	Dummy variable for build back better house, 1 if better, 0 otherwise
BUSINESS-LOAN	Dummy variable for loan purpose, business = 1, 0 other purpose
CONSULT	Dummy variable = 1 if received consultation or visits by health officials, 0 otherwise
COLLATERAL	Dummy variable for loan collateral requirement 1 if required, 0 otherwise
CREDIT	Amount of borrowing
DEBT	Amount of debt incurred after the tsunami
EXPTSUNAMI	Dummy variable = 1, if respondent expects another tsunami within a few years, 0 otherwise
FEAR	A proxy for fear of tsunami (number of months required before returning to the area where the tsunami struck)
GHOST	Dummy variable = 1 if respondent is afraid of tsunami ghosts and spirits, 0 otherwise

INTEREST	Interest rate on loan
LOSSASSET	Percentage of destroyed assets
LOSSFAMILY	Number of family members lost
MEDIASCARE	Dummy variable = 1 if respondent agreed that media has scared visitors away, 0 otherwise
MENTAL	Index of mental health: normal = 0, resolve=1, sad = 2, hallucination = 3, paranoid = 4
MORECASH	Difference between need for more cash aid (NMCASH) and sufficiency of cash aid previously received (SUFCASH)
NMCASH	Liquidity constraint expressed by degree of need for cash
REBUILDING	Dummy variable for visitors' perception of the rebuilding in the area: 1 if there are traces of physical damage, 0 otherwise
SUICIDE	Dummy variable = 1 if knowing other victims who had attempted to commit suicide, 0 otherwise
SUFCASH	Sufficiency of cash aid previously received
STAY-LENGTH	Number of days visitors would prefer to stay
TOTAL-AID	Total amount of financial aid
UNEMPLOY	Number of months being unemployed after the tsunami
UNITY	Variable representing the perception of changes in community unity: 1 if strengthened, 0.5 if unchanged, 0 if deteriorated
VISIT	Number of previous visits in the Andaman area
YB	Pre-tsunami monthly income.

7.   Conclusion

INTRODUCTION

In the wake of a great disaster it is natural to look for hope. We can, we think, at least draw lessons which will help guide us in the future. We can do better next time, we tell ourselves. We hope that the pain that vast numbers of people have suffered will not be in vain. This chapter will consider how realistic such hopes may be in the light of the 2004 Asian tsunami events and consider what lessons may be drawn from the experience of the delivery of aid following the tsunami.

But for those who read these pages hoping for guidelines that can ensure considerable improvements in the delivery of disaster aid in development countries, a warning is in order. One of the main lessons of the delivery of assistance following the 2004 Asian tsunami is that much confusion and conflict is inevitable in the immediate aftermath of such situations. Local emergency institutions in poor countries are almost always greatly over-stretched in crises of this kind. The international community rarely responds much better either. Indeed, our single most important conclusion is that it is local communities – rather than the national or international communities – who are quickest to provide the most valuable practical immediate assistance following a great disaster. The policy implication is that within the extremely limited funding available to support emergency relief measures in poor countries, much greater priority needs to be given to strengthening *local preparedness* rather than funding delayed responses in the aftermath of the event.

It is worth pausing to consider this view. Other approaches need to be considered. One alternative view outlined in the United Nations' first biennial global assessment of disaster risk reduction issued in 2009 is that the emphasis of policy should be on disaster risk reduction (ISDR 2009). According to this view, the emphasis should be less on preparedness and more on action at an even earlier stage with the aim of reducing the risks of disaster and with the ultimate aim of minimizing the risk that a disaster will strike at all. Another view, implicit in the current approach of the international community, is that it is post-disaster responses which are important. According to this view – which embodies a reactive approach to disasters in poor countries – donors should essentially stand ready to respond with various forms of assistance after a disaster has occurred.

Certainly these views need careful consideration. But one of the most important conclusions set out in this chapter is that it is to *local prepared-ness* that governments in developing countries and international donor agencies alike should give more attention. And there are other key lessons as well. In considering these other lessons it will be useful to consider, first, the stages of the initial response to the tsunami disaster, then coordina-tion issues, and third, aid delivery, before finally setting out some main conclusions. A main theme will be that coordination of the relief effort was difficult at every stage and that international donors, especially, need to consider how they might do things better when future megadisasters strike in developing countries.

STAGES OF RESPONSE

Numerous reviews of the overall response to the tsunami disaster noted that the process of providing assistance passed through distinct phases. The sequencing diagram shown as Figure 4.4 in Chapter 4 (Nazara and Resosudarmo) has been widely referred to as a useful schema which illus-trates, in broad terms, how the overall response evolved over time. What the sequencing diagram does not illustrate, however, are the different con-tributions that the various communities and levels of government made at different stages during and following the disaster.

Local Responses

Because the fact is so important, it needs to be appreciated that the first, immediate response to the disaster, almost everywhere, was at the local level. In most places devastated by the tsunami, outside help did not start arriving for at least 24 hours. Indeed, in several places little significant outside help arrived for four or five days – and this, in fits and starts, in an uncoordinated way, as disaster relief systems at the national level began to comprehend the scope of the emergency (Kilby 2007: 124). Numerous community groups and local enterprises in the informal economy, largely out of sight of national agencies and generally invisible to the international community, swung into action immediately. As a Tsunami Global Lessons Learned Project report noted (TGLL 2009: 49): 'The unsung heroes were thousands of small merchants, hoteliers and enterprises situated away from the coast, with the assets, equipment and initiative to commit all to the humanitarian crisis long before outside help was at hand.'

This fact – that the fastest provision of first aid tends to be from the local level – is of central importance in considering future strategies for disaster response in poor countries. The phenomenon has been noted in the case of other disasters in developing countries as well. In India and Pakistan, for example, in October 2005, when a megadisaster caused by an earthquake killed around 75 000 people, it was observed that (Brennan and Waldman 2006: 1769–70):

> International urban search-and-rescue teams arrived within days, but their heroic efforts probably saved relatively few lives: such interventions are generally responsible for only a small part of the public health effort of relief efforts since most survivors are rescued by community members in the first hours or days.

Some of the main implications of this phenomenon, implications which surely need to be considered more carefully by international donor organizations, are taken up below.

National Response

The second set of early responses to the tsunami arrived from the national level. In Sri Lanka and Thailand, accurate details of the local situation began to arrive in the capital faster than was the case in Indonesia. In Indonesia, the terrible news from the distant provincial capital of Banda Aceh trickled into Jakarta only slowly. Key telecommunication and road systems had been severed by the tsunami in Aceh so there was a good deal of confusion at first. In all of the affected countries, it took some days for the under-resourced national emergency systems to comprehend fully the scope of the disaster.

International Responses

International responses to disasters in poor countries usually take some time to arrive. So it was with the provision of international assistance for the Asian tsunami. There are several factors which often lead to significant delays in the response.

For one thing, it often takes time for news to filter out into the western media from remote places in poor countries. And when the Asian tsunami struck, the western media tended to focus on stories about the plight of westerners caught up in the tsunami (Kivikuru 2006). This meant that popular tourist locations in Thailand and Sri Lanka received extensive coverage early on while news from barely known places such as Banda Aceh tended to receive less attention. As one of the main Tsunami

Evaluation Coalition reports (Cosgrave 2005: 6) observed 'Less than 1 percent of those who died were tourists, but these got most of the media attention in donor countries. One study found that 40 percent of western media coverage on people affected by the disaster dealt with tourists.' So the news of the total numbers of dead – and the real scale of the disaster – took time to seep out to western countries where the local media was still caught up in the joyous mood of Christmas rather than focusing on the harsh realities of disasters in distant poor countries. The reaction of many in the Asian region was reflected in the dismay of one Indonesian who recalled that (Tuli: 2007):

> I remember my disbelief when international media attention remained focused on those islands where Western tourists had died. It was like saying locals didn't suffer as much because the colour of their skin wasn't white. Does a darker skin preclude one from feeling pain? Are our dreams and hopes and wishes any less important?

The harsh but honest answer is that for western media agencies reporting from disaster sites, the dreams and hopes and wishes of local people in far-flung places like Aceh and Sri Lanka are indeed less important than the plight of western tourists. Western media firms are commercial organizations. They see their main business as that of providing consumers in rich countries with interesting news, not to provide a voice to people from developing countries.

For another, when news of a disaster arrives it takes time for donor agencies to consider responses, organize campaigns, and raise money. This is true for both non-governmental organizations (NGOs) and for governments. NGOs, if they are swift, can sometimes begin to deliver initial supplies within a week or so, but significant policy responses from international governments generally take longer.

Third, in the case of donor governments especially, most official aid agencies find it difficult to respond quickly. Their operating culture, and the usual planning and disbursement procedures, are not geared for rapid action. Indeed, the culture of the western aid industry is to exercise caution and restraint, to build in strong checks against corruption, and to call for surveys to be prepared before committing themselves to action. All of these things militate against a rapid response.

Staging Issues: Policy Considerations

Some of the policy implications of focusing on the different stages of disaster response are discussed below. But two issues for policy may be mentioned here.

First, the most urgent need in the period immediately after a disaster is for *fast* assistance. The first 24 hours – and indeed the first few hours – are crucial. The medical (and military) concept of 'the golden hour' is relevant in this context. The golden hour refers to the first 60 minutes after a major disaster or medical event and is so called because the victim's chances of survival are greatest if emergency assistance can be provided within that time. In emergency medicine, for example, the golden hour is the first hour after injury during which treatment greatly increases survivability. The idea has been adapted to post-conflict transition terminology where it is often taken to be the first year after hostilities end. Without steadily improving conditions in the first year, popular support declines and chances for economic, political, and social transformation begin to evaporate.

However, despite the great importance of responding to disasters quickly, international donors have given relatively little attention to considering the implications of the need to respond quickly for their usual modes of operation. One step towards improved international disaster response policies would be for the international donor community to understand that the current cumbersome bureaucratic responses are often just far too slow, and to design systems that allow for the rapid provision of aid directly to affected populations.

Second, the lack of recognition given to local responses following the Asian tsunami is worrying. This is, perhaps, a reflection of what Gunnar Myrdal referred to as 'the beam in our eyes' in *Asian Drama*, his major work on Asian development issues (Myrdal 1968: 5–35), where he discussed the tendency of western institutions working on global development issues to see issues in western terms. The recent experience in the provision of international disaster relief following the Asian tsunami suggests that one of the consequences of the beam in donors' eyes is a failure to pay sufficient attention to the key role of national and local communities in disaster-affected countries. Data compiled by the Tsunami Evaluation Coalition (TEC) (Kessler 2006; Marulanda and Rizal 2006) provides valuable information on the size and nature of activities supported by national and local agencies following the Asian tsunami. Commenting on these issues, the TEC (Bennett et al. 2006: 50–51) observed that:

> As might be expected, in the first days and weeks after the tsunami the non-affected community provided assistance and took in the bulk of those displaced. Yet insufficient analysis and acknowledgement of community self-help in disasters has two results: first, it perpetuates the myth of dependency on external aid; second, it shields the aid establishment from the responsibility to build their responses on local capacities. Self-help and hosting of survivors was backed by little financial or material assistance from the governments, and was rarely reported or acknowledged.

The TEC and other reports on these issues serve as an important reminder that a central objective of international donor programs following disasters should be to cooperate with, and strengthen, national and local response programs rather than dominate the recovery effort.

THE COORDINATION PROCESS

The coordination of large, complex aid projects involving numerous actors is always difficult. So it proved with the delivery of post-tsunami assistance in Asia.[1] Coordination arrangements naturally varied from location to location and country to country. In some locations where the number of actors was relatively small, coordination was less of a problem. But generally in countries such as Sri Lanka and Indonesia where the donor presence was large, coordination proved very challenging. Various issues of coordination arose: the multiplicity of actors; lack of coherence; differences in objectives; managing expectations; and oversight of financial arrangements. Each of these is discussed in turn.

Multiplicity of Actors

In countries such as Indonesia, India, and Sri Lanka, the first coordination challenge was to somehow arrange an acceptable level of liaison between the quite bewildering array of organizations who involved themselves in the assistance effort. Participants in a UN workshop in 2005 (as well as many other observers) commented on the problems (UN 2005: 3–4):

> The very large number of often diverse actors created acute coordination challenges, particularly during the first weeks of the response phase. Local authorities, who were in charge of directing the relief efforts, were often weakened by severe human and material losses, and at times had to cope with unclear reporting lines and interference from various government bodies. Many nongovernmental actors, who had little or no experience in humanitarian relief, were unwilling or unaware of the need to coordinate with other partners. In some cases, the very high budgets at the disposal of some NGOs acted as a disincentive to coordinate action. Even large international organizations with a long history of involvement in humanitarian operations, at times took initiatives without consultation with other partners, and in some cases bypassed the government. At the same time, it was recognized that some of the coordination mechanisms that were put in place were dysfunctional, which encouraged some actors to work independently.

In Indonesia, for example, there were numerous multilateral and bilateral donors, a wide variety of national agencies, and by one count over 400

NGOs active in the field (Masyrafah and McKeon 2008: 18). In Tamil Nadu in India, an NGO coordination centre was established with eleven teams to work with a reported 600 NGOs (TGLL 2009: 26). In Sri Lanka, around 180 agencies and NGOs were involved in providing relief as well as the LTTE (Liberation Tigers of Tamil Eelam) separatist group in the north of Sri Lanka (see Chapter 5). Many of these agencies had their own difficult management issues to deal with as well; the BRR in Indonesia implemented over 5000 of its own projects while being required to coordinate the work of numerous other bodies.

The influx into a disaster zone of a multiplicity of extremely diverse agencies of this kind inevitably gave rise to all sorts of difficulties. The arrival of a large number of new staff, most of whom could not speak local languages, placed considerable strain on local systems. For some time after the disaster, basic transport and infrastructure systems were barely functional in some of the affected countries. In Banda Aceh (Wiharta et al. 2008: 88):

> Witnesses report that the airport was a scene of total mayhem, with relief supplies strewn around the runway. Flights landed, tossed out humanitarian aid supplies wherever they could and took off immediately. There did not seem to be anyone in charge. By the end of December 2004 the airport, whose air traffic control tower was damaged, had to handle an average of 132 flights daily. Under normal circumstances, it had to manage only eight flights per day.

The new arrivals needed housing and transport, wanted priority access to communications, sought to hire the best local staff, demanded quick access to senior local officials, and were often under instructions to make arrangements for early high-profile visits by senior officials or politicians from their headquarter agencies or countries (Bennett et al. 2006: 38).

Lack of Coherence

Not surprisingly, under such circumstances it is difficult to arrange coherence of aid programs. Problems of lack of coherence in the global aid industry, and even open competition between aid agencies, have been widely discussed in the development literature. The following observation from an UNCTAD report (UNCTAD 2005: 4) refers to delivery of aid in Africa but it might just as easily have been written about the coordination of post-tsunami assistance in Asia:

> Another major source of the inefficiency and ineffectiveness of much aid is the lack of coherence among donors and their objectives and requirements, and a failure to reconcile these with the needs, priorities and preferences of the

countries receiving assistance. The sheer multiplicity of donors, with different outlooks, accounting systems and priorities have created a landscape of
aid that, at best, can only be described as chaotic. This has in turn stretched
the administrative capacities of the recipient countries to breaking point and
undermined any pretence of local ownership of development programmes. The
institutional capacities of the receiving countries have been further weakened
by the pressures to reduce the size and functions of the state, a prominent
feature of the adjustment programmes driven by international finance institutions. The situation is exacerbated by the presence of numerous new bodies
such as NGOs through which aid is often disbursed with little or no oversight
by the recipient government or other national institutions. Coping with such
a situation would stretch the abilities of the bureaucracies of the Organisation
for Economic Cooperation and Development countries, let alone those of poor
African states.

It is partly because of problems like this that some observers have spoken
of the incoherence of the international humanitarian system.

This problem of lack of coherence was no secret amongst those involved
in the provision of post-tsunami assistance in Asia. The problems –
problems, in a sense, of excess competition between aid agencies – were
discussed in many reports about activities in the field (Bennett et al. 2006;
TGLL 2009). Various attempts were made to improve coordination.
Several of the main multilateral organizations, such as the United Nations
Development Programme and the World Bank, established mechanisms
designed to encourage donors to harmonize the delivery of aid. One of the
best known of these mechanisms was the Multi Donor Fund (MDF) established by the World Bank in Indonesia (MDF 2008; Thornton 2006).[2] Just
as effective were the coordination arrangements established by national
governments. In Indonesia, the *Badan Rekonstruksi dan Rehabilitasi*
(BRR) was established in April 2005; in Sri Lanka, TAFOR (Task Force
for Relief) and TAFREN (Task Force for Rebuilding the Nation) were set
up in early 2005; and other local coordination arrangements were made in
most of the other tsunami-affected countries.

One abiding difficulty with most attempts to improve coherence was the
tardiness of hundreds of aid agencies in participating actively in coordination arrangements. Many individual agencies paid lip service to the need
for coordination but were never keen to be coordinated. According to
the TEC, for example, of the 438 NGOs registered with the Indonesian
government in either Jakarta or Aceh, by mid-September 2005 only 128
had provided their activity reports to the BRR (Bennett 2006: 40). An
important contributing difficulty in strengthening coherence is that multilateral agencies, bilateral agencies, national organizations, and hundreds
of NGOs make up an extremely varied group of organizations. Further,
many of the agencies were under pressure to respond to all sorts of different

internal and external rules and incentives. Donor bilateral agencies, for example, often needed to comply with quite strict administrative requirements and political pressures determined thousands of kilometres away in donor capitals. Because Indonesia had a reputation as a corruption-prone country, most bilateral donors were under instructions from headquarters to maintain tight oversight over the expenditure of tsunami funds in Indonesia. For example, when announcing an increased Australian contribution to Indonesia to support tsunami relief and other activities in early 2005, the Australian Foreign Minister Alexander Downer noted that Australian officials would retain responsibility for spending Australian monies. He said that the Australian government was not prepared to delegate this authority to other agencies.

There is no easy answer to the problem of the excessive competition between aid agencies which often arises during complex international disasters. The incentives for them to cooperate are usually weak. In an ideal world an international or national institution with sufficient powers to induce strong and effective coherence across numerous agencies would be established. But in practice, it is often difficult for developing countries to arrange for effective cooperation from international donors. The establishment of a strong and credible national agency, such as the BRR in Indonesia, is usually a very helpful step in the right direction (Bennett 2006: 39). Multilateral coordination can help as well. But much depends on the goodwill and readiness of numerous, often hundreds, of assistance agencies to cooperate. When incentives to cooperate are weak, then coordination is likely to be difficult.

Differences in Objectives

Differences in objectives between the many organizations providing assistance also became evident. At one level of course, the overriding objective for all agencies was the same – to assist with relief and recovery after the disaster. But a broad objective of this kind can be interpreted in many ways. As noted earlier in Chapter 2, donors often have multiple objectives in mounting relief and assistance programs. Naturally, differences of this kind in objectives became evident at the agency level during the delivery of tsunami assistance. It is clear that many organizations had an eye to self-promotion or to the advocacy of programs endorsed by headquarter agencies. Indeed, it seems clear that many donors provided support in cash or in kind with all sorts of other explicit or implicit objectives in mind.

Differences in objectives with respect to timing, the preferred type of assistance, and various broader issues (relating to conditionalities and advocacy-type issues) all became increasingly evident soon after the relief effort got underway. Differences with respect to timing and the preferred type of assistance are most clearly reflected in the delivery of aid, so these issues are discussed below. But the multiple objectives which various donors had relating to broader issues call for additional comment.

One set of broader issues related to foreign policy.[3] These considerations were perhaps most evident in the American and Australian aid assistance programs. In the case of America, the US response needs to be seen against the growing difficulties that America was having in relations with the Muslim world following the invasion of Iraq over 18 months earlier. By late 2004 there was a growing realization in the US that for geopolitical reasons there was a need to look for opportunities to improve relations with the Muslim world. Thus there was strong political support within the US for a substantial and highly visible American official response to the tsunami disaster in Indonesia. In London, for example, in a news article headed 'US sees aid to Muslim victims as chance to improve image', *The Times* (3 January 2009) reported that[4]

> The United States has a golden opportunity to repair its tarnished image in the Muslim world by leading the relief effort, senior senators said. President Bush stamped his personal seal on America's multimillion-dollar tsunami aid package as the US seeks to turn Asia's humanitarian disaster into a political opportunity . . . . Richard Lugar, Republican chairman of the Senate foreign relations committee, said that the disaster offered a remarkable opportunity for the US to present a compassionate face. . . . Mr Lugar said that aid, so-called soft power, could be a breakthrough for the US in the region. Carl Levin, the senior democrat on Mr Lugar's committee, said 'This is a political opportunity to reach out to the Muslim world and let them know that our humanitarian assistance is across the board, and that we treat the Muslim world as an essential part of the world community.'

President Bush immediately sent the Secretary of State, Colin Powell, to Southeast Asia and despatched the aircraft carrier *USS Abraham Lincoln* to North Sumatra to distribute assistance. During the following few years, numerous senior US officials and leaders visiting Indonesia made frequent public references to the US assistance provided under the tsunami aid program.

Australia, too, had foreign policy reasons to provide a sizeable response quickly, and did so. A little over a week after the tsunami, on 5 January 2005 the Australian government announced an unexpected and greatly expanded program of A$1 billion of new and additional assistance to Indonesia to be delivered (through both loans and grants) over a five-year period (Tomar 2005). It was announced that the assistance would be coordinated through a newly formed Australia–Indonesia Partnership for Reconstruction and Development. The background to this unanticipated initiative was that for some years, Australia's relations both with Indonesia and with several other countries in Southeast Asia had been strained. Various issues, including the events surrounding East Timor's transition to independence, Australia's regional refugee policy, and several other matters had been complicating Australia's relations with the region (Buckley 2005).[5] The rapid and decisive provision of substantial assistance to Indonesia helped Australia rebalance relations with Southeast Asia. The move was seen by the Australian media 'as a foreign policy master stroke in developing close ties with Indonesia in keeping with Australia's status as a regional actor' (Tomar 2005). But there is no doubt, too, that there was widespread and deep sympathy across the Australian community for the pain the tsunami disaster had brought to Indonesia, so the Government's decision received overwhelming public support.

One other aspect of the Australian Government's decision to expand aid to Indonesia immediately after the tsunami should be noted. It was of some significance in terms of foreign policy that the details of the government's announcement made it clear that all areas of Indonesia, not just regions affected by the tsunami, would be eligible for assistance under the expanded program. Although numerous media and official reports included the total amount of A\$1 billion as part of the total international funding provided for tsunami relief, there was in fact no indication in the Australian government's announcement of what share of the package would be devoted to tsunami assistance activities. A Research Note issued by the Australian Parliamentary Library in March 2005 observed that 'It is quite possible that most of the grant aid and loan component will be spent on projects outside Aceh . . .' (Tomar 2005). It therefore seems clear that the Australian government's decision to expand aid to Indonesia substantially in early 2005 was designed to be a significant foreign policy step as well as a rapid response to a large humanitarian disaster in the region.[6]

The second main set of broader issues concerning objectives related to so-called cross-cutting considerations – that is, sectoral issues seen as usually needing consideration when assistance is being delivered. These are matters which it is expected should be allowed for, whenever possible, in the design of all assistance programs. The most important of these in case of post-tsunami aid programs related to peace-keeping and security issues, gender considerations, and the environment – which are discussed in more detail in a later section. Here we simply point out that these added to the set of objectives of the assistance effort.

Thus the many aid agencies which arrived in the tsunami-affected countries to provide assistance brought a varied agenda of cross-cutting objectives with them. In practice, both international and national post-tsunami assistance was provided against a veritable kaleidoscope of objectives.

It is true that immediate humanitarian relief and longer-term rehabilitation and reconstruction were the main objectives for most aid agencies.
However it would be a naive observer who failed to notice that the totality
of objectives underpinning the numerous assistance programs across the
main tsunami-affected countries presented a wide and complex agenda.

Managing Expectations

Part of the job of delivering assistance programs following a disaster is
the management of expectations. If communications, and the associated
information flow between donor agencies and recipient communities, are
not handled carefully, then misunderstandings are likely to arise. And in
retrospect, it can be seen that unrealistic expectations about aid programs
were built up in the aftermath of the 2004 tsunami in Asia. One report
issued from the Office of the UN Special Envoy for Tsunami Recovery
(Wall 2006: 11) noted that:

> The phenomenon of broken promises has become one of the catchphrases of
> the relief effort in Aceh and, to a lesser extent, in Sri Lanka. . . . Typically,
> after the tsunami, an aid organisation would approach a community, carry
> out a needs assessment, or discuss possibilities, and then leave. The organisa-
> tion might think they had merely gathered some information that would form
> the basis for a decision on possible assistance. The community, meanwhile,
> would assume that they had just received a firm commitment for assistance.
> Sometimes the organisation did not return. But the community would wait,
> growing more impatient, sometimes turning away aid from other organisa-
> tions. Organisations that went back to such communities after some time were
> shocked at the hostile reception.

In fact, it appears that misunderstandings resulting from poor communications rather than broken promises were often an important part of the
problem. But 'the perception of broken promises has done a great deal to
shape the perceptions of aid organisations' (Wall 2006: 11).

One incident which attracted international attention at the time was the
decision by a group of 'furious tsunami survivors' in the village of Pasi
in Aceh to reject promised assistance from the UK-based (international
NGO) Oxfam (Hasan 2006). In April 2006 it was reported that the villagers in Pasi 'had agreed to demand a divorce from Oxfam'. Tempers had
exploded several months earlier when an Oxfam officer visiting the village
was attacked by villagers who were frustrated by delays in the provision
of promised housing. Oxfam, in turn, responded quickly to the local problems which were largely due to complex land rights issues as well as scarce
building supplies. Oxfam was certainly not alone in having to deal with
difficult problems of meeting heightened expectations amongst affected

communities. The main significance of this particular incident is that it illustrates the problems which can arise when communications between aid providers and beneficiary communities become difficult.

The proper management of communications, particularly in periods following a major disaster, is a skilled task. In developing countries in Asia in the period after the 2004 tsunami, problems of communication between donors and affected communities were exacerbated by the widespread use of translators and aid jargon, and by the extreme levels of distress widespread in the region. Considerable improvements in communications processes are, in principle, possible. But better arrangements need to be supported by increased funding, a strong political and institutional commitment to the idea of good communications, the recruitment of professionals to design programs, and capacity building for local government officers in such things as accountability and transparency processes to enhance relationships with local communities. Given current constraints on local governments such as limited availability of funding, shortages of skilled staff, and numerous other priorities, it is not clear how quickly progress is likely to be made.

Oversight of Financial Arrangements

The coordination of financial arrangements proved very difficult. There were a range of interrelated problems (see Chapter 3).

First, it was often unclear who had promised what. In complex emergencies it is common for governments to make impressive statements promising significant responses which, on closer examination, are unclear on details. For one thing, as noted in Chapter 3, governments pledged assistance in a mixture of currencies, in a mixture of loans and grants, with all sorts of conditionalities attached, and for uncertain time periods. For another thing, although there was much talk of the generosity of the assistance provided, there is no agreement at all about what constitutes an adequate level of funding in responding to large scale disasters.[7] Across the world, responses tend to be *ad hoc*, determined by the mixture of factors which donors choose to consider at any particular time. From one point of view, the tsunami relief effort was well funded, at least by comparison with many other disasters in developing countries. But when compared with the much more adequate funding provided for disaster relief within rich countries, the funding was meagre.

In addition, unfortunately many of the claims made by donors about transparency and accountability of funding were not fulfilled. The problems were so widespread that there is little point in singling out specific agencies. However some instances of difficulties can be mentioned to illustrate the nature of the issues. For a start, as noted above, ambitious promises raised expectations – but later led to suggestions of 'broken promises'. Further, as noted in Chapter 3, in practice it soon became difficult to follow which agencies were spending how much, and on what. Telford and Cosgrave (2007: 6) concluded that 'the international system for tracking and accounting for funding flows is seriously inadequate'.

A third main problem with funding arrangements was that, too often, national governments and local agencies were denied ownership of the programs. In practice, in the delivery of tsunami aid many donors, especially international agencies, were not willing to hand over financial management of the programs to national agencies. There is a dilemma here to which there is no easy answer. On one hand, in recent years donors themselves have increasingly emphasized the importance of country ownership in the delivery of aid. The need to strengthen national ownership in the management of aid was one of the key themes of the Paris Declaration on Aid Effectiveness agreed to in early 2005 by all major OECD donors and representatives from many developing countries.[8] On the other hand, international donors are also under strong pressure from headquarter agencies in capitals to ensure high standards of accountability and transparency (also emphasized in the Paris Declaration). It is therefore perhaps not surprising that foreign aid officials, faced with all sorts of problems of accountability when disbursing funds under high-risk conditions in the field, were reluctant to give up responsibility for financial controls. But it is also not surprising that officials in recipient governments felt that this approach reduced national ownership of activities in their own countries.

DELIVERY OF ASSISTANCE

Initial problems of planning for aid coordination were soon reflected in practical difficulties in the delivery of aid in the field. Various issues arose: different donors wanted to supply different types of aid; the staging of the provision of aid varied depending on the preferred type of aid; there was constant need to make allowances for cross-cutting issues; at every stage, issues of financial control were important as well. All of these issues combined to make the overall coordination of aid delivery difficult.

Types and Timing of Aid: Relief, Rehabilitation, Reconstruction

The delivery of physical assistance following a large scale disaster is an extremely complex logistical operation. As we have seen, in the first few hours after the tsunami disaster it was local, often informal and *ad hoc* responses that provided immediate assistance. But as official relief mechanisms began to get underway, the problems of coordinating the movement of supplies and people quickly multiplied. The types of aid provided during the different relief, rehabilitation and reconstruction phases varied considerably so different approaches to coordination were needed (Figures 2.1 and 4.4 above). Some aid providers (such as the US Navy and the INGO Médecins Sans Frontières) had the objective of providing humanitarian and relief aid for a relatively short period of perhaps a few months and then winding down their activities. Other agencies took a longer-term view, placing more emphasis on the goal of providing medium or long-term support for reconstruction and rehabilitation over time. These differences in timing were naturally reflected in the preferred type and sector of assistance as well.

In the initial period of the official response, the most urgent priority was the provision of emergency relief and humanitarian assistance. As the scale of the disaster became clear it was realized, first, that the needs for immediate assistance were very large, and that second, the main relief phase would stretch out for much longer than first anticipated.

It was largely unavoidable that during the early relief stage, coordination of activities was very difficult. On one hand, large numbers of aid workers representing many different agencies arrived on the scene offering supplies of all sorts of goods and services. On the other hand, the needs of the disaster-affected local communities were not clear. The first wave of assistance brought supplies of items such as food, water, clothing, temporary shelter, and emergency medical supplies. These were provided by official international, bilateral and national civilian agencies, domestic and international NGOs, and by police and military personnel as well. The American government, for example, despatched an aircraft carrier while the Australian government sent several destroyers to deliver assistance in Aceh. The coordination of civilian and military agencies was not easy. In a review of the implications of using foreign military assets as part of the international response after a major natural disaster, Wiharta et al. (2008: xiii) observe that:

> Coordination between civilian humanitarian actors and military assets has been one of the greatest challenges created by the increasing deployment of foreign military assets. The differences in cultures, priorities and operating modes between military personnel and civilian actors have an impact not least on information sharing between the civilian and military spheres. Information sharing is crucial to the success or failure of any relief operations.

Clearly, it is extremely difficult to coordinate the activities, for example, of helicopters from offshore foreign warships staffed by personnel who communicate in English with assistance delivered by local NGOs who work in local languages.

Numerous reports indicate that the most urgent needs of affected communities were generally catered for. However it seems clear that some key social and psychological priorities were neglected. One urgent need which received somewhat haphazard attention was for survivors to find out what had happened to other members of their families who had disappeared – either carried away by the tsunami and saved, or just as likely, drowned. Numerous attempts were made, of course, to reunite families. However in some cases it took weeks or months for family members to find each other. In other cases, survivors had many months of uncertainty before having to accept that their loved ones had probably died. Further, many survivors suffered debilitating periods of trauma in the wake of the disaster. The need to address these problems as priority issues was acknowledged but in practice often received low priority.

Within a month or so, initial planning for longer-term rehabilitation and reconstruction activities got underway. One of the most urgent needs was for housing so numerous agencies developed housing programs. Many reports suggest that the arrangements made by different agencies for the supply of housing varied widely. On the one hand, there was pressure from tsunami survivors living in temporary accommodation to be rehoused as soon as possible. On the other hand, there were all sorts of potential risks involved in constructing new housing too quickly. Problems which delayed housing programs included planned changes to government regulations following the tsunami, disputes over land title, uncertainties over housing designs, lack of infrastructure, and disagreements between aid donors as to who was responsible for what.[9]

A second priority for rehabilitation activities was to move quickly to try to reinvigorate local private sector and informal commercial activities. Local livelihood programs were one of the main ways by which many assistance agencies tried to do this (ILO 2005; Nowak and Caulfield 2008: 25–37). The immediate impact of the tsunami on local economies which received a direct hit was to destroy virtually all commercial activities. In most cases, survivors lost all income-earning assets (fishing boats, local vehicles, stalls and small shops, and the like) immediately. Most local commercial activity ceased entirely, creating instant widespread unemployment and loss of almost all income. The economic shock was remarkable. To be sure, there was a small revival of some economic activities once aid flows got underway. However, much aid expenditure went on goods and services purchased elsewhere. Much of the aid spending did little, in the short term, to directly reinvigorate the local informal economy.

But although most disaster relief in developing countries has traditionally been in kind, this does not have to be the case. In fact, cash for work (CFW) programs soon became a prominent part of the tsunami response in some parts of Asia (Doocy et al. 2006: 278):

Many organisations launched cash interventions after the Asian tsunami and large-scale CFW programmes were widespread in Aceh, Indonesia, and Sri Lanka, with tens of thousands of beneficiaries participating in CFW programmes operated by multiple international non-governmental organisations (INGOs) and the United Nations Development Programme (UNDP), sometimes in partnership with local non-government organisations (NGOs). In the post-tsunami context, where livelihoods were destroyed and assets lost, CFW programmes provided income, contributed to community rehabilitation, helped to meet financial needs and had positive social effects in tsunami-affected communities. While CFW programmes have been utilised in a variety of contexts, they have never been implemented before on the scale observed following the Asian tsunami.

Cash-based programs have pros and cons (Harvey 2006; Harvey 2007; Kelaher and Dollery 2008). Disadvantages of cash-based approaches for emergency relief include difficulties in targeting, the possibility of misuse of cash, and the risks of conflict between recipients who are eligible and those who are not. In situations where supply channels have been severely disrupted cash payments may simply bid up prices of available goods rather than help meet needs. As against this, advantages include the speed with which help can be delivered, the sense of self-reliance that cash gives to recipients, and the multiplier effects that additional spending has on local economies.

Longer-term planning for activities such as physical and social infrastructure take some time. Official assistance agencies – caught up as they are in the byzantine red tape of coordination mechanisms, conferences, planning, studies of all kinds, and contract administration – find it hard to be nimble. Thus the first major meetings to discuss the international response to the disaster were not held until February 2005; some major national organizations such as the BRR in Indonesia were not established until April 2005; and planning for several of the larger infrastructure projects did not get underway until the end of 2005, almost twelve months after the tsunami. Some observers saw these responses as 'leisurely'.

By early 2006 the initial relief stage of assistance was largely complete and there was increasing emphasis on rehabilitation and reconstruction. Significant progress in the provision of housing had been made. Throughout 2006 and into 2007 the overall approach to the delivery of post-tsunami assistance underwent a significant change. Larger scale infrastructure projects began to get underway, well-developed housing programs were in the process of implementation, and activities to encourage livelihood activities were receiving strong support (Thorburn 2009). Reliable data on overall spending is not available. However a broad guess would be that by the end of 2007, three years after the disaster, perhaps half of the funding originally promised by international donors had been spent.

During 2008 and into 2009, both international and national agencies were moving to scale down post-tsunami programs. Many housing programs had been completed; livelihood and business programs were being phased out; and while spending on remaining infrastructure projects continued at a fairly high level, plans were to ensure that the main projects would be substantially completed by the end of 2009.

Cross-cutting Issues

Cross-cutting issues were recognized as requiring attention as soon as the large-scale relief effort got underway. Four cross-cutting issues, in particular, were seen as being of high priority: peace-keeping; social participation; women and children; and the environment.

In the case of both Indonesia and Sri Lanka, and to a lesser extent Thailand, the tsunami arrived at a time when local security issues were posing major problems for national policy makers. In Indonesia, Acehnese resentment at heavy-handed rule from distant Jakarta had been simmering for years. The local Free Aceh Movement had mounted worrying challenges to national authority within the province of Aceh (He and Reid 2004). In response, the Indonesian government had established a significant military presence which, in turn, had fuelled local resentment. In Sri Lanka, the problem was rather different. Tension, and open clashes, between the central government and the LTTE had severely tested the authority of the central government. Whilst in Indonesia the security problems in Aceh were at the periphery, in Sri Lanka security issues concerning the LTTE had become an overriding concern for national government. In contrast, in neither Thailand nor India were security concerns of this kind significant issues in providing post-tsunami relief.

It was quickly realized, in both Aceh and Sri Lanka, that immediate priority needed to be given to negotiate peace agreements in the bitter local conflicts that had been underway before the tsunami. The cessation of conflict was important, of course, so that aid could be provided to disaster-affected areas. In addition, many people hoped that in the period of local anguish following the disaster, there might perhaps be a window of opportunity to establish lasting peace agreements as the war- and disaster-affected communities resolved to look to the future rather than the past.[10] In Sri Lanka however, little significant progress towards a peace settlement was made (see Chapter 5). A little over a year after the tsunami, open hostilities between the central government and the LTTE were resumed. But in contrast, in Aceh, following the tsunami there was a renewed willingness on all sides to look for compromises. International delegates joined with high-level negotiators from Jakarta, including Vice-President Jusuf Kalla, to broker a peace agreement announced in August 2005.[11] In the eyes of many observers, the peace settlement in Aceh reached shortly after the tsunami demonstrated that sometimes traumatic events such as national disasters can open the way to dramatic political and social changes. Some specialists in peace and governance issues therefore urge that security issues should be included on the agenda of key cross-cutting issues in the wake of major disasters in developing countries.

Social participation was recognized as important because social barriers caused by factors such as gender, age, religion or occupation can restrict access to assistance in the wake of a disaster. Commenting on the need for attention to social participation, former UN Special Envoy for Tsunami Recovery Bill Clinton said that[12]

> Without a dedicated effort to change historical patterns of inequity, tradition- ally marginalised or disenfranchised groups will continue to lack both the political awareness and power to demand their fair share of recovery resources. . . . And the problem can be compounded by a post-disaster influx of new assist- ance providers who have little knowledge of the context in which they are oper- ating, including structures of inequality, chronic poverty and vulnerability.

In India, for example, more than a quarter of the population affected by the tsunami belonged to underprivileged and marginalized social groups. They included people working in the fishing sector who lost their jobs when fishery activities came to a halt in the wake of the disaster, landless labourers, and salt-pan workers, many of them women (TGLL 2009: 38). Steps are needed, therefore, to ensure that local people in communities affected by disasters in developing countries are consulted on relief and rehabilitation programs. In the language of the international aid commu- nity, local people need a voice.[13]

Issues affecting women and children received close attention from donors as well (Nowak and Caulfield 2008). Numerous reports from agen- cies in the field drew attention to the various ways that women, as well as the children they often cared for, were disproportionately affected by the tsunami and disadvantaged during the subsequent relief efforts. Women and children were disadvantaged from the moment the disaster struck. Tsunami survival rates were significantly higher for men than for women and children. Post-tsunami data show that up to twice as many women were killed as men.

Nowak and Caulfield (2008: 32), for example, observed that:

> There has been a disproportionate negative impact on Acehnese women follow-
> ing the earthquake and tsunami. This imbalance decreased women's opportu-
> nities to have a voice in the planning and reconstruction of their communities.
> Even more striking is the point raised by a woman activist in the Aceh Women's
> League, who noted that women were not only excluded in the post-tsunami
> relief process, but they were not considered in the implementation of the peace
> accord. Since women's role in the peace was not acknowledged they have no
> role as participants in the peace process.

And Telford et al. (2006: 35) reported that:

> The raw death toll tells only part of the story. Disproportionate numbers of the
> most vulnerable people died. . . . More women than men died. This was high-
> lighted early on when Oxfam announced that, in the villages it had surveyed,
> there were three times as many adult male survivors as female ones.

It seems that one of the main reasons for this, quite simply, is that men had
a better chance of escaping the flood waters than women. Men were able
to run faster or climb trees more easily than women who, in any case, were
often encumbered by the need to look after children. It is clear that women
in many of the affected communities faced a wide range of problems,
ranging from lack of access to aid programs, legal rights and housing, to
domestic violence (IDLO and UNDP 2007). The sad truth is that when
terrible disasters in developing countries strike suddenly, it is often a case
of 'women and children last'.

The indications are that men often fared better during the later aid
delivery phase as well. Several surveys of the assistance effort were critical
of the relative lack of attention to gender issues in aid delivery (Bennett
2006: 58; Clinton 2006: 6–7). Positions of leadership in the tsunami-
affected communities were generally held by men. Men tended to speak
for the communities, not always properly representing the special needs
of women and children. Issues such as lack of privacy and security, and
the dangerous living conditions found in some temporary barracks,
often affected women and children more than men. Men could generally
more easily spend much of their time away from the confines of the barracks than could women and children. Men often found it easier to take
advantage of new job opportunities that opened up as the rehabilitation
programs got underway.

Environmental matters attracted considerable debate at times as well.
Some research workers drew attention to the protection that natural
defences provided against the tsunami in Sumatra and argued that
'healthy coral and mangrove are reported to have saved lives during the

recent tsunami' (Montgomery 2006: 69). They urged that lessons from this experience should be incorporated into the design of rehabilitation programs. Other environmentalists were concerned that the building boom expected to occur as housing reconstruction activities got underway would lead to the uncontrolled exploitation of valuable forestry resources. It seems clear that the sharp increase in the demand for timber for housing did indeed encourage careless logging practices. Indriatmoko (2006), for example, reported that during 2005 in North Sumatra:

> Lowland forest and mountainous forest have become highly exploited due to the high increase of timber demands during the reconstruction period. . . . Prolonging politically armed conflicts hampered the natural resource management in Aceh. . . . armed rebels dominated the utilization and exploitation of natural resources including forests. [The] Helsinki MOU, 2005, has brought negative impacts to forest, since many irresponsible parties make use of the situation to freely enter the forest and cut the trees . . .

Certainly, as post-tsunami reconstruction programs picked up pace in 2005 and 2006 the demand for timber and other inputs for building activities increased. Environmental groups, in turn, became increasingly concerned about the impact on natural resources that the building boom was beginning to cause. They pressed for more effective regulation but their calls were not especially effective in face of the strong pressures to provide new housing quickly. A third concern of environment groups was that proper environmental planning be undertaken before settlements of thousands of houses in new locations be approved. Aid agencies acknowledged the need to consider the environmental impact of new settlements. But this concern, too, needed to be balanced against the increasing resentment from tsunami survivors over delays in providing housing. It was not always easy to reach agreement on the trade-offs between these multiple objectives.

Financial Considerations

Practical problems related to the physical delivery of aid interacted with difficulties in the financial management of programs as pointed out earlier in the section on financial arrangements. Sometimes delays in the physical delivery of aid led to financial problems, and sometimes issues of financial management caused slippages in the physical delivery of aid.

As we have seen, most donors chose to provide much of their assistance in kind. In-kind delivery of aid has the advantage (from the point of view of donors) that the provision of the assistance can be closely controlled. Donor staff in the field can report back to headquarter agencies that aid flows, including financial arrangements, have been carefully monitored.

In-kind delivery also means that donor agencies become closely involved in the numerous decisions which affect trade-offs between the speed of delivery of the aid, the quantity and the quality.

Delays in spending, which caused increasing frustration amongst tsunami survivors as time passed, soon became an issue. Four main problems contributed to the delays. First, many financial managers wanted to be sure that control mechanisms were satisfactory, and particularly that proper safeguards existed to provide checks against corruption. As noted earlier (Chapters 2 and 3), these issues received particular attention from the donor community in Aceh because Indonesia is widely regarded as a corruption-prone country. Similarly, the issue of proper controls over expenditures was seen as important in Sri Lanka.

Second, trade-offs between providing assistance quickly and emphasizing quality were naturally reflected in expenditures. As time went on and delays in spending became a matter for public comment, one line of defence which some donors adopted was to emphasize the importance of quality. Proper targeting of assistance was one aspect of quality which some donors wanted reassurance on. Another was their concern to ensure that cross-cutting issues were properly addressed. The motto of 'build back better' was frequently mentioned by officials and international NGOs alike, partly as justification for falling short of the enthusiastic expectations that some tsunami survivors originally had that facilities such as new housing would be supplied promptly. But on occasions, groups of tsunami survivors expressed their own views about the 'build back better' approach by demonstrating and throwing rocks at the offices of local aid agencies.

Yet another reason for shortfalls in expenditure was the delays in project preparation and construction caused by all sorts of red tape. Delays in gaining approvals to access land for housing and infrastructure were particularly common. And to add to the problems, according to numerous reports, the caution that many officials had in cutting corners was exacerbated by the widespread publicity given to the penalties for corruption. Many officials were said to be cautious about issuing project clearances, signing contract agreements, or approving expenditures whenever there was even the slightest doubt about the legality of doing so.

A fourth and major factor was the sharp increase in costs of important inputs which took place shortly after the disaster. The local economic effects of a major disaster are, not surprisingly, extremely destabilizing. As noted earlier, the immediate impact is to cause great damage to the local economy and, in effect, destroy most local economic activity. But as soon as there is an influx of external assistance, a sharp increase in demand for particular types of local goods and services occurs. Depending on local circumstances, this phenomenon can pose significant challenges to policy makers and therefore warrants some additional comment.

Impact of Financial Flows: A Construction Boom

A surge of financial flows is to be expected as aid arrives following a natural disaster. Physical asset replacement involving the supply of capital items (such as fishing boats and nets) that can be imported (either from overseas or from elsewhere within the country) is relatively easy and can be arranged as assistance in kind. This type of aid often does not involve financial transactions. Indeed, fishery equipment was replaced quite rapidly and, by and large, quite effectively in Indonesia, Sri Lanka and Thailand. However, large scale reconstruction is different. A large proportion of reconstruction usually involves the replacement of houses, buildings, bridges, roads, and other infrastructure. This effort leads to a sudden increase in demand in local markets for construction materials and labour inputs.[14] Thus the negative economic shock due to the initial disaster is often followed by a positive 'demand shock' in the construction sector. In other words, there is often a 'construction sector boom'.

A boom of this nature usually leads to cost increases. The magnitude of the demand shock depends on the scale of the disaster and the consequent size and pace of the reconstruction program. The degree to which costs increase depends on both the size of this demand shock and on the supply responsiveness of the inputs needed in the construction sector.

If the effects of a disaster are small relative to the size of the national economy, the supply of inputs that the construction industry needs (both materials and labour) will tend to be relatively elastic. More generally, this will tend to be the case both for specific categories of construction materials in abundant supply and for relatively unskilled labour. If all the inputs in demand are internationally 'tradable' and can be imported at more or less world prices, the extra demand will probably not lead to major price or cost increases. Many construction materials are indeed tradable – that is, they can be easily imported from world markets – at more or less unchanged prices. For these materials, the impact on world prices of even large increases in demand caused by a local construction program would tend to be small.[15]

However it is rarely the case that all of the inputs needed in a reconstruction program are in elastic supply. Because the supply of some non-tradable factors (skilled labour is a good example) is usually quite inelastic in the short run, their prices tend to rise as demand increases. Clearly, the stronger the boom in local construction, the greater will be the inflationary impact.[16] Shortages of non-tradable factors are likely to be more marked in the short run than in the long run.[17] In the case of skilled workers for example, this is true for two reasons: first, because over time, more skilled workers can usually be recruited to ease the shortages; and, second, because in the medium term, increasing numbers of unskilled workers can learn specialized construction skills and will thus expand the supply of skilled labour available. But many factors, particularly specialized types of labour, must often be supplied from local or at least domestic sources (and are therefore 'non-traded').[18]

Construction Cost Escalation

The different experiences in Indonesia, Sri Lanka, and Thailand demonstrate how the interaction between higher demand and supply elasticities took place in different places following the tsunami. In Aceh, the cost of building a new 36-square metre house increased from an initial estimate of US$3000 to around US$5000 by end-2005. The increase was driven both by rising labour costs – somewhat moderated by the increased willingness of labour to move into the province of Aceh following the establishment of peace – and, even more importantly, by price increases in domestically sourced building materials such as timber.[19] According to USGAO (2007: 17):

> World Bank data provided by USAID show that construction costs increased as a result [of the increased demands for construction and labour]. For example, between October 2004 and October 2005, the average wage for bricklayers, plumbers, and construction supervisors in Aceh increased 55 percent, 72 percent, and 81 percent, respectively. USAID expects that ongoing demands for materials and labor will continue to create inflationary pressures.

Overall '. . . some key project activities in Indonesia and Sri Lanka – particularly its signature projects intended to generate increased visibility for U.S. assistance – have experienced increased estimated costs, are behind initial schedules, and in the case of Indonesia have been reduced in scope' (USGAO 2007: 31).

In Sri Lanka, too, total construction costs for houses planned for tsunami-affected families rose quickly. Costs were estimated to have risen by 30–50 per cent by August 2005, and, by September 2006, had increased over initial estimates by 60–80 per cent or more. While prices of some materials did increase in Sri Lanka, cost increases were mainly driven by higher wages for skilled labour (such as carpenters, painters, and masons) whose wages doubled in some locations (Weerakoon et al. 2007). Skilled construction labour was in scarce supply in many tsunami-affected locations so workers had to be brought in from outside the affected areas.

While the tsunami destroyed the livelihoods of many people and created local unemployment, most of the unemployed people (for example, local fishers, farmers, small traders, and others) had few or no construction skills.

In contrast, in Thailand construction costs actually declined during 2005 following the tsunami. Nidhiprabha (2007: 11) explains this phenomenon by emphasizing the role of local factor supply elasticities due to unemployment and excess capacity in the depressed construction sector of Thailand when the tsunami hit:

> The reconstruction activities certainly increased demand in the affected regions for construction materials and labour. This was seen in the opening of a large number of construction material shops in the affected areas. However, higher demand did not lead to price increases. Here it is important to note that the tsunami-affected areas were not very far from the metropolitan Bangkok region, and the overall reconstruction activity was small relative to the size of the Thai economy. What was particularly important was that the higher demand came in the context of a depressed construction sector at the national level, reflecting the overall slowdown in economic activity, which was tending to push prices down. There was considerable excess capacity in the main input markets for construction. Substantial excess capacity in the steel industry led to declining prices of steel products used in construction, while prices of wood and wood products rose less than five per cent over prices in December 2004. Even though higher oil prices exerted some upward pressure on most materials, prices of essential raw materials such as cement and steel remained subdued during the reconstruction period. Overall, the magnitude of the demand effect was not sufficient to increase prices because there was an elastic supply of construction inputs.

Thus the particular economic circumstances in Thailand, which had yet to fully recover from the 1997 economic crisis, meant that inflation in construction costs in the tsunami-affected areas in Thailand were only moderate.

Dutch Disease and Reconstruction Following Disasters

This discussion of the impact of the local construction booms following the Asian tsunami has marked similarities to issues discussed in the well-known 'Dutch Disease' literature. Whenever a particular sector in a particular economy experiences a marked boom, the demand for inputs used in that sector (both factors of production and materials) tends to increase. This increased demand, in turn, tends to cause negative impacts for other industries that compete for the inputs used in the booming sector. The increased prices of inputs raise costs and reduce profitability in the competing (non-booming) industries. The resulting negative impact

on the non-booming sectors is known as 'Dutch Disease', so named after
the experience in the Netherlands of de-industrialization in the wake of
large inflows of export revenues from North Sea Oil in the late 1970s.
The broad lesson is that in general, when countries receive large capital
inflows, including foreign aid flows, expenditure is often concentrated in
certain sectors. These sectors sometimes experience a marked boom while
competing non-booming sectors may need to deal with negative Dutch
Disease effects which flow from the resulting cost increases.[20] The cost
increases observed in the construction sectors following the Asian tsunami
are a reflection of these Dutch Disease effects associated with absorption
of financial inflows into the regional economy.

Certain features associated with this phenomenon of aid funds inflow
to finance construction following natural disasters have important policy
implications. Suppose, for simplicity, that two main types of inputs – tradable (imported) goods and non-tradable (domestic) goods[21] – are required
to support a construction boom (and, more generally, asset replacement
following the loss of assets as a result of the tsunami). Suppose, also, that
these inputs are used in fixed proportions. Given world prices of imported
tradable goods, a given unit of foreign currency will buy a fixed quantity of
imported inputs irrespective of the exchange rate of the recipient country.[22]
But the amount of domestic non-tradable inputs that a unit of foreign
currency can purchase depends on both the nominal exchange rate and on
the domestic price of those inputs. The cost escalations which reflect the
Dutch Disease are closely associated with the local prices of these domestic
(non-traded) inputs.

If the nominal foreign exchange rate is fixed, the amount of local construction that can be financed for any given amount of foreign aid (say,
US$1 million) will be lower and the higher the domestic rate of inflation
will be.[23] The country's exchange rate policy, therefore, becomes an important matter to consider. A policy of propping up the nominal exchange
rate by 'leaning against the wind' in foreign exchange markets (as appears
to have occurred, for example, in Sri Lanka following the tsunami) makes
it much harder to fund rehabilitation or reconstruction programs with any
given amount of foreign aid.[24] By contrast, domestic inflationary pressures
can be partially mitigated by trade liberalization which tends to reduce the
costs of tradable goods (including imported intermediate goods used in
construction and other aid activities).

Distributional issues also need to be considered. The sensitive matter of
the 'fair use' of aid often arises in the wake of a disaster. It is a fact of life
that some people tend to benefit more than others when a Dutch Disease
phenomenon occurs. Because of this, allegations that local traders said
to be 'monopolists' are indulging in activities believed to be 'profiteering'

and are 'exploiting disaster victims' are not unusual. In fact, it is true that following a disaster such as the tsunami, the local inflation of prices for inputs in short supply (such as skilled labour and certain materials) can create something of a bonanza for suppliers of these inputs. Inflation therefore tends to create a redistribution of construction-targeted aid funds, sometimes seen as an unfair windfall gain, to suppliers of these inputs. The result, within any given budget, is that plans about the scale of construction need to be revised downwards when the costs of construction rise, and, consequently, the expectations that have been raised amongst aid-beneficiary groups tend to be disappointed.[25]

Given these problems there is surely a case for relieving supply bottlenecks by encouraging more imports, including the import of skilled labour. This approach would help reduce cost pressures and support faster construction programs. Further, an expanded reconstruction program would inject much-needed funds into the depressed local economy (see the comments about sharp decreases in incomes in Box 2.2 earlier) and would help generate jobs for unemployed local people, many of whom often lack the skills to participate in the construction boom. The extra expenditure from both imported skilled labour and locally employed labour would, in turn, have a wider multiplier effect, lifting overall demand in the local economy. This was observed to be an important aspect of the revival of the regional economy in Aceh following the tsunami.

Trade-off: Pace and Amount of Reconstruction

How quickly should reconstruction proceed in the wake of a disaster? Should planners aim, as many locally affected people often prefer, to repair the damage and to build new houses, schools, and roads as quickly as possible? Or is it better to go more slowly, and to aim to 'build back better', as many donors decided to do in Indonesia and Sri Lanka following the Asian tsunami?

Those who prefer the more measured 'build back better' approach argue that if too much construction is undertaken too quickly, the regional construction boom is likely to impose unacceptable burdens on over-stretched local administrative, technical, and economic systems. They point to the risks of severe localized Dutch Disease effects as inflationary pressures mount, and also to the risks of leakages of funds if contracting processes are not carefully managed. The argument in favour of phasing in reconstruction projects over time is that if the demand for inputs is allowed to increase in a measured way, supplies of these inputs will be more elastic. The result, it is suggested, will be that both cost increases and the leakage of construction funds will be correspondingly lower. A more phased approach also allows time for training programs to be provided to local people in at least low-skilled construction activities which has both a cost reducing effect and a job-creating effect.[26] The overall result of this approach is that more capital assets can be replaced for a given amount of funding. However, a slower pace of reconstruction imposes various costs: it delays the creation of the flow of valuable services from the capital assets so that services are forgone for a longer time. Ideally, a balance needs to be struck between the high costs associated with a rapid pace of capital asset replacement and the losses due to delayed reconstruction. It is best that a program of reconstruction be planned to allow for the costs and benefits associated with different reconstruction projects. This way, rankings can be established on an economically and socially sound basis.

There are also political economy factors to bear in mind when considering the pace of reconstruction. Foreign aid donors do not hang around forever. Unless funds are put to good use quickly the funds may be diverted to other activities as donors' priorities change. There is some evidence that this happened in the use of donor funds in Indonesia and Sri Lanka following the Asian tsunami. Domestic funding can also be diverted as well. Delays in reconstruction may lead to funds being used in ways that do not really meet the needs of the worst-affected groups. In other words, the costs of delays in reconstruction may fall largely on poor and politically weak groups. This issue is particularly important because a financing gap can lead to a rationing of funds. This indeed appears to be the case in Sri Lanka where reconstruction activities were heavily concentrated in politically favoured regions dominated by the majority community.

Finally, there are two points that need to be noted. One is that the negative effects of the Dutch Disease phenomenon during a construction boom following a natural disaster should not be exaggerated. The most direct negative impact of a localized construction boom would be on competing industries outside the local reconstruction areas (probably also in the construction sector in nearby regions). But this negative effect is likely to be relatively short lived.[27] By its very nature, this type of boom is temporary. It reflects activities that rehabilitate the productive base of the economy including key economic infrastructure such as roads, bridges, and ports. A boom of this kind provides lasting benefits that enhance the future profitability of all sectors across the local economy. The main challenge for policy makers is to maximize the benefits that flow from the boom without dissipating reconstruction funds in ways that lead to too high windfall gains for people who were not directly affected by the disaster.

Secondly, it needs to be remembered that cost increases of the kind discussed above, which are well above economy-wide average inflation levels, are inevitable. They need to be expected and budgeted for when estimating funding requirements for construction programs. Unless this is done, funding gaps will emerge. Indeed, it is surprising that the international disaster management industry apparently did not anticipate this situation in the wake of the Asian tsunami in December 2004.

LESSONS OF EXPERIENCE

There is a very extensive international literature which discusses lessons learnt from delivering aid during natural disasters.[28] Numerous official documents discuss disaster risk reduction policy in broad terms (ISDR 2009), and many reports were issued by different agencies which discussed their experiences of delivering post-tsunami aid in Asia (ILO 2006; Clinton 2006; Schwartz 2006). Depending upon the detail, it is possible to list hundreds of lessons reported by monitoring and evaluation teams working in different sectors. Rather than survey this literature in detail, the aim here is to set down the most important broad lessons which emerge from the experiences surveyed in this book. Eight main lessons are summarized in Box 7.1.

LOOKING AHEAD

The 2004 Asian tsunami was the greatest natural disaster in recent times. It posed challenges that were unprecedented in scale and scope for both national agencies and the international community. The delivery of a very large aid program of perhaps US$17 billion of tsunami assistance in total across various countries by thousands of agencies was an extraordinary effort. Many lives were saved. Much long-term assistance was delivered. One clear conclusion, therefore, is that the major assistance program was highly successful in achieving the goal of providing widespread help following the 2004 tsunami disaster in Asia.

But there is another important conclusion which should be noted as well: the international donor community should aim to do better.

Here it is important to emphasize the need to recognize the critical role of local agencies and communities in delivering relief during the critical early phase of a natural disaster. International agencies should aim to strengthen their capacity to cope with natural disasters and see their own efforts as complementing them. When megadisasters strike in poor countries, international donors do not always cooperate as well as they should – either with national governments or with each other. Too many agencies from too many countries with too many goals compete rather than cooperate to provide aid. The result is that scarce coordination resources

BOX 7.1   SUMMARY OF MAIN LESSONS

1. **Objectives**   The very large number of different donors involved in the delivery of assistance following the Asian tsunami, as well as other actors such as the media and policy makers, had many differing objectives. The effective delivery of humanitarian emergency relief was one of these objectives, but only one.

2. **Local responses**   The fastest relief after the Asian tsunami was usually provided by local communities. The key role that local communities play in providing fast relief needs more recognition; strategies to improve the capacity of local communities to cope in times of disaster should receive high priority.

3. **Coordination**   The overall coordination of the tsunami aid effort was often very difficult. A large number of different agencies was involved. The early establishment of credible national and international agencies with recognized standing can help improve coordination arrangements.

4. **Stages**   Responses, and the role played by different actors, varied over time. In planning, it is important to distinguish between the relief, rehabilitation, reconstruction and post-assistance stages.

5. **Supply-oriented donors**   Donors often tended to be supply-oriented rather than demand-responsive. Mechanisms are needed to ensure that local communities affected by a natural disaster have adequate opportunities to indicate what they see as their priority needs.

6. **Finance**   The details of arrangements for the provision of international finance were often problematic. The performance of the international donor community sometimes fell below the standards generally expected in the delivery of international aid in terms of speed and scale.

7. **Cost increases**   Local Dutch Disease effects, reflected in sharp increases in some costs for items in short supply, occurred in some areas after the tsunami. Aid planners should allow for sharp cost increases, particularly in the construction activities, when drawing up assistance programs.

8. **Methods of spending**   Assistance following the Asian tsunami was delivered in many different ways. The way in

> which aid is provided has many implications for, amongst other things, the speed of delivery and effectiveness of the assistance. Donors should consider carefully the best way of providing help; choices include whether the aid should be in cash or in kind, and what form in-kind aid might take.

in recipient countries are stretched close to breaking point, seriously undermining the efficacy of the relief and reconstruction effort. While the international donor community can congratulate itself for a job well done in responding to the 2004 Asian tsunami, the international community should also recognize that greatly improved systems of international donor coordination are needed.

Sadly it is inevitable that megadisasters will continue to threaten the lives of hundreds of thousands of people in developing countries in the coming decades. National governments must pay a great deal more attention to developing strategies to deal with them that are broad-based, participatory and cost-effective. And donors, too, need to improve planning and delivery systems both to help developing countries themselves prepare for the inevitable disasters that will occur, and to ensure that the donor community can respond in a far more effective way when disaster strikes.

NOTES

1. For references to the very considerable literature on coordination issues which arise in the delivery of post-tsunami aid, see the annotated document review prepared by Cosgrave and colleagues (Cosgrave et al. 2009). See also the useful discussion in Masyrafah and McKeon (2008: 24–34).
2. Numerous reports on the operations of the World Bank Multi Donor Fund (MDF) are available on the MDF website at http://www.multidonorfund.org/index.html, accessed 17 July 2009.
3. Myrdal (1968: 10–16) presents a prescient discussion which emphasizes security concerns of western countries at the end of the 1960s that influence the approach of western countries towards developing countries.
4. Roland Wilson, 'US sees aid to Muslim victims as chance to improve image', *The Times*, 3 January 2005. Similar reports were carried widely in other international media outlets. For example, Richard W. Baker (2005), special assistant to the US President at the time, discussed the issues in an op-ed piece in the *Canberra Times* noting that the subject needed to be 'carefully and sensitively handled'.
5. Bennett et al. (2006: 40) note that in the period following the tsunami, 'The interface between the Government of Indonesia and international actors was somewhat problematic. The role of the UN in East Timor was still fresh in the minds of many government officials . . . .'
6. Additional details of the main changes in the Australian assistance program in Indonesia in the post-tsunami period are provided in a recent OECD review of the Australian aid program (OECD 2009: 97–104).

7. The notion of 'generosity' is something of an issue. Edward Aspinall (2006) spoke of 'the orgy of self-congratulation about "Australian generosity" that quickly dominated discussion of [the Indian Ocean tsunami] in this country'. See also the discussion in Appendix 3.1 above.
8. http://www.oecd.org/dataoecd/11/41/34428351.pdf
9. A Fact Sheet issued by USAID in July 2005 noted that in Sri Lanka, 'logistics, lack of supplies, ethnic tensions, low-levels of development, and local regulations, in particular in the buffer zone, have impeded the progress of the transitional shelter sector in eastern Sri Lanka'. See USAID (2005).
10. For references to the very extensive literature on the issue, see Cosgrave et al. (2009).
11. The World Bank Decentralisation Support Facility provided regular reports on the level of conflict in Aceh Province. See the references to the World Bank reports for the period from mid-2005 to mid-2008 provided in Cosgrave et al. (2009: 307–19), items 537–66.
12. Quoted in TGLL (2009: 37–38).
13. For a discussion of 'voice' in the context of delivering public services in developing Asian countries, see Schiavo-Campo and Sundaram (2000: 509). See also Wall (2006) for a discussion of information and communication issues.
14. In the case of Sri Lanka, for example, estimates indicated that at least 100 000 additional workers were required, including about 13 000 masons, 2000 carpenters, 2500 painters, and nearly 54 000 unskilled labourers (Jayasuriya et al. 2005: 38).
15. This is the so-called 'small country' case in economic analysis where, because the economy of a country is small compared to the world economy, economic changes within the relevant country do not affect world prices of tradable goods.
16. It should be noted that references to inflation in this context refer to one-off price increases rather than a sustained process of continuing increases in the general price level which extends over a period of time.
17. Recent experience in Pakistan, the US (hurricane Katrina), and even in Indonesia after the Yogyakarta earthquake in 2006 indicates that sharp construction cost increases in disaster zones are common.
18. For various reasons, such as local political factors, it may not be possible sometimes to import certain factors of production. In the case of the construction sector, for example, it is usually possible, in principle, to import skilled labour from other countries. In Sri Lanka following the tsunami, there was a suggestion that skilled labour shortages in the construction sector should be met by importing skilled labour from India. However this proved to be politically unacceptable.
19. The reasons for the sharp (and somewhat surprising) increase in the price of timber are discussed by Nazara and Resosudarmo (2007).
20. See Corden and Neary (1982) and Corden (1984) for an outline of a basic analytical model for Dutch Disease. A booming sector also generates expenditure effects which raise the overall demand for goods and services. But higher demand does not always translate into higher prices in the case of (internationally) tradable goods. Generally, such goods can be imported at more or less exogenously fixed world prices while domestically produced and consumed goods (non-tradable goods) tend to experience off-setting price increases. Hence, tradable goods experience cost pressures from booming sectors but do not get much of an offsetting effect from higher income–expenditure related demand increases. As a result the relative price of non-tradables to tradables increases. This fall in the relative profitability of tradable industries is the standard 'real exchange rate appreciation' that is a necessary and unavoidable outcome of foreign capital absorption by the domestic economy. This can be minimized in the short term through foreign exchange market interventions and other sterilization measures, but cannot be entirely avoided.
21. Explanation of terms: (1) Here, there is a distinction between 'tradable' and 'non-tradable' goods. These goods have the very important difference that 'tradable' goods (for example, oil) are traded freely in world markets and thus have their prices set in world markets. However, 'non-tradable' (or 'non-traded') goods are not traded in world markets and have their prices set within a country. (2) For most countries, there

are two types of 'tradable' goods – 'imported tradables' (also known as 'importables') and 'exported tradables' (also known as 'exportables'). (3) However, whether any tradable good is an 'importable' or 'exportable' good depends on the particular country being considered – for example, oil is an 'importable' (or imported tradable) for Japan but is an 'exportable' (or exported tradable) for Saudi Arabia.

22. The assumption is that the recipient country is a 'small' country in world markets so its international transactions do not have a significant impact on world market prices.

23. The regional economy of the disaster affected area may be considered as a distinct entity within the broader national economy that has a fixed exchange rate with the rest of the economy. Then, the same considerations apply for funds coming into the region from within the country itself.

24. In the immediate aftermath of the tsunami in Sri Lanka there were euphoric expectations of massive capital flows, peace, and economic prosperity. In this atmosphere, the Sri Lanka rupee appreciated (see Figure 5 in Weerakoon et al. (2007)). Subsequently, the government appeared to have used tsunami aid funds to prop up the currency for political reasons. Such a policy also implies slower absorption (expenditure) of foreign assistance, which reduces domestic cost pressures.

25. In the longer term, higher expenditures by the 'profiteering' groups who gain these higher incomes will tend to raise costs throughout the economy, thereby tending to squeeze profits in export and import competing industries. In contrast, the availability of services from reconstructed infrastructure and other assets has an offsetting impact in the future on costs, facilitating increased supplies. Thus, investment in domestic capital stock tends, in the first instance, to produce a real exchange rate appreciation. Later, improved international competitiveness may be expected once the capital assets begin to provide services used in the tradable industries.

26. The incentives for people to take up training in new skills depend on expectations and incentives. In Thailand, Nidhiprabha (2007) observed that many people were reluctant to undertake training programs to acquire new skills because they expected to go back to their previous jobs in fisheries and tourism relatively quickly. On the other hand, anecdotal evidence from Sri Lanka suggests that many unemployed people were willing to undertake training in simple construction sector skills.

27. This is a more general point that applies to the spending of all types of financial flows – including development aid – that expand the productive capacity of an economy. It should also be mentioned that all economic agents are likely to perceive that the boom is a temporary phenomenon. The boom is therefore unlikely to generate future unemployment later due to downward rigidity of wages and prices when the boom ends.

28. See, for example, the extensive list of reports and conclusions from workshops listed on the Tsunami Evaluation Coalition website: http://www.tsunami-evaluation.org/ Other+Evaluations+and+Reviews/Lessons+Learned.html, accessed 31 July 2009.

REFERENCES

Aspinall, Edward (2006), 'Selective outrage and unacknowledged fantasies: rethinking Papua, Indonesia and Australia', online Austral Policy Forum 06-15A, 4 May 2006, Nautilus Institute, RMIT, http://www.globalcollab.org/Nautilus/ australia/apsnet/policy-forum/2006/0615a-aspinall.html/?searchterm=Aspinall, accessed 25 September 2009.

Baker, Richard W. (2005), 'Right time for US to show its heart', *Canberra Times*, 12 January.

Bennett, Jon, W. Bertrand, C. Harkin, S. Samarasinghe and H.Wickramatilake (2006), *Coordination of International Tsunami Assistance in Tsunami-affected Countries*, London: TEC.

Brennan, Richard J. and R.J. Waldman (2006), 'The south Asian earthquake six months later – an ongoing crisis', *New England Journal of Medicine*, **354** (17), 1769–71.

Buckley, Ross (2005), 'Whatever Howard's motives, generosity was a master stroke', *Canberra Times*, 17 January.

Clinton, William J. (2006), 'Key propositions for building back better', United Nations, http://ochaonline.un.org/OchaLinkClick.aspx?link=ocha&docid=100 5912, accessed 4 September 2009.

Corden, W. Max (1984), 'Booming sector and Dutch Disease economics: survey and consolidation', *Oxford Economic Papers*, **36** (2), 359–80.

Corden, W. Max and P.J. Neary (1982), 'Booming sectors and de-industrialisation in a small open economy', *Economic Journal*, **92**, 825–48.

Cosgrave, John (2005), *Tsunami Evaluation Coalition: Initial Findings*, London: Tsunami Evaluation Coalition, www.tsunami-evaluation.org/NR/rdonlyres/576D8E84-27DB-44DC-8663-83AB9D5BF614/0/lowresA520060221.pdf, accessed 15 July 2009.

Cosgrave, John, E. Brusset, M. Bhatt, L. Fernandez, Y. Deshmukh, Y. Immajati, R. Jayasundere, A. Mattsson, N. Muhaimin and R. Polastro (2009), *A Ripple in Development? Document Review*. Annotated Bibliography prepared for the Joint Follow-up Evaluation of the Links between Relief, Rehabilitation and Development (LRRD) in Responses to the Indian Ocean Tsunami, Stockholm: SIDA, www.sida.se/publications, accessed 10 September 2009.

Doocy, Shannon, M. Gabriel, S. Collins, C. Robinson and P. Stevenson (2006), 'Implementing cash for work programmes in post-tsunami Aceh: experiences and lessons learned', *Disasters*, **30** (3), 277–96.

Harvey, Paul (2006), 'Editorial: mini special issue on cash transfers', *Disasters*, **30** (3), 273–76.

Harvey, Paul (2007), *Cash-Based Responses in Emergencies*, HPG Report 24, January, London: ODI.

Hasan, Nurdin (2006), 'Angry Aceh tsunami survivors demand split from aid agency', Agence France-Presse, 14 April, www.reliefweb.int/rwarchive/rwb.nsf/db900sid/SODA-6NX4ET?OpenDocument, accessed 20 September 2009.

He, Baogang and A. Reid (2004), 'Special issue editors' introduction: four approaches to the Aceh question', *Asian Ethnicity*, **5** (3), October, 293–300.

IDLO and UNDP (2007), *Perempuan Aceh di hadapan hukum setelah konflik dan tsunami berlalu: Laporan case study*, http://www.idlo.int/publications/17.pdf, accessed 9 September 2009.

ILO (2005), *Working Out of Disaster: Improving Employment and Livelihood in Countries Affected by the Tsunami*, Bangkok: International Labour Office.

ILO (2006), *Lessons Learned and Good Practices from the ILO Aceh Programme*, Jakarta: International Labour Organization.

Indriatmoko, Yayan, H. Adnan, H. Komarudin and Y. Siagian (2006), 'Resilience, rights and resources: two years of recovery in coastal zone Aceh: tsunami, conflicts and forestry in Aceh: a brief review', Briefing Note, Bogor: World Agroforestry Centre, CIFOR, November, http://www.worldagroforestrycentre.org/SEA/W-New/datas/Aceh30Nov06/19%20Tsunami,%20conflict%20and%20forestry%20in%20Aceh.pdf, accessed 15 October 2009.

ISDR (2009), *Global Assessment Report on Disaster Risk Reduction*, Geneva, Switzerland: United Nations.

Jayasuriya, Sisira, P. Steele and D. Weerakoon (2005), *Post-Tsunami Recovery:*

Issues and Challenges in Sri Lanka, Report presented to the Prime Minister of Sri Lanka, November, Colombo: Institute of Policy Studies.

Kelaher, David and B. Dollery (2008), 'Cash and in-kind food aid transfers: The case of tsunami emergency aid in Banda Aceh', *International Review of Public Administration*, **13** (2), 117–28.

Kessler, Earl (2006), *Local Response: Overview*, Bangkok and London: ADPC and TEC.

Kilby, Patrick (2007), 'The strength of networks: the local NGO response to the tsunami in India', *Disasters*, **32** (1), 120–30.

Kivikuru, U. (2006), 'Tsunami communication in Finland: revealing tensions in the sender–receiver relationship', *European Journal of Communication*, **21** (4), 499–520.

Marulanda, Liliana and S. Rizal (2006), *Local Response: Indonesia*, Bangkok and London: ADPC and TEC.

Masyrafah, Harry and J.M.J.A. McKeon (2008), *Post-Tsunami Aid Effectiveness in Aceh: Proliferation and Coordination in Reconstruction*, Wolfensohn Center for Development Working Paper 6, Washington: The Brookings Institution, http://www.brookings.edu/~/media/Files/rc/papers/2008/11_aceh_aid_masyrafah/11_aceh_aid_masyrafah.pdf, accessed 26 September 2009.

MDF (Multi Donor Fund) (2008), *Investing in Institutions: Sustaining Reconstruction and Economic Activity: Four Years after the Tsunami*, Jakarta: World Bank, http://go.worldbank.org/IIC768ARX0, accessed 15 July 2009.

Montgomery, Roger D. (2006), 'The next Sumatra tsunami: who will live and who will die?', *Asian Affairs*, **XXXVII** (1), 50–71.

Myrdal, Gunnar (1968), *Asian Drama: An Inquiry into the Poverty of Nations*, New York: Pantheon.

Nazara, Suahasil and B.P. Resosudarmo (2007), *Aceh-Nias Reconstruction and Rehabilitation: Progress and Challenges at End of 2006*, ADBI Discussion Paper 70, Tokyo: ADBI.

Nidhiprabha, Bhanupong (2007), *Adjustment and Recovery in Thailand Two Years after the Tsunami*, ADBI Discussion Paper 72, http://www.adbi.org/files/dp72.thailand.tsunami.adjustment.recovery.pdf, accessed 31 October 2009.

Nowak, Barbara S. and T. Caulfield (2008), *Women and Livelihoods in Post-Tsunami India and Aceh*, Working paper no. 104, Singapore: Asia Research Institute, National University of Singapore, http://ssrn.com/paper=1317142, accessed 25 July 2009.

OECD (2009), *Australia Development Assistance Committee (DAC) Peer Review*, Paris: Organisation for Economic Co-operation and Development.

Schiavo-Campo, Salvatore and P. Sundaram (2000), *To Serve and To Preserve: Improving Public Administration in a Competitive World*, Asian Development Bank, Manila, http://www.adb.org/Documents/Manuals/Serve_and_Preserve/default.asp, accessed 31 October 2009.

Schwartz, Eric (2006), 'Keynote address of Eric Schwartz', European Forum on International Disaster Response Laws, Rules and Principles, 25 May, www.ifrc.org/docs/pubs/idrl/euro-forum-ppt/eschwartz.pdf, accessed 24 June 2009.

Telford, John, J. Cosgrave and R. Houghton (2006), *Joint Evaluation of the International Response to the Indian Ocean Tsunami: Synthesis Report,* London: Tsunami Evaluation Coalition.

Telford, John and J. Cosgrave (2007), 'The international humanitarian system and the 2004 Indian Ocean earthquake and tsunamis', *Disasters*, **31** (1), 1–28.

TGLL (Tsunami Global Lessons Learned Project) (2009), *The Tsunami Legacy: Innovations, Breakthroughs and Change*, TGLL Project Steering Committee, http://www.reliefweb.int/rw/rwb.nsf/db900sid/MUMA-7RF7PQ?OpenDocument, accessed 26 August 2009.

Thorburn, Craig (2009), 'Livelihood recovery in the wake of the tsunami in Aceh', *Bulletin of Indonesian Economic Studies*, **45** (1), 85–105.

Thornton, Paul (2006), 'The multi-donor trust fund for Aceh and Nias', paper prepared for the 2006 Asian Regional Forum on Aid Effectiveness: Implementation, Monitoring and Evaluation, Dhaka: Verulam Associates, http://www.adb.org/Documents/Events/2006/Aid-Effectiveness/country-papers/INO-MDF.pdf, accessed 8 August 2009.

Tomar, Ravi (2005), 'Australia's $1 billion tsunami-related aid package to Indonesia: progress on the eve of the March ministerial meetings', Research Note, 7 March, Canberra: Australian Parliament, Department of Parliamentary Services, http://www.aph.gov.au/library/pubs/RN/2004-05/05rn36.pdf, accessed 16 March 2009.

Tuli, Priya (2007), 'On Boxing Day, the tsunami and scrooge', *JakartaPost.com*, 30 December, accessed 15 December 2008.

UN (2005), *Regional Workshop on Lessons Learned and Best Practices in the Response to the Indian Ocean Tsunami: Report and Summary of Main Conclusions*, Medan: Indonesia, June, http://www.tsunami-evaluation.org/NR/rdonlyres/33531D5E-07AE-4FBB-9B96-532B52BECF05/0/lessons_summary.pdf, accessed 25 August 2009.

UNCTAD (2005), 'Economic development in Africa – doubling aid: making the "big push" work', Document TD/B/53/4, 26 July, Geneva: UNCTAD Secretariat.

USAID (2005), 'Indian Ocean – earthquakes and tsunamis', Fact Sheet #39, July 7.

USGAO (2007), *Foreign Assistance: USAID Signature Tsunami Reconstruction Efforts in Indonesia and Sri Lanka Exceed Initial Cost and Schedule Estimates, and Face Further Risks*, Report to Congressional Committees, February, www.gao.gov/cgi-bin/getrpt?GAO-07-357, accessed 17 June 2007.

Wall, Imogen (2006), *The Right to Know: The Challenge of Public Information and Accountability in Aceh and Sri Lanka*, New York: Office of the UN Secretary General's Special Envoy for Tsunami Recovery, www.wpro.who.int/NR/rdonlyres/94653175-72B4-4E69-9075D1921FF119FA/0/the_right_to_know.pdf, accessed 18 August 2009.

Weerakoon, Dushni, S. Jayasuriya, N. Arunatilake and P. Steele (2007), *Economic Challenges of Post-Tsunami Reconstruction in Sri Lanka*, Tokyo: Asian Development Bank Institute, http://www.adbi.org/discussion-paper/2007/08/31/2354.sri.lanka.post.tsunami.reconstruction/, accessed 31 October 2009.

Wiharta, Sharon, H. Ahmad, J.-Y. Haine, J. Löfgren and T. Randall (2008), *The Effectiveness of Foreign Military Assets in Natural Disaster Response*, Stockholm: Stockholm International Peace Research Institute, http://books.sipri.org/files/misc/FMA/SIPRI08FMA.pdf, accessed 16 July 2009.

Wilson, Roland (2005), 'US sees aid to Muslim victims as chance to improve image', *The Times*, 3 January.

Index